Ordinary and Presumptive Trauma

Ordinary and Presumptive Trauma offers a sociopolitical account of trauma grounded in the lived experiences of oppressed and socially disadvantaged peoples. In doing so, this book seeks to articulate a theory of trauma that generates space for the recognition of historical and ongoing political violence, the collective healing of harmed people, and the bridging of psychological theories with social justice scholarship and activist traditions.

Ordinary and Presumptive Trauma is uniquely situated at the crossroads of two worlds that often struggle to coexist, but that have the potential to grow significantly in conversation with one another. Accordingly, this book provides a multifaceted approach that appeals to a wide readership in multiple disciplines, such as psychology, Women's and Gender Studies, Ethnic Studies, Queer Studies, and more.

Samuel Z. Shelton holds an M.A. degree in Women, Gender, and Sexuality Studies. Their teaching and scholarship address topics in Critical Trauma Studies, Critical Disability Studies, Queer and Trans studies, and transformative justice movements.

AF763718

Ordinary and Presumptive Trauma

Exploring the Psychological Impacts of Oppression

Samuel Z. Shelton

Routledge
Taylor & Francis Group
NEW YORK AND LONDON

Designed cover image: Illustration by Jean Shelton

First published 2027
by Routledge
605 Third Avenue, New York, NY 10158

and by Routledge
4 Park Square, Milton Park, Abingdon, Oxon, OX14 4RN

Routledge is an imprint of the Taylor & Francis Group, an informa business

© 2027 Samuel Z. Shelton

The right of Samuel Z. Shelton to be identified as author of this work has been asserted in accordance with sections 77 and 78 of the Copyright, Designs and Patents Act 1988.

All rights reserved. No part of this book may be reprinted or reproduced or utilised in any form or by any electronic, mechanical, or other means, now known or hereafter invented, including photocopying and recording, or in any information storage or retrieval system, without permission in writing from the publishers.

For Product Safety Concerns and Information please contact our EU representative GPSR@taylorandfrancis.com. Taylor & Francis Verlag GmbH, Kaufingerstraße 24, 80331 München, Germany.

Trademark notice: Product or corporate names may be trademarks or registered trademarks, and are used only for identification and explanation without intent to infringe.

ISBN: 978-1-041-20384-1 (hbk)
ISBN: 978-1-041-20301-8 (pbk)
ISBN: 978-1-003-71619-8 (ebk)

DOI: 10.4324/9781003716198

Typeset in Palatino
by Apex CoVantage, LLC

This book is an expression of the best versions of myself, and it is an act of love for the people I strive to build just and accountable relationships with. In writing this dedication, I express a deep, unyielding gratitude for the people who, above all others, have helped me to become the human that I am today – one who is more capable of feeling and expressing love because of what they have nurtured within me. I recognize as well that I am moody and stubborn, and that their compassion has been a testament to their refusal to give on me, even when I have given up on myself. My greatest partner and wife, Casey: you are the ever-burning lighthouse that guides me through storms to calmer waters. I would have crashed long ago without your flame to keep me afloat. My unrelenting mother, Jean: everything I am comes from what you gave me. I could never have hoped for a better caregiver or mentor to guide me forward when I did not know the way.

Contents

Land Acknowledgement

I wrote this book as a settler occupying stolen lands once home to the Chepenafa or "Mary's River" band of the Kalapuya peoples. By choosing to attend Oregon State University to earn my graduate degree in Women, Gender, and Sexuality Studies, I rooted my future in a place that still bears the historical trauma of Indigenous people who, not even 200 years ago, were forcibly removed to reservations by settlers laying claim to what is now known as Corvallis, Oregon. I continue to seek out understanding and accountability for my participation in the continuation of settler colonialism, and I ask the same of you during your engagements with this text and beyond.

Stirring

When you visit my stirring,
weary mind deep into the night,
it occurs to me:
There is a place
not too far away from here
where two ancient rivers flow deep
side-by-side until
they meet for a moment,
in the roots of a tree
spanning the steady distance between them.

No, the rivers never do cross, but
the roots of the tree reach down, conveying life
from the one and from the other
into an amalgamation of living cells
nourished by an eternal longing for lost
connection.
In its simple, indescribable magnificence,
the tree becomes love and joyousness,
an erotic sensation for two waters split

Apart

by a world intent on pulling order from the chaos
of its existence. You see,
the two rivers were once an ocean,
united in a wholeness now unknown,
and then they weren't anymore.
The landscape was changed violently,
bent to a will swollen, fit to b u r s t.
And yet,

they flow by an unconquered tree,
spanning their great distance,
in open defiance of
Those who proclaim themselves Lord.

I wonder if they are us,
Or if we once were them.
Oh, how we used to be whole.

I miss the part of you that yearns
to again be a part of me.
You know, we once shared a body
and everything else.
But then,
like an ocean forced
into two rivers flowing steady,
we become two,
and never touched again.
Was it my fault? Was it yours?
Or, was it something beyond our control,
something we were taught by
Those who proclaim themselves Lord?

One day, we will swell over our banks
swallowing the great distance
between all of us.
That time could be now,
if enough of us really wanted it.

But if it is not,
if we are yet to flow alone
for a time,
then we must find a tree
to span our longing
with roots growing, running deep into our currents
so that we can imagine a world
where everything is all of us
all of the time.

A world where a tree standing in open defiance
of the hatred, violence driving us

Apart

doesn't stand alone,
but grows beneath the roof
of a great forest
like in the stories our loved ones, lost ones
used to tell us late into the night
to quiet our stirring, weary minds.

My mind will stir until I am with you –
Until I am you
once again
in a world where there are
None who proclaim themselves Lord

1

Ordinary Trauma: The Psychic Harms of Oppression

In 2015, The Icarus Project published a community guidebook titled *Madness & Oppression: Paths to Personal Transformation and Collective Liberation* – a captivating resource that they describe as a *Mad Maps Guide*. In their words, Mad Maps are "documents that we create for ourselves as reminders of our goals, what is important to us, our personal signs of struggle, and our strategies for self-determined well-being." Founded in 2003, The Icarus Project is a collective of advocates, activists, and other people who "experience the world in ways that are often diagnosed as mental illness." Much of their community-based work has to do with building liberatory spaces for people diagnosed as "mentally ill" and promoting socially just alternatives to the medicalization, pathologization, and oppression of "mentally ill" people. *Madness & Oppression* is a text that comes directly from and exemplifies the mission of The Icarus Project: as a "guide," it moves readers through the complex, embodied experience of oppression and offers a lens or language that readers can use to make sense of and process their personal experiences in an oppressive, traumatizing society. This resource bridges the personal and the sociopolitical, asking illuminating questions along the way, such as "What does oppression feel like?", "How does oppression affect the way you perceive yourself?", and "Where can we begin to address oppression within our communities?"

DOI: 10.4324/9781003716198-1

Just a few years later in June 2017, generationFIVE published *Ending Child Sexual Abuse: A Transformative Justice Handbook*. This handbook takes a critical, radical stance on resisting child sexual abuse that promotes collective healing and systemic change over surveillance, policing, or incarceration. The vision of transformative justice advanced in this text proposes that child sexual abuse won't be solved by locking "bad people" away because "incidences of child sexual abuse do not happen in a vacuum" (II); this issue is systemic, and it requires interventions that go beyond individual harm doers. Like The Icarus Project, generationFIVE is a collective of people working towards social justice in an oppressive society. Many of the people involved in the organization are victims/survivors of child sexual abuse, and much of their work centres building communities of resistance. Their mission is to "end the sexual abuse of children within five generations" as they work together "to interrupt and mend the intergenerational impact of child sexual abuse on individuals, families, and communities." Their Transformative Justice Handbook also functions like a sort of guide that outlines the issue of child sexual abuse, explains why more traditional, carceral responses do not work, and introduces alternative strategies for community-building and collective action.

About a decade earlier, the group Asian Communities for Reproductive Justice (now Forward Together) created the text *A New Vision for Advancing Our Movement for Reproductive Heath, Reproductive Rights, and Reproductive Justice*. This groundbreaking work carefully lays out the reproductive justice framework and the rationale for it as well as the histories of racism and White supremacy in reproductive rights, particularly pro-choice, movements. Founded by women of colour feminists, reproductive justice movements centre a framework that roots reproductive freedoms in the totality of people's lived experiences and identities, including, among other things, race, class, gender, sexuality, age, and immigration status. Since 1989, ACJR "has been at the forefront of building a Reproductive Justice Movement that places the reproductive health and rights of Asian women and girls within a social justice framework" (2005: 1). As with The Icarus Project and generationFIVE, members of this organization draw on their experiences to envision and advance towards a world liberated from multiple forms of oppression, particularly those impacting Asian women and girls. They also recognize that more traditional approaches, such as the pro-choice framework, have not been effective in addressing the root causes of inequity and injustice for multiple reasons, such as the failure to attend to *intersectionality*.

These critical resources share a lot in common: their focus on transformative social justice, their resistance to dominant narratives and practices, their multifaceted and intersectional frameworks, and so on. Furthermore, each of them is also grounded in experiences of *trauma* and committed to transforming the traumatic harm of oppression into sources of understanding, empowerment, and motivations for social change. Though they may not use the language or lens of trauma directly, these resources are inseparable from traumatic histories of inequity and injustice. For The Icarus Project, Mad Maps are tools for collectively resisting dominant understandings of "mental health" and "mental illness" that have been used to categorize, contain, and regulate those of us who exist on the thin line between brilliance and madness. Similarly, generationFIVE's notion of transformative justice takes on both the trauma of child sexual abuse and the traumatizing practices of the police/carceral state. The reproductive justice movement came about as the result of the trauma women of colour experienced, first from the assault on their reproductive liberties and second from White activists who refused to think/act beyond their racial position.

It is hard not to feel the traumatic experiences underlying each of these texts as well as the authors' desire to produce trauma-informed, healing-centred approaches to social change and transformation. But what exactly is trauma in relation to systems of oppression? Why is trauma not a more common term in conversations about social justice when it carries such potential to generate knowledge from the shared experience of structural violence? Further, definitions of and approaches to healing from trauma repeatedly neglect critical theories of power and activist histories. Much of the time, liberation from systems of oppression is seen as somehow separate because trauma is *individualized* and *depoliticized*, and so the lived experiences of traumatized/harmed people are removed from the social contexts in which they occurred. But what would it mean to describe trauma through liberation in conversation with anti-oppressive theories and activist histories?

Medicalization, Pathologization, and the Sociopolitical Nature of Trauma

The third edition of the *Diagnostic and Statistical Manual of Mental Disorders* (DSM-III) from the American Psychiatric Association defines traumatic events as those producing feelings of helplessness and/or terror that exist "outside the range of usual human experience" (1986). The fourth edition of the DSM removed this requirement that traumatic events be extraordinary, defining them instead as those moments of "actual or threatened death or serious injury, or other threat to one's physical integrity" (2000). Traumatic events, in this updated definition, started to centre around concerns of longevity or control over an individual's body; rather than being instances of terror that surpass usual human experience, traumatic events came to refer to moments that threaten continued human existence – experiences in which the traumatized person's life or autonomy are seriously brought into question. The subsequent edition of this text, the DSM-V, offers an even more expansive definition of trauma, including a wider range of potentially traumatic events and a recognition that trauma can be experienced directly or secondarily (i.e. *vicariously*) through various forms of exposure to other people's encounters with trauma:

> Exposure to actual or threatened death, serious injury, or sexual violence in one (or more) of the following ways: directly experiencing the traumatic event(s); witnessing, in person, the traumatic event(s) as it occurred to others; learning that the traumatic event(s) occurred to a close family member or close friend (in case of actual or threatened death of a family member or friend, the event(s) must have been violent or accidental); or

> experiencing repeated or extreme exposure to aversive details of the traumatic event(s).
>
> (2013: 271)

However, even as the DSM-V provides a broader and more expansive account of trauma, its clinical/psychiatric approach leaves much to be desired because it mischaracterizes or at least obscures social, political, and historical conditions underlying traumatic experiences within this unjust and indisputably violent society. Of particular concern to me here are the ways in which pervasive social issues connected to multiple, interlocking systems of power are packaged and sold off as individual problems necessitating individual, often therapeutic solutions. By defining traumatic events solely in relation to mental afflictions and individual experiences, these definitions do make specific interventions possible, such as counselling and crisis response, and my purpose is not to argue that such interventions are unimportant. However, through *medicalizing* and *pathologizing* trauma, these discourses also subvert the possibility of recognizing traumatic events as iterative, collective, and systematic; that is, as the ordinary outcome of systems of oppression.

Medicalization and pathologization refer to interrelated processes of reducing sociopolitical issues, which are the outcomes of inequity and injustice within a society, to individual-level problems to be "cured" or "fixed" through individual solutions, such as changes in behaviour, medications, and therapies (Clare 1999, 2017; Durazo 2006). In this sense, medicalized and pathologized discourses about trauma make sense of harmful experiences through the lens of individual lives in isolation from broader social systems. Accordingly, it becomes difficult to understand traumatic events and their associated bodily repercussions as emerging from and bound to an oppressive social landscape that normalizes and distributes harm towards particular groups of people. Much of the time, discussions about social justice and activism are all but entirely absent from trauma studies, and the people invested in contributing their knowledge to the literature about trauma have often not developed a critical social justice lens. For these reasons, discourses concerning trauma too frequently become depoliticized and privatized (Naples 2003; Tseris 2013).

At the same time, many social justice theorists and activists organizing against systems of oppression have been hesitant to draw on trauma as an analytical tool that could inform and guide struggles for social transformation. A part of this hesitancy comes from the clinical/psychiatric discourses surrounding trauma that cause it to appear less useful for and even threatening to social justice movements. Indeed, the medicalization and pathologization of trauma, which place the individual and therapeutic at the centre, go against the tendency of activists to focus on larger social issues and systems impacting members of disadvantaged groups. Individualized and depoliticized accounts of trauma struggle to account for the ways that systems of oppression generate structural violence that affects groups of people based on their social positions within the matrix of domination (Collins 1990; Young 2011).

Despite this ongoing dissonance, I seek to demonstrate in this chapter that when trauma is strategically put in conversation with critical social justice frameworks, it can be a powerful tool of analysis and an undertapped source of resistance to systemic harm. When detached from the medicalizing and pathologizing discourses that have taken a hold of it, a politicized theory of trauma, what I term *ordinary trauma*, can act as a bridge to join individuals together and help them make sense of their experiences with systems of oppression. The exploration of trauma and social justice I develop throughout the pages of this book builds upon existing frameworks, but it also critiques and pushes back against them in search of a definition of trauma as political, cultural, and sociohistorical (Barlow 2018; Keating 2004; Levins Morales 1998; Treleaven 2018). For as Goodkind et al. (2012: 1023) write, "It is clear that trauma and suffering often result from political, economic, and institutional forces," even if those forces are not always recognized or named.

In *An Archive of Feelings: Trauma, Sexuality, and Lesbian Public Cultures*, Cvetkovich (2003: 2) expresses a strong feeling of ambivalence about the risks of using the language of trauma that I share:

> Despite the risks involved in taking on a discourse that has been dominated by medical and pathologizing

> approaches, I have been drawn to the category of trauma because it opens up space for accounts of pain as psychic, not just physical. As a name for experiences of socially situated political violence, trauma forges overt connections between politics and emotions.

When I started this project, I felt uneasy and unsure about utilizing the concept of trauma as the guiding language of my writing for the same reasons that Cvetkovich describes as well as others that I will address shortly. Despite this trepidation, I continued to use the concept of trauma because it generates an understanding of violence and harm as *multidimensional*, as crossing between the physical, emotional, and spiritual aspects of our being. Accordingly, one of the claims I make throughout this text is that by thinking about systemic inequity and injustice as *traumatic*, we can gain a better sense of the complicated and multifarious ways in which systems of power assault, constrain, and regulate our existence. I argue that a lens of trauma can help to restore a wholeness to our lived experiences and being that systems of power seek to steal away. I also deeply appreciate Cvetkovich's definition of trauma as a term for experiences of "socially situated political violence" because this description works to bridge and even dissolve the distance between the individual and the social, the personal and the political, the private and the public – all of which are more closely related than dominant discourses have been led to believe.

In addition to feeling drawn towards the discursively loaded concept of trauma, I also share with Cvetkovich the intention to do more than just expand the definition of trauma to include varied issues of social (in)justice. Writing specifically about the persistent disappearance of sexual violence from discourses about trauma that produces a need to repeatedly "break the silence," Cvetkovich (2003: 3) says that we need "a quite different approach [than efforts at inclusion], one that can recognize trauma's specificities and variations." Therefore, when Cvetkovich is discussing "lesbian sites of trauma," the effort is not to equate these sites with other sites of trauma (e.g. masculinized sites of trauma), but rather to figure out "how these lesbian sites give rise to different ways of thinking about trauma and in particular to a sense of trauma as connected to the textures of everyday experience." I too am interested in taking a different approach to thinking about trauma that is grounded in specific, lived experiences of inequity and injustice – one that doesn't necessarily seek to integrate them together into some grand narrative of trauma, but rather allows for difference in the place of similarity and complexity in the place of simplicity.

The tendency to collapse trauma into narratives of sameness is, I believe, yet another reason why advocates and activists have been hesitant to utilize the concept of trauma, and it is a tendency I strive to work against in this project. Like Audre Lorde (1984), Kimberlé Crenshaw (1991), Vivian May (2015), and other critical intersectionality theorists, I recognize difference as both necessary and useful to the task of expanding thought and action toward meaningful nuance that resembles the complex reality in which we live. The importance of attending to difference, especially where differences are constituted by and constitutive of power, raises the stakes of this re/claiming of trauma as a potentially resistant and liberatory concept – by which I mean to say that trauma carries a sordid history that we must reckon with moving forward. Trauma has never functioned as a "disencumbered term," but rather one that has always carried racialized, gendered, and classed meanings (Stevens 2009).

Though many feminist, anti-racist, disability, queer, and Indigenous activists, among others, have employed trauma to advocate for equity and social justice, systems of power have also shaped dominant understandings of trauma to advance particular modes of violence (such as exploitation, marginalization, regulation, and containment) and to make them less legible as forms of injustice. Angela Carter (2019: 19) maintains that we live in a *traumatocracy*, or a "socio-political discursive regime wherein the rhetorics and narratives of Trauma/PTSD are utilized to mobilize certain figures and forms of U.S. citizenship." In other words, whose experiences get counted as trauma, under what conditions, and what resources people gain access to are mediated by politically inflected constructions of difference rooted in systems of oppression. Under this traumatocracy according to Carter, hierarchies of recognition and validation emerge as pillars through which systems preserve their interests and ensure their reproduction.

The most socially legible or recognizable accounts of trauma are those which can be utilized to draw attention away from social conditions of inequity and injustice by positioning trauma within individual bodyminds and/or isolated situations; that is, those that serve to uphold a medicalized and pathologized view of trauma and, therefore, to promote individual changes or interventions rather than social critique. As an example of this, David Treleaven (2018: xxi) explains his experiences in a programme called Somatic Experiencing:

> The course taught me about the way the body responds to trauma, including safe and practical ways to work with survivors. It's a powerful methodology that shaped my thinking. . . . But I also felt something was missing in this work. While the teachers spoke about the biological roots of trauma, they never discussed its *social* roots – including systems of power that correlate with trauma. I was being trained to think about trauma solely as an individual experience disconnected from the larger world.

This experience is relatively common, and I have encountered it myself on many occasions. The high incidence of people being trained to think about trauma just in terms of individual experience and biology saddens, infuriates, and frightens me. This training or conditioning is illustrative of how systems of oppression covertly influence our perceptions: when people are instructed to recognize and respond to trauma without an awareness of social injustice, social change becomes disconnected from or irrelevant to the conversation, thus allowing the oppressive social conditions underlying traumatic experiences to persist unabated and unacknowledged. However, Goodkind et al. (2012: 1023) teach us that "[r]epresentations of suffering must be grounded in people's experiences, rather than attempting to understand them through general abstraction, categorization, and labelling." In other words, we cannot understand trauma outside of the lived experiences of people's lives – experiences that we must contextualize and understand as part of a larger narrative of oppression. My purpose in the upcoming sections of this chapter, and throughout this text more broadly, are to name some of these social conditions and theorize their functions as part of a political ordering of trauma within the traumatocracy.

Ordinary Trauma, Systemic Oppression, and Dehumanization

To begin the work of situating my sociopolitical and historical analysis of trauma, I return to the DSM-III's account of trauma as those experiences, personal or shared, which exceed or burst "outside the range of usual human experience." Many have pushed back against this definition of traumatic events as *extra-ordinary* by pointing out that the everyday experiences of violence under systems of oppression can feel just as traumatic as events which occur in exceptional moments. Feminist theorists like Cvetkovich (2003), Brown (1995), and Ahmed (2017) have written about the insidiousness and familiarity of traumatic harm by naming the normalization of traumatic events in the lives of disadvantaged people, most notably men's violence against women. For instance, acts of sexual or domestic violence for many people are daily occurrences and can often produce feelings of helplessness and terror from both the threat of harm and the perpetration of abusive actions. Living with a violent partner can make traumatic harm feel frequent and even normal. Relatedly, people living in militarized zones might experience the trauma of warfare as a routine part of their lives, which Judith Herman (1992b) claims as one reason why the condition of "outside the range of usual human experience" was removed from the fourth edition of the DSM.

Such clear examples make a compelling case for trauma as not quite extraordinary – indeed, Brown's writing (1995) is titled "Not outside the range" – and they make it possible to talk about the connection between trauma and systems of power without losing sight of the ways that traumatic experiences reverberate through individual bodyminds. For the authors cited here, the humanity of disadvantaged people pushes back against the idea that trauma has to be an extraordinary aspect of human experience. Indeed, if trauma must be "outside the range," then it cannot account for the lived experiences of people who experience trauma in usual, frequent, or sometimes even predictable moments. A problem take shape in the form of whose experiences get counted as "usual human experience" and whose get counted as something else, typically something lesser or something not as fully "human." As I argue in the upcoming pages and chapters, this question of humanity comes to centre around issues of power and dominance.

While there is much value to be found in efforts to broaden the definition of traumatic events to include these more "usual" or common traumatic experiences, I seek to make a different kind of intervention: I argue that trauma may very well exist outside the range of usual *human* experience, but the people for whom trauma is not an extraordinary experience – those for whom trauma may be as near as an intimate partner – are disproportionately viewed as less-than-fully human due to their social positions within a social hierarchy defined by systems of oppression. The experience of trauma for such people does not undermine the condition that it be extraordinary human experience; to the contrary, it reveals the persistent ingrained dehumanization of them as well as the social positions with which they have been identified. Systems of power encourage us to believe they have something other than ordinary "human" experience – that they are outsiders to humanity because some aspect(s) of their existence transgress normativity and mark them as less than, abnormal, and/or unnatural (i.e. queer), or at the very least less able to live up to standards of human exceptionalism.

This outsider or "other" position where trauma becomes "usual" is the space of oppression. Expounding this point, Laura Brown (1995: 101) writes that "the range of human experience becomes the range of what is normal and usual in the lives of men and the dominant class: white, young, able-bodied, educated, middle-class, Christian men." Furthermore, Carter (2019: 61), expanding on Brown, states that "[t]he trauma that is recognized is trauma that disrupts particular lives – lives that should *not* be disrupted." Lives recognized and accepted as fully human. The traumatic events people experience become more acceptable as they become regarded as less-fully human under systems of oppression and, therefore, in the thinking of socially advantaged subjects. In the following chapter, I examine the implications and processes of dehumanization as they are related to trauma, but for now, my argument is that *traumatic experiences become ordinary parts of people's lives as they become regarded as less-than-fully human under systems of oppression*.

According to this argument, trauma is bound up in humanity, specifically in the ways that we come to recognize/not recognize the humanity of ourselves and other people like or not like us. When regarded as fully human, people typically experience trauma as an *extraordinary* facet of their lives – as something arising from isolated, clearly identifiable, and temporally and spatially bounded moments. Andrea Bell (2017) writes that "[w]hen many people think of trauma, they tend to think about shock trauma: a single, overwhelming incident that's larger that our ability to cope." Shock trauma, while valid and real, originates from a narrative of social advantage wherein traumatic harm is not woven into ongoing or iterative, everyday experiences. In the "Shock Trauma" narrative, a traumatic experience or event takes place and then it concludes, although the impacted individual(s) may carry it with them for a much longer time.

Systemically disadvantaged people who are seen as less-than-fully human, however, often experience trauma as an *ordinary* aspect of our lives – as something that is continuous and tied to multiple, iterating experiences of harm that carry across space and time. And, in their ordinariness, trauma experiences become interconnected rather than individual or isolated, and they start to vibrate on a collective level. Rachael Alaia (2019) states that

> On a collective level, systemic complex trauma may look like hoarded wealth and mass inequity, widespread domestic abuse and sex trafficking, religious indoctrination and forced colonization, feminicide and transphobia, institutional racism and police violence,

> generations of ethnic wars and genocide. And, it may also look like ecocide and climate collapse.

To recognize trauma as ordinary is to critically attend to these multiple ways in which society has been set up to normatively distribute these and other experiences of harm and suffering, such that certain people become more vulnerable to trauma and differently impacted by the environments in which they exist. This structuring of harm benefits those few people settled atop social hierarchies through the routine traumatization of the many forced down towards the bottom, thus making it that ordinary trauma becomes expected and accepted as normal.

For example, in their introduction to *Keetsahnak*, an anthology about missing and murdered Indigenous women, girls, and two-spirit people, Anderson (2018: xxiv) effectively argues that this ongoing crisis impacting Indigenous people all across North America is grounded in the everyday realities of *settler colonialism* (the system of oppression suppressing Indigenous peoples' sovereignty and livelihood): "We wish to foreground that the MMIWG2S crisis and related trauma is part of a daily, lived experience for Indigenous women and families." Later in the anthology, Helen Knott (2018) explains her embodied reaction to this ongoing ordinary trauma: "Every time I see a photo of an Indigenous woman or girl who has gone missing, I feel my spirit tighten inside of me." This crisis has been taking place for centuries, it impacts large numbers of Indigenous people, and it is neither accidental nor reducible to individual experiences. Moreover, the widespread absence of concern or resistance to this crisis outside of Indigenous communities – the fact that in my entire 3½ years working at a shelter for victims/survivors of sexual and domestic violence, I never learned about the connections between settler colonialism and gendered violence – reveals the function of settler normativity and structural violence in discourses of trauma and practices of crisis response.

Further, the silence surrounding the MMIWG2S crisis reveals how the conceptualization and social framing of trauma readily stray from objectivity and political neutrality into alignment with prevailing forms of inequity and injustice. Maurice Stevens

(2009: 1) argues that trauma has never been disencumbered of political meaning:

> As one might expect, trauma has also been racialized, sexualized, gendered, and classed from its inception. In fact, from its first applications in the explanation of symptoms deriving from railway accidents, trauma has never really functioned transparently or equitably and has never been an unencumbered descriptive term.

In other words, trauma has not just become tangled with power over the course of its history, but rather power has been present from the earliest uses of trauma as a theoretical concept. Indeed, my need to carve out this space for social justice theory in the discourses of trauma, in this space where such considerations are frequently absented, demonstrates the urgency of attending to these harmful meanings and intentionally dismantling or transforming them. For trauma to be useful in the ways social justice activists need it to be, it must first be torn apart and then sewn back together in queer new forms – and we must always remember the stitches.

Privatized, medicalized, and pathologized narratives of trauma centre extraordinary trauma and marginalize/silence ordinary trauma precisely because the latter is a manifestation of the dehumanization of people based on their social positions and, therefore, is an expected by-product of systems of power; that is, while extraordinary trauma is most often attributed to something beyond the affected person's control and something for which they can readily be forgiven (e.g. a car accident, a natural disaster), the same is not true for ordinary trauma. Systems of oppression condition us to regard ordinary traumatic experience as an expected outcome of who someone is and/or what they do; power naturalizes or normalizes ordinary traumatic experiences among dehumanized people, and in doing so, functions to limit and contain resistance to the social/political order. It encourages us to internalize the belief that "this is just how things are" and to doubt that change is necessary and possible.

Ordinary trauma comes from systems of oppression that dehumanize and harm oppressed people, but in order to excuse and invisibilize such violence, these systems make it seem as if harm was inevitable or that oppressed peoples are to blame for the harms they experience. For instance, discourses of *biological determinism* and *gender fatalism* make violent futures appear inevitable because of an imagined biological and/or psychological inferiority (Ahmed 2017). Emma Jane Tseris (2013: 2), for instance, writes:

> [A] large proportion of interventions for trauma, despite the use of the word *trauma*, continue to be informed by assumptions about the biological basis of women's emotional distress – assumptions that privilege diagnostic assessments as the foundation of effective work – that increasingly rely on neurobiological understandings that frame interventions and devalue interventions that involve social change and activism.

Tseris (2013: 5) elaborates that increased attention to neuroscience and the medicalization/pathologization of trauma "often implies a deterministic relationship between experiences of abuse and deficits" while neglecting the sociopolitical conditions of inequity and injustice. In doing so, the context in which the trauma came into being, along with the distributions of power underlying it, fades from view so that the individual comes under interrogation rather than an oppressive social order. This perceptual shift comprises a refusal of the urgent need for social transformation and redistributions of power in favour of a more simplistic, regulable account of individual deviation/transgression. Writing about racism, Bell (2010: 3) explains that "[a] myopic focus on the individual, idiosyncratic, and unique preclude[s] a critical view of racial dynamics across time and space that would explain more accurately events in context." Bell's claim is true of ordinary trauma as well as the many intersecting systems of oppression that underlie it.

This concept of ordinary trauma is needed because prevailing discourses about trauma still ignore, discount, reject, or otherwise leave unacknowledged/unconsidered the implications of systems of oppression for lived experiences of traumatic harm. Hala Khouri (2019) asserts this issue: "What the trauma informed framework often fails to explicitly name is systemic or institutionalized trauma." This noteworthy omission continues in many places despite the pervasiveness of discourses of trauma as well as the abundance of literature about social justice. Indeed, conversations about trauma circulate all over the place from social media to clinics to buses to classrooms – to the point where trauma's meaning has become so muddied that Lauren Berlant (2011: 10) advocates for an different concept altogether: *crisis ordinariness*. Berlant says that while trauma does occur all of the time, is present all around us, and is embedded in the everyday realities of people's lives, the discourse circulating about trauma render it both extraordinary and excessive; for Berlant, the idea of crisis, which she argues is "embedded in the ordinary," better represents the harmful experience of life under oppressive social systems, like neoliberalism.

While I agree with her premise here, I am not ready to give up on trauma as an analytic tool and resource for understanding; I am yet unwilling to concede trauma to the digestive tracts of power because I believe it still holds vital nourishment for myself and for the people I love. Like Cvetkovich (2003), I maintain that reclaiming trauma means turning it over onto its head, theorizing from the particular, the intimate, the ordinary, and positioning it in relation to the most impacted peoples instead of the most advantaged; we need to make trauma our own, and we need to stop squeezing ourselves into somebody else's narrative. We must venture from the margins to the centre until the centre shifts entirely.

Extraordinary Versus Ordinary Trauma

A primary distinction between extraordinary trauma and ordinary trauma has to do with the influence systems of oppression exert over individuals' experiences of harm: extraordinary trauma is most often accidental and the outcome of individual choices, such as enduring a life-threatening injury when hiking across the Grand Canyon or playing in a full-contact sport. Ordinary trauma, on the other hand, is an outcome of being positioned on the disadvantaged side of systems that produce widespread inequity and injustice, such as when families lose their homes or get evicted from their apartments as the result of economic injustice within capitalism that leads them into poverty. In this sense, extraordinary trauma tends to emerge from accidental/unintentional experiences, whereas ordinary trauma is always connected to historically mediated and socially distributed experiences of harm (i.e. systems of power working as they were meant to). As a result, people can most often (but not always) identify extraordinary trauma as emanating from particular moments. Conversely, at a community-based workshop I attended a few years ago about trauma and trauma-informed care, people spoke of ordinary trauma as manifesting in a fear of police, in being "triggered by whiteness," and in anxiety over being taken from their parents by Immigration and Customs Enforcement (ICE). One participant powerfully stated, "most of my trauma is just being black."

Extraordinary trauma is immediately noticeable as such because it stands apart from other experiences, but ordinary trauma is so normalized that people may just accept it without a second thought, and we may think "this is just the way things are, this is just a part of life." With extraordinary trauma, there is time to stop, notice, and reflect on harmful experiences – there is a moment to catch your breath and leave or move away from the traumatic event – but ordinary trauma is much more anaerobic, and the people who become familiar with it can often hardly process things before something else happens. In an interview about racial trauma, Erlanger Turner (cited in Meadows-Fernandez 2017) states, for instance, that "it's hard to recover from one incident before another occurs." This compressed or non-existent recovery time is present as well with other sorts of trauma rooted in oppression. Realities of ordinary trauma are much more continuous or at least scattered across time and place, in the same way that power is not consolidated in any single location but dispersed throughout society and ever-present (Spade 2011).

I am not claiming that one form of traumatic experience is necessarily more or less extreme than another, or that one ought to be prioritized above the other; rather, my assertion is

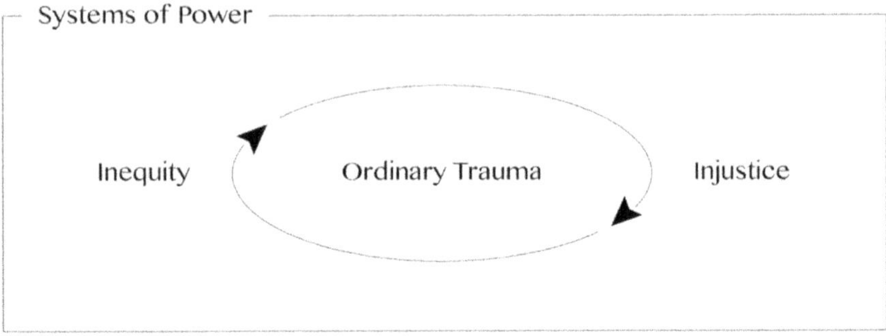

FIGURE 1.1 A representation of the relationship between trauma, systems of power, and inequity/injustice. Ordinary trauma emerges as systems of power both normalize and violently distribute inequity and injustice in favour of particular people at the expense of other, less advantaged, systemically dehumanized people.

that extraordinary trauma tends to make disruptions or points of departure between expectation and lived experience while ordinary trauma emerges in the spaces where lived experiences of harm come to be *expected*, even if they are not acknowledged as such by the impacted person. Extraordinary trauma carries an element of surprise that ordinary trauma more often lacks or subdues. In the place of surprise and disruption, ordinary trauma is bound up in an overarching narrative of dominance that both rationalizes and invisiblizes violence, often to the point where actions, processes, systems, and structures that cause harm are easily able to refuse accountability. Figure 1.1 provides a visual representation of the relationship between trauma and systems of oppression.

One of my goals in offering a theory of ordinary trauma is to critique the dividing line between trauma and not trauma; to unsettle normative constructions of trauma in our traumatocracy. Carter (2019: 84) asserts that "[j]ust as all disability is constituted through the (false and oversimplified) binary of disabled or abled, embodiments of trauma are also constituted through the unmarked binary of traumatized or untraumatized." Through diagnostic criteria and other sorts of assessments, such as those provided in the DSM-V, dominant imaginaries of trauma come to embrace a line of demarcation between legitimate traumatic experiences/traumatized people and others that do not belong and are, therefore, regarded as unworthy or recognition and consideration. People often have a "very powerful and felt sense that we know what we mean" when we talk about trauma (Stevens 2009) – a sense of where that line falls and who belongs on which side of it – yet the boundaries of trauma are actually murkier, more fluid, than many of us are prepared to admit.

This theory of ordinary trauma seeks to create space to recognize things that are often not recognized as traumatic as well as people removed from the dominant conceptualization of trauma; it is a space-making concept as well as a narrative concept that situates experience holistically, so that we can more accurately theorize the connection between more extreme modes of violence and everyday forms of violence to which many of us become accustomed. In bridging these experiences, the concept of ordinary trauma aims to disrupt our certainty, especially as it originates from power, by centring the experiences and needs of people on the margins, the people who, much of the time, we do not think of when we define trauma – the ordinarily forgotten and displaced people existing along the periphery, in the shadows of consciousness.

To be clear, the distinction I am drawing between ordinary trauma and extraordinary trauma has little to do with the severity of harm. Both can take on more severe and less severe forms, and the severity of either is experienced relative to the impacted people. Sexual violence, for instance, is almost always ordinary trauma whether it comes in the form of catcalling, sexual commodification, or sexual assault. For me, the differences between these types of trauma are more dependent on how acts of violence get reinterpreted under systems of oppression as normal, acceptable, and excusable. It also has to do with the way that certain bodyminds become marked as abusable and violable, if not outright deserving of the trauma(s) they are subjected to, and how other bodyminds are given the authority to commit traumatizing acts against them. As I will discuss in the upcoming chapter about dehumanization, a significant underlying factor here are constructions of *innocence* and *guilt*, which influence how people are seen as deserving of harm and punishment versus care and support (Kandaswamy 2006).

Furthermore, ordinary trauma is always iterative and never isolated. Even sexual assault and rape, which may seem extreme/severe, are ordinary because they are embedded in cultures that normalize their presence and, oftentimes, are more willing to blame and punish harmed people than to hold people accountable for harming others. Much of the time, the very idea of punishing people for committing sexual assault is viewed as worse that the sexual assault itself, which is a point I will discuss more in Chapter 4 when I write about victim-blaming and fragility. The people most likely to be exposed to sexual violence (women, queer/trans folks, Indigenous people and other people of colour, disabled peoples) continually have our bodies violated and/or taken from us by those more advantaged. Think about how often people from these oppressed social locations are treated as if our bodies exist solely or primarily for the sexual pleasure of someone else. Think about how often we are treated like deviants, freaks, subordinates, or property. Think about how being treated in this way can easily translate into more severe forms of sexual trauma, such as incest or corrective rape (Levins Morales 1998).

Throughout their book about sexual violence and the colonization or North America, Andrea Smith (2005) repeatedly comes back to the disturbing idea that Indigenous women become "inherently rapable" under White supremacy as means of promoting conquest and empire. *Rapable* literally means capable of being raped – as in people can acceptably and typically without consequence commit sexual violence against them. The term "rapable" only makes sense within a context of ordinary trauma wherein sexual and other forms of systemic harm/structured violence are pervasive and not immediately regarded as wrong. Ordinary trauma means that violence, inequity, and injustice have become an aspect of the everyday lives of disadvantaged peoples, often woven into our normal routines, presumed to be present at all times, or at least potentially so.

As another example, I think about the episode of *Designing Women* that was concerned with HIV/AIDS and the deaths of queer folks, whose existence is often portrayed as un-human to the point of not being worthy of continued life, in need of containment, and even marked for death. One of the main characters asserts, "As far as I'm concerned, this disease [AIDS] has one thing going for it: it is killing all the right people" (1987). Traumatic experiences become ordinary when people who bear witness to them are supported in saying "[they are] killing all the right people." This history and ongoing harm of the HIV/AIDS crisis, the policing and incarceration of queer and trans folks, and the sustained efforts to refuse queer and trans identities all speak to the ways in which systemic harm against people deviating from sexual and gender norms is rationalized and embedded in the social order (Spade 2011). The "Civil Right Removal Act" passed in 2025 by the Iowa Legislature removes protections for and legalizes discrimination against people based on gender identity. This passing of this act as well as the fact that it is plausible demonstrates the extent to which queer and trans people are acceptably harmed, the degree to which we are made to expect violence against us and live with the knowledge that so many others don't even see us as worthy of basic civil rights, such as housing or work.

This hateful sentiment appears throughout the history of the United States in the government's ongoing legacy of abandoning people to die (e.g. by the gutting of Medicare and Medicaid), of doing almost nothing to regulate corporate exploitation of those struggling to access basic human needs, of building hateful ideologies in order to promote violent political agendas, and so on. The central argument I am making here is that systems of power serve to establish and direct ordinary trauma by inequitably distributing harm, access, and care. They consolidate power by normalizing, invisiblizing, and rationalizing the abuse and violation of oppressed peoples coded as less-than-fully human. White supremacy, settler colonialism, patriarchy, ableism, capitalism, heteronormativity, xenophobia, and other systems of oppression create shared experiences of trauma among socially and materially disadvantaged people as they work to ensure that actual or threatened death and the potential for harm are almost always present.

In talking about shared experiences of harm, I want to recognize that oppressed peoples do not have identical experiences – there is a lot of variation in the harms that different systems of oppression inflict as well as in individuals' experiences under any specific system. In the example of physical or sexual violence against queer and trans people, not everyone within this group has experienced the same kinds of violence or to the same degree. However, I will describe in the upcoming chapters how witnessing or learning about acts of violence against people with shared social positions can often lead to the realization of shared vulnerabilities and fears, particularly the harrowing feeling that "it could have been me." I describe such a realization as *transference*: the lingering echoes of ordinary traumatic harm can resonate or transfer between oppressed peoples given that the origin of the harm is shared between the individual harmed person and the witnesses or observers who identify with that person. This concept aligns with Prentis Hemphill's crucial recognition that "[t]rauma does not live neatly in one body. It necessarily spreads. It spreads relationally and it spreads across time" (2023). With ordinary trauma, individual people may directly experience harm, but the harm is never contained or limited just to them.

Transference is another characteristic of ordinary trauma, for whether or not we are directly traumatized, disadvantaged people often cannot fully protect ourselves or others from the traumatization of people like us, people who could have been us. In a later chapter, I discuss how victim-blaming and other defensive tactics emerge as a tool of othering that allows for distancing from the realization of how close we are to harm. These defensive tactics, in part, reduce or defer the psychic impacts of transference and therefore can be important survival strategies for oppressed people. However, they can also inhibit critical connection between oppressed people and, in doing so, serve to uphold systems of oppression by reinforcing or naturalizing logics of dominance. Accordingly, defensive strategies like victim-blaming both emerge from the threat of ordinary traumatic harms and extend the potential for such harms to continue on into the future.

Structural Violence and Integration

Ordinary trauma describes the complicated, systemic ways that disadvantaged/oppressed people's experiences of traumatic harm become unquestioned, normalized, and expected within the existing social and political order; put in another way, ordinary trauma names how traumatic harm becomes an ordinary fact of disadvantaged peoples' lives. This theory is one that endeavours to recognize the systemic, structural realities of oppression: it maintains that the sources of trauma in disadvantaged people's lives are tied to the ways in which society has been arranged to dehumanize, violate, exploit, and eventually dispose of us. Describing the concept of "structural oppression," Iris Young (2011: 41) explains that oppression

> refers to systemic constraints on groups that are not necessarily the result of the intentions of a tyrant. Oppression in this sense is structural, rather than the result of a few people's choices or policies. Its causes are embedded in unquestioned norms, habits, and symbols, in the assumptions underlying institutional rules and the collective consequences of following those rules. . . . We cannot eliminate this structural oppression by getting rid of the rulers or making some new laws, because oppressions are systemically reproduced in major economic, political, and cultural institutions.

The harms of oppression are beyond any individual person; harmed people and harm doers alike are acting within a social context that has already been set up to inequitably distribute harm and access to resources. This statement is not about excusing people's actions or the importance of accountability, but rather it is a recognition that ordinary trauma arises from structural oppression and, therefore, needs systems-level solutions in addition to individual and/or community approaches. While ordinary trauma may include specific people, it is not reducible to those people – it includes the broader historical, social, and political conditions that underlie and contribute to experiences/enactments of harm. Being "structural" means that ordinary trauma isn't accidental but intentionally *manufactured* through "unquestioned norms, habits, and symbols," each of which contribute to the (re)construction of power and privilege across normative lines (Spade 2011).

The notion of *complex trauma* comes closest to aligning with this understanding of ordinary trauma, for it recognizes traumatization as the accumulation of objectionable and harmful events in an individual's life rather than as an outcome of a single shattering moment. Bessel van der Kolk (2005: 402) explains that complex trauma is meant to describe "the experience of multiple, chronic and prolonged, developmentally adverse traumatic events, most often of an interpersonal nature (eg, sexual or physical abuse, war, community violence) and early-life onset." According to this definition, complexity comes from the inability to identity a precise moment or a single causal precursor to traumatization as a result of histories of repeated abuses and/or violations. Moreover, I would add that complexity refers to the non-linearity of healing and restoration from traumatic harm as well as to variability in individuals' reactions to trauma as they work through and make sense from their experiences.

However, the idea of complex trauma, as it shows up in the clinical and psychiatric literature, still falls short in explanatory power because it is treated as both exceptional and individual, rather than *mundane* and grounded in oppressive social arrangements. Accordingly, trauma becomes complex because of the twists and turns of individual histories and mental states, while the intricate and difficult-to-grasp workings of systems of power are left to exceed the boundaries of this concept. Even when psychiatrists/clinicians willingly acknowledge the impact systems of power have on individual bodyminds, their approach to healing typically remains fixated on "curing" individual bodyminds (e.g. giving people tools to process living under oppressive systems). And even though some therapists do actively take part in social movements, resistance to injustice goes beyond the scope of their responsibilities. My goal is stating this point is not to undermine the value of therapy or psychiatry – indeed, they are vital sources of healing and survival for many people – but rather to name the need for more, especially when dealing with ordinary trauma.

Judith Herman (1992a), who first developed the concept of complex trauma, explains it as the result of prolonged and repeated exposure to traumatic harms wherein the harmed person is trapped in some state of imposed captivity, such as in the cases of domestic violence and child abuse. In this sense, the complexity of trauma is partly the outcome of being unable to escape; the captivity in itself constitutes a form of psychic damage that exacerbates specific acts of violence, abuse, and neglect. While it is true that complex traumatic harm does often involve some form of extended captivity, I want to challenge Herman's claim that "prolonged, repeated trauma can occur only where the victim is in a state of captivity, under the control of the perpetrator" (377a). This quote does a few things that distinguish complex trauma from the account of ordinary trauma I offer here.

First, it suggests that captivity is primarily the outcome of interpersonal relations instead of the broader social, political, and historical forces working to normalize and promote violent forms of interaction. Consequently, her framing of complex trauma, like dominant accounts of trauma more generally, becomes estranged from critical analysis of structural oppression, meaning that it leaves too limited a space in which to consider the implications of structural violence. For disadvantaged people, captivity is often an unavoidable and normalized state of being, regardless of whether there is a specific person seeking control through dominance. Second, from this understanding, preventing the continuation of complex trauma becomes a matter of removing individuals from the captivity of harm doers – a matter of changing their personal relationships. Again, this analysis fails to address the ways that we are all directed towards violence by systems of oppression, such that even when disadvantaged people do escape violent relationships, it can often be expected or presumed that the violence against them will continue, especially if they occupy multiple devalued social positions. For they are not just captives of abusive others; they are captives of structural oppression.

In addition to these divergences from complex trauma, ordinary trauma is also distinct from *collective trauma* (even though it is typically collective and/or communal in nature). Defining collective trauma, psychologist Charles Figley (2019) writes:

> Unlike individual trauma, which affects a single person or small group, collective trauma is experienced by a larger

> population. This makes the induction and reduction process for collective trauma different: Individuals can be diagnosed with post-traumatic stress disorder, but we don't have an equivalent diagnosis for collective trauma. Our knowledge about collective trauma and how to treat it is not as expansive as individual trauma.

Ordinary trauma is more than just the collective experience of traumatic harm, for this term does not take into account power relations existing among harmed people or the differences in their social position. Ordinary trauma asserts that the harmed people have been, in some way, made vulnerable to trauma, that they were systemically targeted or structurally set up to be more intensely impacted and frequently less able to access resources for healing and transformation. Collective trauma does not have this same requirement or even necessarily a capacity to recognize power.

Furthermore, even within the experience of collective trauma, there is often great variation between harmed peoples, which means that while some people may come into a space of ordinary trauma, others may not. I think here about the differences in traumatic experiences based largely on race, class, gender, and ability seen in the aftermath of Hurricane Katrina and other "natural" disasters. I think about how the structural oppression of capitalism and White supremacy and ableism caused the hurricane's enormous damage to be experienced disproportionately by the city's most disenfranchised residents, who were both neglected and actively betrayed by the government and left to fend for themselves; how they became expected causalities while the more advantaged people were provided with pathways to life (Capeheart and Milovanovic 2007; Giroux 2006). Collective trauma was certainly present here, but harm was not equally distributed. For some, the trauma was extraordinary and shocking, but for others, it was an extension of other pre-existing injustices – extreme and exceptional, to be sure, but build from an already established foundation of inequity.

Furthermore, one of the most central areas of departure between ordinary trauma and other forms of trauma has to do with the *integration* of harm. Ogden (2006: 66) says that: "Trauma refers to any threatening, overwhelming experiences that we cannot integrate." This general sentiment is echoed across trauma theorists (e.g. Treleaven 2018): traumatic experiences are those which stand out, that cannot be forgotten, that do not make emotional or spiritual or logical sense; those experiences that our bodyminds refuse to accept as a part of us and, therefore, work to expel in a multitude of ways, such as through self-harm or physical illness. However, in the instance of ordinary trauma, this notion of integration becomes an issue: it is precisely because *traumatic experiences make sense*, because we can explain them and point to a source, because they can fit neatly into our expectations, because they do not just happen to us in exceptional/extraordinary moments – it is because we *can* integrate these harms, are expected/pressured to integrate them, that trauma materializes.

Within the "traumatocracy" (Carter 2019), things that are regarded as difficult or impossible to integrate are oftentimes considered legitimate; the difficulty of integration becomes a key determination of which harms are acceptable/unacceptable. Conversely, the things people are accused of holding onto for too long, the things that people refuse to or just will not "get over" despite expectations for them to move on, the things people should not remember or are compelled to leave in the past in order to "move on with their lives" – these are the things that tend to constitute ordinary trauma. From a different vantage point, these are the things that society integrates too readily, because society was and *is* structured to integrate them, to hold them indefinitely as part of its normal functioning.

What does integration mean in the contexts of ordinary trauma? Simply put, ordinary trauma transpires where the integration of harmful experiences is expected and governed by violent social structures, structures which were created to uphold particular distributions of power relative to race, class, gender, sexuality, ability, and other sites of oppression. The presence of ordinary trauma reveals the ways in which people have been systemically conditioned to integrate harm – to perceive specific forms of violence (i.e. structural violence) as unworthy of critical attention or radical response beyond perhaps a momentary charitable recognition. In this sense, can integration be a form of traumatic experience *in itself* wherein inequity and injustice become so ingrained in the social order as to also become integrate-able with our past experiences of harm in a society that devalues and hates oppressed people? Shouldn't we actually strive to politicize and defy integration as a means of *dislodging* and *dismantling* the normativity underlying ordinary trauma?

If the problem of ordinary trauma can be summed up by the fact of what people can integrate and are expected to integrate, then the healing and transformation of trauma has to involve a sustained movement against integration that compels people to re-examine what we have allowed to become part of us, who we have allowed ourselves to become in the presence of our own and other people's suffering. Expelling the social conditions that promote ordinary trauma requires that we actively question how it is that inequity and injustice have become so normalized and justified that people can readily absorb them into their view of the world. Dis-integration, therefore, is a viable, necessary aspect of healing and transformation away from systems of oppression. This refusal of integration requires us to develop an alternative understanding of *resilience* that promotes our collective liberation over repeated exposures to oppressive harms.

Resilience as Oppression Versus Resilience as Connection

When trauma becomes ordinary, rather than being granted compassion, validation, support, and relevant resources for healing, harmed peoples are treated as if they are making too big a deal out of their experiences. In place of authentic healing and transformation, systems of oppression that underlie ordinary trauma compel disadvantaged people to absorb harm into our bodies, minds, and spirits and become accustomed to holding it in increasing quantities. The compulsory absorption and sustained holding of harm reveal power's warped meaning of *resilience*, which has, much of the time, come to refer to detrimental, disabling processes of forced integration and forced assimilation – processes of pressuring us to take things into ourselves instead of refusing to hold them any longer. Sara Ahmed (2017: 189) explains:

> We can see how resilience is a technology of will, or even functions as a command: be willing to bear more; be stronger so you can bear more. We can understand too how resilience becomes a deeply conservative technique, one especially well-suited to governance: you encourage bodies to strengthen so they will not succumb to pressure; so they can keep taking it; so they can take more of it. Resilience is the requirement to take more pressure; such that the pressure can be gradually increased.

Here we come upon another notable aspect of ordinary trauma: through governing concepts like integration/resilience, ordinary trauma is contained, commanded, and compelled such that it can be steadily amplified. The more that people are expected to bear, the more harm can be done to them, the worse the exploitation and violence affecting them can become. If dis-integration is a form of resistance to power, then the systemic corruption of resilience is how power conditions and coerces people out of this practice; resilience is suppressing and silencing, it contains and isolates to generate complicity. The fact of being resilient indicates sustained survival, a refusal to succumb or surrender to oppression, but in indicating these things, it also reveals a system or structure that has not changed, a world that has remained essentially the same in its willingness to harm oppressed peoples.

Dominant discourses of resilience too readily align with the neoliberal imperatives towards hyperindividualism or personal responsibility in the sense that they pressure harmed people to take charge of their own healing and wellness while requesting as few social or structural supports as possible. Oftentimes, key social supports come with expectations that they be "earned" or only accessed by "deserving" people (i.e. those with the proper social positions and who have experience accepted forms of harm). Jijian Voronka (2019: 9) writes:

> Resiliency places responsibility on individuals to activate and self-govern wellness, which complements neoliberal healthcare reform. Resiliency policy and practice models offer cost saving measures for public health and social care systems by diverting patients out of formal medical systems and into self-help, positive thinking, and affective governances, while normalizing the uncertainties associated with global neoliberal capitalisms.

The manufactured need for resilience comes into being because of what we are expected to hold, what other people will not hold with and/or for us, even when they have participated in constructing a need for holding it. Resilience as a tool of neoliberalism is disciplinary in the Foucauldian sense: it normalizes the imperative to self-govern wellness through alignment with dominant modes of being, doing, thinking, and feeling. This self-governing, in turn, excuses dominant social institutions, governments, and corporations, as well as advantaged people, from being accountable for harms they cause, and, by doing so, resilience generates social and material resources for dominant groups.

Robin James (2015: 7) argues that neoliberal modes of resilience generate surplus value for power:

> Instead of expending resources to *avoid* damage, resilience discourse *recycles damage into more resources*. Resilience discourse thus follows a very specific logic: first, damage is incited and made manifest; second, that damage is spectacularly overcome, and that overcoming is broadcast and/or shared, so that; third, the person who has overcome is rewarded with increased human capital, status, and other forms of recognition and recompense, because; finally, and most importantly, this individual's own resilience boosts society's resilience. The work this individual does to overcome their own damage generates surplus value for hegemonic institutions.

Through this logical script, the spectacle of overcoming harm through resilience transforms harm into something profitable that simultaneously maintains the expectation of individual responsibility for self-governing health and wellness and benefits systems and structures of power – often the same ones that caused harm in the first place – through the acquisition of surplus resources. Society's resilience here refers to the capacity to postpone or limit social change, to keep functioning as it currently is by absorbing greater levels of harm. Importantly, resilience is what must emerge in the absences of collective access and care – we become resilient through a traumatizing process of surviving inequity and injustice, of remaining alive against our manufactured disposability and disadvantage.

The neoliberal idea of resilience is one of repetition, of surviving over and again, that creates an illusion of progress. It is only by moving beyond discourses of resilience or fundamentally altering them that we can dismantle ordinary trauma and systemic or structural oppression. I think considering the etymology of resilience is useful here: resilience comes from the Latin word *resilīre* meaning to jump or leap back, which we could interpret as either to recoil or to rebound. In relation to ordinary trauma and systems of oppression, resilience often means leaping back into traumatizing conditions of inequity and injustice after recoiling from harm – that is rebounding to the world as it is to likely be harmed again. The very idea and expectation of resilience expose systems and structures that we must force ourselves back into in the first place, for if they were not already damaging us, we would not need to become resilient living under them.

David Treleaven (2018: 126) asserts that "resilience isn't meant to be a way to bypass areas of pain in our life. It also isn't meant to be a practice to cover over inequities or oppressive violence." And while I understand and do agree with his assertion on a particular level, I also recognize that this is precisely *the task* of resilience under neoliberalism, White supremacy, heteropatriarchy, ableism, and other oppressive systems. Actually, the next sentence in this quote captures the role of resilience I am describing here: "Instead resilience increases our capacity to be present with life as it is." Internally, such a capacity to be present is a valuable tool for survival, but externally, it too often manifests as complicity and stalled resistance, for the ability to be present under oppressive conditions too readily translates to a lessened impulse to advocate and mobilize for social change. Or, to recall Ahmed's words from above, learning to be present by developing resilience is a "deeply conservative technique" through which we come "to bear more."

However, in light of Treleaven's words and those of other theorists and activists whom I cite momentarily, I want to consider how resilience can be reclaimed, transformed into a healing, liberatory concept. I think it could be constructive to distinguish between resilience as a *tool of oppression* vs. resilience as a *tool for generating life* in response to oppressive systems or even more generally. Notably, the former account of resilience is one that promotes debility and death because it keeps on reproducing harm to limit the extent to which people can act out against systems of oppression; it increases our capacities to absorb or hold harm rather than our capacities to reduce and unmake harm. Thus, this version is neither restorative nor transformative, even as it pretends to be so. The alternative version, however, resilience as a tool for generating life, could be both restorative and transformative, but only if resilience underwent several substantive changes in meaning.

I am interested in advancing an understanding of resilience as a tool of recovery and critical learning from hardship in the context of loving, dependable, and accountable relationships and communities; resilience as the story of how we learn to show up for ourselves and each other within and beyond those moments where harm is present. I wonder whether instead of merely jumping back into adversity or oppressive environments, we could learn to persistently leap forward into accessible and just communities that provide us with things we need to imagine different worlds. Resilient in the sense that our creativity and radical dreaming stay with us for as long as we need them. Resilience as a tool of sustaining the radical imagination, which describes

> a process by which we collectively map 'what is,' narrate it as the result of 'what was,' and speculate on what 'might

> be' . . . which is a crucial aspect of the fundamentally political and always collective (though rarely autonomous) labour of reweaving the social world.
>
> (Haiven and Khasnabish 2010: iii)

Oppressive resilience exists in those contexts where we are expected to recover from harm and suffering that does not go away but rather intensifies and is perpetuated again and again on purpose. Could a more transformative resilience be that which increases our capacity to refuse or dismantle things contributing to what Mimi Khúc (2014) refers to as our *structured unwellness*? Janie Victoria Ward (2018) writes that resilience "is a process in which people dynamically and positively adapt within the context of adversity." It strikes me that "adapt" here could follow the same lines of thought as Ahmed's critique of resilience (e.g. we adapt to the weight of harm so that we might bear more), but could we not also think of adaptation as how we make sense of the shifting realities of oppression such that we can transform the spaces and the people around us? Havi Carel (2008: 81) states:

> Adaptability takes place on physical, psychological, social, and temporal levels . . . it is not a smooth process but a series of dialectic encounters of a body with an environment, of a demand with failure, and of failure with the need for modification.

What if liberatory resilience is actually the process of adapting to failure, of adapting by not modifying ourselves and instead carving out a liveable space in rejection? Returning to the earlier conversation about integration, is there a possibility of understanding resilience as a process of becoming more experienced in *dis*integration, in not succumbing to expectations of silence and forgiveness? Resilient in our resistance?

A resilient resistance, I believe, is an opportunity for us to form spaces of togetherness that welcome failure, that encourage failure even, so long as we are in a meaningful practice of unlearning harm and studying compassionate accountability and love. In such spaces, we could ask ourselves what it would mean to "shift understandings of survival and resilience from individual assets to spaces of solidarity, collective action, and culture-building and community identity" (Aubrecht and La Monica 2019). In other words, we could diverge from neoliberal discourses of resilience as a possession and source of self-control or governance and move toward an understanding of resilience as something created in communities filled with people invested in one another's life and well-being. For as Lucién Demaris (n.d.) tells us: "What makes a community of individuals resilient is not self-mastery or will – it is the quality, strength, and inclusivity of our relational bonds." Or, in the words of Judith Hermann (1992b), "[t]rauma de-humanizes the victim; the group restores her humanity."

I describe collective resilience as a built capacity to provide restorative and transformative access and care to ourselves and the people in community with us through critical attention to the sources of our harm and through commitments to share responsibly in the processes of liberatory world-building. At times, collective resilience might involve providing collective care through something like an accountability circle. At other times, it might mean showing up for an event or demonstration in whatever ways we are able. It might also mean providing a community garden or food pantry or fighting for affordable food and housing. Any actions which reduce the presence of harm and promote continued life among those most impacted by systems of oppression. As I reach the end of this conversation about resilience, I want to conclude with the words of Cara Page (2013) who shares with us her definition of collective resilience:

> Being able to transform inside of perhaps the worst conditions, but still on a cellular level being able to respond to, intervene, or transform what has been done to us or on us. And so as a Black Queer woman working in these movements understanding the possibility for us in the worst possible conditions to remember that we deserve dignity, honor and a way to look at how we can sustain our well being, in a society that has almost normalized our physical, emotional and spiritual degradation. That in and of itself is collective resilience.

References

Ahmed, Sara. *Living a Feminist Life*. Durham: Duke University Press, 2017.

Alaia, Rachael. "The Trauma of Western Culture and the Crisis of Climate Change." *Medium*. https://medium.com/@contact.rachael.alaia/the-traumas-of-climate-collapse-372109272dac (published August 30, 2019).

American Psychiatric Association. *Diagnostic and Statistical Manual of Mental Disorders* (3rd ed.). Washington, DC: American Psychiatric Publishing, 1986.

American Psychiatric Association. *Diagnostic and Statistical Manual of Mental Disorders* (4th ed.). Washington, DC: American Psychiatric Publishing, 2000.

American Psychiatric Association. *Diagnostic and Statistical Manual of Mental Disorders* (5th ed.). Washington, DC: American Psychiatric Publishing, 2013.

Anderson, Kim. "Introduction." In *Keetsahnak: Our Missing and Murdered Indigenous Sisters*, edited by Kim Anderson, Maria Campbell, and Christi Belcourt, xxi. Alberta: The University of Alberta Press, 2018.

Asian Communities for Reproductive Justice (ACJR). *A New Vision for Advancing Our Movement for Reproductive Health, Reproductive Rights and Reproductive Justice*. Oakland, CA: Asian Communities for Reproductive Justice, 2005.

Aubrecht, Katie and La Monica, Nancy. "Complexities of Survival and Resilience." *Canadian Journal of Disability Studies* 8, no. 4 (2019): 1–3.

Barlow, Jameta Nicole. "Resorting Optimal Black Mental Health and Reversing Intergenerational Trauma in an Era of Black Lives Matter." *Biography* 41, no. 4 (2018): 895–908.

Bell, Andrea, "Love and Connection: How Trauma Can Bring Us Closer Together." *Good Therapy*. https://www.goodtherapy.org/blog/love-connection-how-trauma-can-bring-us-closer-together-0905174 (published September 5, 2017).

Bell, Lee Anne. *Storytelling for Social Justice: Connecting Narrative and the Arts in Antiracist Teaching*. New York: Routledge, 2010.

Berlant, Lauren Gail. *Cruel Optimism*. Durham: Duke University Press, 2011.

Brown, Laura. "Not Outside the Range: One Feminist Perspective on Psychic Trauma." In *Trauma: Explorations in Memory*, edited by Cathy

Caruth, 100–112. Baltimore: The John Hopkins University Press, 1995.

Capeheart, Loretta and Milovanovic, Dragan. *Social Justice: Theories, Issues, and Movements*. Rutgers University Press, 2007.

Carel, Havi. *Illness: The Cry of the Flesh*. UK: Acumen, 2008.

Carter, Angela. "Disabling Trauma: Toward a Crip Critique of Post-Traumatic Stress Disorder." Ph.D. Dissertation. University of Minnesota, 2019.

Clare, Eli. *Brilliant Imperfection: Grappling with Cure*. Durham: Duke University Press, 2017.

Clare, Eli. *Exile and Pride: Disability, Queerness, and the Liberation*. Durham: Duke University Press, 1999.

Collins, Patricia Hill. *Black Feminist Thought: Knowledge, Consciousness, and the Politics of Empowerment*. New York: Routledge, 1990.

Crenshaw, Kimberlé. "Mapping the Margins: Intersectionality, Identity Politics, and Violence against Women of Color." *Stanford Law Review* 43, no. 6 (1991): 1241–1299.

Cvetkovich, Ann. *An Archive of Feelings: Trauma, Sexuality, and Lesbian Public Cultures*. Durham: Duke University Press, 2003.

Demaris, Lucién. "About Us—Relational Uprising." Accessed August 20, 2025. https://relationaluprising.org/mission (n.d.).

Designing Women. "Killing All the Right People." October 5, 1987.

Durazo, Ana Clarissa Rojas. "Medical Violence against People of Color and the Medicalization of Domestic Violence." In *Color of Violence: The Incite! Anthology*, edited by Incite! Women of Color Against Violence, 179–190. Durham: Duke University Press, 2006.

Figley, Charles. "Confronting and Treating Collective Trauma." *U.S. News and World Report*. https://www.usnews.com/news/best-countries/articles/2019-05-02/commentary-countries-need-to-treat-the-trauma-of-large-scale-attacks (published May 2, 2019).

generationFIVE. "Transformative Justice Handbook." *Generationfive.org*. http://www.generationfive.org/the-issue/transformative-justice/ (published June 2017).

Giroux, Henry. "Reading Hurricane Katrina: Race, Class, and the Biopolitics of Disposability." *College Literature* 33, no. 3 (2006): 171–196.

Goodkind, Jessica, Meredith, Hess Julia, Gorman, Beverely and Parker, Danielle. "'We're Still in a Struggle': Diné Resilience, Survival, Historical Trauma, and Healing." *Qualitative Health Research* 22, no. 8 (2012): 1019–1036.

Haiven, Max and Khasnabish, Alex. "What is the Radical Imagination? A Special Issue." *Affinities: A Journal of Radical Theory, Culture, and Action* 4, no. 2 (2010): i–xxxvii.

Hemphill, Prentis. "Transforming Our Systems, Transforming Ourselves: The Pivotal Role of Healing in Social Change Work." *Non-Profit Quarterly*. https://nonprofitquarterly.org/transforming-our-systems-transforming-ourselves-the-pivotal-role-of-healing-in-social-change-work/ (published February 13, 2023).

Herman, Judith Lewis. "Complex PTSD: A Syndrome in Survivors of Prolonged and Repeated Trauma." *Journal of Traumatic Stress* 5, no. 3 (1992a): 377–391.

Herman, Judith Lewis. *Trauma and Recovery*. New York: Basic Books, 1992b.

The Icarus Project. "Madness & Oppression: Paths to Personal Transformation & Collective Liberation." *NYCIcarus.org*. http://nycicarus.org/images/MadnessAndOppressionGuide-compressed.pdf (published 2015).

James, Robin. *Resilience & Melancholy: Pop Music, Feminism, Neoliberalism*. John Hunt Publishing, 2015.

Kandaswamy, Priya. "Innocent Victims and Brave New Laws: State Protection and the Battered Women's Movement." In *Nobody Passes: Rejecting the Rules of Gender and Conformity*, edited by Matt Sycamore, 83–94. Emeryville: Seal Press, 2006.

Keating, AnaLouise. "'Making New Connections': Transformational Multiculturalism in the Classroom." *Pedagogy* 4, no. 1 (2004): 93–117.

Khouri, Hala. "Trauma and Social Justice: Why We Can't Talk About One Without Including the Other." *Off the Mat*. https://www.offthematintotheworld.org/blog/2019/3/21/trauma-and-social-justice-why-we-cant-talk-about-one-without-including-the-other (published March 21, 2019).

Khúc, Mimi. "Critical Feeling." *Forum for Theological Exploration*. https://fteleaders.org/blog/critical-feeling (published December 17, 2014).

Knott, Helen. "Violence and Extraction: Stories from the Oil Fields." In *Keetsahnak: Our Missing and Murdered Indigenous Sisters*, edited by Kim Anderson, Maria Campbell, and Christi Belcourt, 147–160. Alberta: The University of Alberta Press, 2018.

Levins Morales, Aurora. *Medicine Stories: History, Culture and the Politics of Integrity*. Cambridge: South End Press, 1998.

Lorde, Audre. *Sister Outsider: Essays and Speeches*. New York: Ten Speed Press, 1984.

May, Vivian. *Pursuing Intersectionality: Unsettling Dominant Imaginaries*. New York: Routledge, 2015.

Meadows-Fernandez, Rochaun. "The Little Understood Mental-Health Effects of Racial Trauma." *TheCut.com*. https://www.thecut.com/2017/06/the-little-understood-mental-health-effects-of-racial-trauma.html (published June 23, 2017).

Naples, Nancy. "Deconstructing and Locating Survivor Discourse: Dynamics of Narrative, Empowerment, and Resistance for Survivors of Child Sexual Abuse." *Signs* 28, no. 4 (2003): 1151–1185.

Ogden, Stormy. "Pomo Woman, Ex-Prisoner, Speaks Out." In *Color of Violence: The Incite! Anthology*, edited by Incite! Women of Color against Violence, 164–169. Durham: Duke University Press, 2006.

Page, Cara. "Kindred Collective: Cara Page." *Kindred Southern Healing Justice Collective*. http://www.healingcollectivetrauma.com/cara-page.html (published 2013).

Smith, Andrea. *Conquest: Sexual Violence and American Indian Genocide*. New York City: South End Press, 2005.

Spade, Dean. *Normal Life: Administrative Violence, Critical Trans Politics, and the Limits of Law*. Durham: Duke University Press, 2011.

Stevens, Maurice. "From the Past Imperfect: Towards a Critical Trauma Theory." *Letters* 17, no. 2 (2009): 1–5.

Treleaven, David. *Trauma-Sensitive Mindfulness: Practices for Safe and Transformative Healing*. New York: W.W. Norton & Company, 2018.

Tseris, Emma Jane. "Trauma Theory Without Feminism? Evaluating Contemporary Understandings of Traumatized Women." *Affilia: Journal of Women and Social Work* 28, no. 2 (2013): 1–12.

van der Kolk, Bessel. "Developmental Trauma Disorder: Towards a Rational Diagnosis for Children with Complex Trauma Histories." *Psychiatric Annals* 33, no. 5 (2005): 401–408.

Voronka, Jijian. "Storytelling Beyond the Psychiatric Gaze: Resisting Resilience and Recovery Narratives." *Canadian Journal of Disability Studies* 8, no. 4 (2019): 8–30.

Ward, Janie Victoria. "Lessons in Resistance and Resilience." *Diversity and Democracy* 21, no. 1 (2018).

Young, Iris Marion. *Justice and the Politics of Difference*. Princeton: Princeton University Press, 2011.

2

Dehumanization: The Process of Making Trauma Ordinary

Dehumanization and Normalized Violence

In the previous chapter, I wrote about ordinary trauma as a matter of humanity: the peoples exposed to ordinary trauma – people whose encounters with traumatic harm are normalized, expected, perhaps even presumed – are routinely *dehumanized*, treated as if their humanity is questionable or somehow lesser than that of advantaged peoples. Systems of oppression effectively, and usually subconsciously, influence how people are perceived and valued as human and which come to be regarded as less-than-fully human. Speaking on a panel at the Women in the World Summit in 2018, actor Terry Crews offered his insight into how men are conditioned to view women as not "even all the way human" (cited in Aggeler 2018), which, according to him, is part of what makes acts of sexual objectification thinkable. Crews goes on to explain the deep aversion that many men feel when women do things that make them appear more human, such as when someone working in a strip club starts to talk about their life outside of that environment.

For Crews, men's ordinary, persistent failure to view women as "all the way human" is what enables them to participate in sexual objectification and, by extension, more severe acts of sexual aggression. I do not mean to argue that sex work is inherently

DOI: 10.4324/9781003716198-2

traumatic or that all sex workers have been traumatized – indeed, sex work is legitimate, provides a valuable service, and deserves respect as much as any other profession, despite the paternalistic responses from people speaking for sex workers (Daring 2018). Yet, I find that there is value in examining how widespread processes of dehumanization, such as sexual objectification, increase the likelihood of people encountering and interacting with one another in relatively prescribed ways that tend to be marked by unequal power relations. Furthermore, although Terry Crews offers the example of his experiences as a man attending a strip club, his discussion about masculinity and the dehumanization of women extends to other gendered spaces as well as other systems of oppression.

While there might be disagreement about what does and does not constitute trauma – it truly is subjective and relational – people who cause ordinary harm to others almost always have some preconceived image of the harmed person as an object existing for their own pleasure or fulfilment, or they produce that understanding through the traumatizing act. For example, in sexually assaulting another person, harm doers (typically men) seek to assert their control over and further dehumanize/disempower another (typically women, queer, or trans folks); sexual violence in this sense has an intrinsic connection to dominance and is not just about sex or pleasure (NCADV 2018). Systemic dehumanization is one way disadvantaged people become objects of what Lorde (1984) names the *pornographic*, which describes a denial of power through the suppression of true sensation and feeling. For acts of sexual violence, the harmed person ultimately becomes regarded as a less-than-fully human object existing for the gratification of the harm doer rather than a complete and fully human person.

Sometimes, harm doers intentionally target the people that they have come to view as less-than-fully human because they feel entitled to the "objects" of their desire or because their socialization into a position of dominance encourages them to view these others as existing for their gratification or benefit. At other times, dehumanization is about gaining access and superiority to somebody who was previously out of range. Trauma simultaneously emerges from and reinforces dehumanization of oppressed peoples as advantaged people and social institutions aim to secure the control systems of power promised to them. As I discuss more in the chapter about fragility, trauma can also be a consequence of resistance to normative hierarchies wherein advantaged people violently lash out in response to unfulfilled promises of dominance, obedience, and/or access to dehumanized others – in other words, ordinary trauma can be the *punishment* imposed on oppressed people who attempt to move against or refuse the sense of entitlement that systems of oppression cultivate in more advantaged people.

In each of these examples, ordinary trauma is bound to assertions and refusals of humanity: oppressive constructions of humanity serve to empower some people while making others more vulnerable to traumatic harm. Systems of oppression influence ideas about humanity as a means to distribute harm away from people atop social hierarchies towards oppressed people at the bottom. This effect is not just true of heteropatriarchy and men's treatment of women, but rather manifests in unique, specific ways across multiple different systems and structures. For instance, disability justice activist Stacey Milbern (cited in Berne et al. 2018: 247) asserts: "for people with disabilities it feels like survival every day is just about proving your humanity." Similarly, Connor (2014: 120) writes: "Akin to racism, sexism, heterosexism, and ageism, ableism signifies the belief that people lacking one or more characteristics do not qualify as fully human." As a result of not qualifying as "fully human," the logics of power teach us that oppressed people may justifiably be exposed to ordinary harm in the forms of marginalization, exploitation, domination, and so on.

Further, we need to think about this issue *intersectionally*, by giving critical attention to how systems/structures of oppression overlap and interlock, such that people will be differently impacted based upon the multitude of their identities. An able-bodied, transwoman of colour for example will be subjected to dehumanization differently from a White poor disabled man, even though they may both experience ordinary trauma. Accordingly, dehumanization is a convoluted, contextual, and compounding process: the unbalanced extent to which people are perceived as fully human is not static or constant, but shifts according to the situations people find themselves in as well as the needs of power, which can produce temporary and contextual recognitions of humanity. For example, White men may be more willing to accept the humanity of White women in order to shore up racial power, to create a united front in the name of White supremacy. Similarly, White women might extend recognition to women of colour in moments when solidarity against male dominance requires collective resistance, but then withdraw such recognition later on, choosing to return to the ranks of racial power rather than continuing a humanizing praxis of accountability (Russo 2016).

However, such contextual humanity, which can itself become an aspect of ordinary trauma when it is taken away, is never enough for true equity or social justice, for liberation is neither fleeting nor temporary but all-encompassing and transformative. The end of ordinary trauma solely comes from the true, lasting abolition of dehumanization and *human exceptionalism* for all people. Human exceptionalism refers to an oppressive belief that humans are not only different from nature but also superior to it – that in some way the world was created for humans and, therefore, that we are entitled to control and possess other life forms (Russell and Semenko 2016). Dehumanization carries the power to distribute/normalize ordinary trauma because to be regarded as less-than-fully human is to be defined as less deserving of power and control in a society built on logics of human exceptionalism. I discuss this concept more in the following section of this chapter.

The perpetual assault systems of power wage against the humanity of oppressed people are both absolute and unforgiving, but the degree to which individual people internalize this view of humanity is much more complex and shifting. For all people existing within our unjust and inequitable society, dehumanization is a relational construct, meaning the degree to which people become recognized as fully human or less-than-fully human emerges from both their positionality and the positionalities of the people around them as well as the pieces of them that transcend systems of oppression. Within social hierarchies, people are unlikely to view themselves or similarly positioned people as less-than-fully human – although internalized dehumanization/oppression is a harsh reality, so much so that Beth Berila (2015) argues it should be regarded as a form of ordinary trauma in itself.

As a queer and trans person, I am privileged enough to be able to recognize the humanity in other queer and trans folks in a way that many straight cisgender people are conditioned not to. My positionality, in this sense, empowers me to view queer and trans people in a different way than people who occupy other social positions, people who are conditioned to view queer and trans folks as something less than human. Susan Stryker (1994: 238), for instance, writes that: "I find a deep affinity between myself as a transsexual woman and the monster in Mary Shelley's Frankenstein. Like the monster, I am too often perceived as less than fully human due to the means of my embodiment." This perception is something I have been able to resist and unlearn as I have come to embrace my own gender and sexuality.

Yet, the more advantaged aspects of my social position, such as my Whiteness, create unique barriers to seeing the humanity of, for instance, Black, Indigenous, and other people of colour. While I am personally committed to racial justice and I do not willingly harbour racial prejudices, White supremacy seeps into my core, as it does all White people. In order for me to see people of colour as fully human, I have to make conscious efforts to grapple with and overcome my internalized racism, and I have to acknowledge the extent to which my life has been structured by the ordinary abuses and violations of White supremacy. I have to actively choose humanity above power, and I must do it over and over again. This struggle is the uphill climb or liberation for advantaged people: we have to keep striving to move forward or we will be yanked back by the "gravitational pull" of systems of oppression (Crass 2013, cited in Russo 2016).

At the same time as people tend to see humanity in others at/above their position, the many different hierarchies of advantage twist and turn around one another so that nothing is ever so simple. Indeed, intersectionality makes it so that even people who share some things in common, such as experiences of violence or exploitation, do not always extend recognition of humanity to one another. *Horizontal hostility* (Lorde 1984) names how advantaged people turn disadvantaged people against each other in order to maintain their power. For example, wealthy people actively strive to convince poor White workers that the source of economic insecurity is (Brown) immigrants and other people of colour, instead of corporate exploitation, market deregulation, and union busting. Even though poor Whites and poor people of colour share a similar economic position, poor Whites are encouraged to see poor people of colour as less deserving of honest work, as thieves, and as criminals. This intersection of capitalism and White supremacy increases the chances that poor Whites regard people of colour as less human than them despite a shared experience of economic exploitation; they are viewed as dangerous threats in need of removal rather than potential allies with shared experiences.

Given that ordinary trauma comprises a relational failure to honour and generatively respond to harm and suffering because of stolen humanity, the only pathway out of ordinary trauma is the reclamation and reparation of stolen humanity: the repair of lost connections through the restorative and transformative power of love. Patricia Berne (cited in Berne et al. 2018: 241) explains that liberation is a matter of love:

> I believe liberation is intimately tied to the experience of being human, to every cell of our beings saturated in love – self-love and love for others – liberated from the shaming enforced by ableism and other systems of oppression. And liberated *to* be responsible for creating a culture, a world, which values all communities.

The logic of dehumanization, coupled with the false vision of human exceptionalism, is how we justify loving other people less, to the point where we can rationalize our complicity and involvement in their suffering. Genuine, humanizing love is the energetic force that brings us back from this isolation, which liberates us to be responsible and accountable to one another.

Paulo Freire (2000 [1970]: 79), author of the revolutionary, groundbreaking text *Pedagogies of the Oppressed*, describes liberation as "the process of humanization" – a critical process which he maintains is an act of transformative dialogue across difference that requires love. Love is the political force animating all movements for justice (hooks 2000). It reminds us of our interdependence and it gives us the resources to act from that interdependence instead of in denial of it (Mingus 2017); love creates communities where connection and life flourish because we dare to witness ourselves in other people and them in us by crossing over power lines in order to prioritize alliance and relationships above power hording or isolation (brown 2019; Carrillo Rowe 2008; Price 2011). In short, love is the freeing capacity to be fully human together. It counteracts dehumanization, "which marks not only those whose humanity has been stolen, but also (though in a different way) those who have stolen it, [and] is a distortion of the vocation of becoming more fully human" (Freire 2000 [1970]: 44). In a later chapter, I will describe the expression and practice of love in connection to what I define as *authentic humanity* – the pursuit of which unifies us and empowers us to come together in the shared pursuit of life, self-actualization, and collective liberation.

Human Exceptionalism

If we accept that the dehumanization of oppressed peoples is what makes ordinary trauma socially acceptable, then we must also accept that there is a pre-existing hierarchy between the human world and the natural world. Systems of power enforce a separation of humanity from all else, living and unliving, and in doing so seek to fill humans with a belief in their right to dominion over that which we become alienated from. This "privilege of dominion" extends to all of nature as well as to people that are determined to be less removed from nature. It is what has allowed for the clear-cutting of forests, the theft and pollution of water, the hunting and killing of other life forms to the verge of extinction, and numerous other environmental degradations (Clare 1999; LaDuke 2017; Simpson 2017); it is simultaneously a crucial factor upholding every major system of oppression in operation today. Without the logics of human exceptionalism, oppression stops making sense because oppressive systems depend upon the devaluation of the natural world to distinguish and classify humans.

Throughout history, stories of great humans – most often great men – have celebrated their command over nature and *her* bounty. These stories have been deeply entwined with stories about the physical or sexual domination of women, especially Indigenous and other women of colour who are regarded as differently connected to and symbolic of the land – for example as more animalistic, less "civilized," less intelligent, and/or more overtly sexual beings (Smith 2005). Feminists have often interpreted distinctions between nature and culture as simultaneously being about gendered relations between women and men (Lloyd 2005), with the masculine construction of culture subordinating the feminine and the natural. This claim is certainly an interesting argument given that nature is often depicted as a woman (e.g. mother nature or mother earth). In this line of argument, fears of nature are feminized, and it is the masculine prerogative to emerge as the conqueror or saviour via domination of the natural world.

However, I argue that men's domination over the natural world is more than just a metaphor for men's domination of women. The systematic devaluation of the "less-than-fully human" world[1] contributes to harmful discourses of human exceptionalism that cut across systems of oppression in interesting and complex ways. A particular manifestation of power emerges from the logic of human exceptionalism and the belief in Man's destiny to control the world, yet, as I have been arguing, not all people are seen as exceptionally human. As with women, so too are people of colour, poor people, queer and trans folks, and disabled people, among others, perceived as more strongly bound to the less-than-fully human world and, therefore, less deserving of the privileges of humanity.

Oftentimes, the fabricated chains binding oppressed people to the denigrated natural world revolve around the image of animals or savages unable to control their beastly dispositions. Convicted felon Donald Trump's decision to refer to immigrants as animals and to talk about his ancestors as "taming a continent" and to routinely mock people with disabilities – all of these come from the deeply ingrained and widespread belief that oppressed people just are not human in the same way as others, and it is this harmful belief that underlies power and precedes the development of ordinary trauma. Constance Russell and Keri Semenko (2016: 212) maintain that "most of us also are living in profoundly anthropocentric cultures wherein humans are viewed as the center of the universe and inherently superior to, and rightly dominant over, all other species." Anthropocentrism manifests from human exceptionalism, which sets the stage for oppressed people subjected to dehumanization to be subjugated/conquered alongside other life forms including the land.

The concept of human exceptionalism proposes that at the same time as oppressed people come to be regarded as less-than-fully human, so too do advantaged people gain access to recognition as more-fully human in opposition to the dehumanization of others. *Exceptional* humanity, the kind that comes with power and dominance, is built from the humanity stolen from disadvantaged people. Young (2011: 41–42) writes:

> The systemic character of oppression implies that an oppressed group need not have a correlate oppressing group. While structural oppression involves relations among groups, these relations do not always fit the paradigm of conscious and intentional oppression of one group by another[, but] for every oppressed group there is a group that is *privileged* in relation to that group.

And for every dehumanized social position, there is a social position whose occupants claim, both explicitly and through more subtle behaviours, to be more-fully human. Importantly, this distribution of humanity is not dependent upon advantaged peoples' active suppression of dehumanized others; dehumanization is built into the social structure itself – into education, the workforce, the legal system, the home, religion, and so on. So, while advantaged people may not always directly participate in the routine dehumanization and othering of oppressed people as part of the ongoing performance of their positions (e.g. through misogynistic jokes and queer and transphobic discourses [Pascoe 2007]), they are still structurally elevated to positions of dominance. The fragility of this positioning is, as I will describe in a later chapter, frightening and, because it is founded on the ongoing dehumanization of others, a common source of feelings of insecurity that precede acts of violence against the oppressed.

The Four Pillars of Dehumanization

Discourses of human exceptionalism supposedly grant people rights to occupy land, extract resources from the natural world, and destroy wildlife habitats or ecosystems, and a wide range of other destructive practices. As social groups undergo processes of dehumanization, they become subjected to the more-fully human person's will as it pertains to the natural world: through dehumanization, advantaged people and social institutions come to see oppressed people as resources and exploitable labour to be claimed by individuals granted a recognition of fuller humanity. In this way, dehumanization warps perceptions of oppressed people from autonomous living beings into animals or objects which can be manipulated, exploited, and violated to varying levels. The outcomes of this traumatizing transformation are at least four, which I will now describe (see Table 2.1).

Pillar 1: Stolen Cultures, Traditions, Histories, Knowledge

First, advantaged groups lay claim to that which, in the imaginary of human exceptionalism, belongs to humanity. They strip dehumanized people of lands, cultures, traditions, histories, and other unique characteristics of their communities and identities. They destroy historical relations, kinship networks, and familial bonds. They assault transgressive ways of knowing common to

TABLE 2.1 Four Pillars of Dehumanization

1. Stolen Cultures, Traditions, Histories, Knowledge
2. Excessive Exposure to Human Waste and Pollution
3. Heightened Culpability for Social Problems
4. Compulsory Sacrifice for Human Betterment

oppressed peoples and separate them from the sources of their knowledge (e.g. by separating them from their familiar land bases and languages). In doing all of these things, dehumanization reaches deeper and spreads further: as dehumanized groups are robbed of what the colonizer/oppressor/violently human perceives as potentially connecting them to humanity, so too are they robbed of recognition as sharing in the human spirit residing within and across all people. Thus, authentic connection between regarded-as-fully human people and dehumanized others becomes more challenging and exceptional. In my naming this first consequence, I claim that dehumanization, as a tool of social and political domination, "has as much to do with destroying [people's] sense of purpose – their confidence in their world-view and meaning system – as it does with physical conquest" (Sousan Abadian, cited in Lambert 2008).

We can readily observe this outcome in relation to the violences of settler colonization, such as the occupation of Indigenous lands, forced migration and displacement, and boarding or residential school systems – each of which was at least in part about eradicating Indigenous identities, histories, kinships, languages, and ways of being and knowing (Child 1999; Gould 1992; Leo 2018; Miranda 2013; Simpson 2017). Sousan Abadian (cited in Lambert 2008) says that:

> [T]he collective traumas of colonization affected nearly 100 percent of indigenous peoples. Healthy child-rearing practices were disrupted or warped by involuntary boarding schools. Native spiritual practices and traditions were banished, and missionaries often replaced them with foreign religious forms that tore apart the community's social cohesion. It is like an epidemic hitting a society when its doctors and healers have been exterminated. No one escaped the ravage.

Ordinary trauma in the context of widespread colonial dehumanization included the active, ongoing assault on Indigenous kinship and family systems as well as religious and epistemic violence through the coercive administration of settler worldviews and moralities. Similarly, the institution of slavery in the United States, which was a predecessor for modern day institutions of law enforcement/incarceration (Davis 2015; Smith 2006), relied heavily on trafficking Black people from their ancestral lands, from their families and communities, from a sense of their physical, spiritual, and sexual autonomy, and from most other things that would potentially individualize and humanize them; indeed, "chattel" slavery, by definition, means reducing a group of people to *property*, objects to be bought, sold, owned, and bred. Even following the abolition of formal chattel slavery after the Civil War, dehumanized Black people continued to be treated as "partial people" who were subservient to Whites and who needed Whites to help them overcome their own "lazy" and "degenerate" natures.

This first pillar can also take the form of denying oppressed people's knowledge, both about themselves and about the world around them, and presuming that advantaged people know more or understand things more rationally. Medical paternalism, for instance, is the practice of assuming that recognized experts/officials – typically socially advantaged and dominant people – are more equipped to make medical decisions than the peoples impacted by those decisions to the point where they are denied access to bodily autonomy (Moen and DeWolfe 2019). For women, medical paternalism can be the refusal to acknowledge or treat women's pain based on the assumption that women are weak or exaggerating their pain. Accordingly, women are not recognized as the experts of their own bodies and embodied needs, but more often seen as unreliable narrators of their experiences, as people who should be doubted or questioned. Similarly, the politicization of birth control and abortion is, in part, about control over women's bodies and the unwillingness of men to accept that women are fully capable of making informed decisions about their reproduction.

At this political moment in particular, it is also important to think about medical paternalism in relation to trans people and our bodies. Largely in an effort to shore up political power and draw attention away from the economic exploitation of oligarchs and billionaires, politicians are pushing a conservative, oppressive political agenda that steals decision-making power from trans people. The dehumanization and vilification of trans people (e.g. false narratives that trans people are just men trying to get into women's restrooms) leads to a belief that we should not be in control of our bodies as well as policies that illegalize or make inaccessible the things that extend trans lives. *Gender-affirming care,* which refers to anything that allows us to feel more at home in our bodies and more genuine in our gender expression, becomes unacceptable within a transphobic society because it emerges from our knowledge that the gender binary doesn't work for everyone, that people can experience gender in resistant and queer ways, and that gender is not fixed at birth. The refusal to listen to trans people's lived knowledge, the oppressive practices that remove agency from trans people, are foundations of our systemic dehumanization.

Pillar 2: Excessive Exposure to Human Waste and Pollution

The second pillar of systemic dehumanization is that advantaged people, social institutions, and governments expect/force oppressed people to disproportionately bear the unwanted by-products of humanity. That is, not only do oppressed people forcibly have their humanity stolen away, but they are also treated like receptacles for destruction, pollution, and waste. Environmental racism, for instance, is an informative intersection between the devaluation of the natural world and Black, Indigenous, and other people of colour. Robert Bullard (2003: 50) writes that

> People of color around the world must contend with dirty air and drinking water, and the location of noxious facilities such as municipal landfills, incinerators, hazardous waste treatment, storage and disposal facilities owned by private industry, government and even the military. These environmental problems are exacerbated by racism.

I would add that much of the reason people of colour are put into contact with these things to begin with has to do with the impact of racism, colonialism, and capitalism. It is not just that racism makes the problem worse, but rather that it a core component of environmental and climate inequities. Bullard (2003: 49) also explains that:

> The systemic destruction of indigenous peoples' land and sacred sites, the poisoning of Native Americans on reservations, Africans in the Niger Delta, African-Americans in Louisiana's "Cancer Alley," Mexicans in the border towns, and Puerto Ricans on the island of Vieques, Puerto Rico all have their roots in economic exploitation, racial oppression, devaluation of human life and the natural environment, and corporate greed.

The existence of environmental racism simultaneously indicates that the devastation of the natural world in the name of improving particular human lives is, at least to a certain degree, acceptable, and that routinely exposing Black, Brown, Indigenous, and other people of colour to pollutants, toxins, waste is better than exposing White communities to these by-products. Put in another way, communities of colour, which disproportionately include poor people and immigrants, and the lands where they live are perceived as acceptable sacrifices where the betterment of White people's lives requires environmental destruction.

By disproportionately locating sites of environmental injustice in/near communities of colour (and thereby reserving ecological benefits for more advantaged/humanized White people), environmental racism effectively defines people of colour as existing, at least in part, for the benefit of White people, whose overall quality of life is improved by the diminishing of racial minorities (LaDuke 1999). As with the dominion over nature, the dehumanization of peoples of colour, and any trauma they experience as a result, serves the greater purpose of elevating people seen as more fully human and is therefore justifiable (LaDuke 2017). Other instances of this second outcome can be seen in the ways governments seek to disappear or dislocate homeless people away from public spaces; the ways advantaged people dispose of garbage and the people expected to clean up (e.g. wives and mothers, but also sanitary workers and maids); and the people we deem acceptable loses in the current environmental/ecological crisis (Levins Morales 1998).

It is important to recognize the immediate and long-term impacts of this increased exposure to human waste and pollution. The long-term health implications range from higher rates of cancer and terminal diseases to birth differences or abnormalities to varied kinds of debility, such as difficulty in breathing or loss of body parts or functionality. For instance, discussing the history of unsafe, unethical mining practices in the Western United States on Indigenous lands, including the failure to clean up sites and reduce exposure to harmful environmental contaminants like uranium, Lewis et al. (2017: 130) assert that

> Recent results show that Native Americans living near abandoned uranium mines have an increased likelihood for kidney disease and hypertension, and an increased likelihood of developing multiple chronic diseases linked to their proximity to the mine waste and activities bringing them in contact with the waste.

Data also suggests that other significant health disparities likely exist as well, such as higher incidences of cancer. Women of All Red Nations (W.A.R.N.) – an organization of Indigenous women who struggled against things like uranium mining and sterilization – also identified a strong correlation between proximity to uranium mines and miscarriages, premature births, and birth deficits/differences (W.A.R.N. 2017). Accordingly, exposure to pollution and waste directly affects how oppressed people are able to persist into the future as well as the health and well-being of future generations.

There are also significant negative cultural outcomes, including the destruction or damaging of sacred lands or communal spaces; shifts in the emotional and spiritual energy of families and communities as they adapt to things like environmental racism; and the further loss of cultural knowledge and tradition as elders and other community members disappear or die at younger ages. There is also the fundamental shift in worldview that can arise from existing so near to pollution and waste while knowing that others can live in clean spaces, raise their children further away from toxins, and experience the beauty of the world and the benefit of human production. More immediate impacts include things like a heightened experience of mental unwellness as people make sense of their ordinary trauma and develop new believes about their futures; distress as nutritious food, drinkable water, safe and affordable housing, and other material needs become more scarce; and loss of kinship and connection as people do what needs to be done for their survival. Not to mention the direct impact of the

Pillar 3: Heightened Culpability for Social Problems

The third pillar of dehumanization is that oppressed peoples tend to be held responsible for issues impacting their own communities, more privileged groups, and society as a whole. Pervasive social issues are routinely attributed to oppressed people's presence and actions, and the dominant solutions to these issues often take the forms of correction, containment, removal, and even extermination. Social Darwinism, biometry, eugenic rhetoric, discourses of "population management" – all blame oppressed people for what's wrong with the world and for obstructing the full realization of humanity with their immorality/degeneracy and the strain they place on social/material resources (Subramaniam 2014). Misplaced culpability ultimately serves to draw attention away from the harms caused by advantaged peoples and institutions that consume and hoard with little to no concern beyond their own self-interest. In doing so, it promotes the belief that human life would be better off without certain groups of people, or at least with fewer of them.

Acting upon such beliefs, advantaged peoples – as well as others conditioned into logics of oppression – have done truly terrible things, ranging from the theft of reproductive freedoms through forced/coerced birth control or sterilization (ACJR 2005; Roberts 1997; Smith 2005), to the theft of bodily autonomy through criminalization/incarceration (Smith 2006; Spade 2011), to ongoing acts of land theft and genocide, such as those taking place against Palestinians or people in Ukraine. There is an underlying assumption that oppressed people, in related but distinct ways across race, class, gender, sexuality, ability, etc., are dirty, sinful, violent, unintelligent, and/or immoral; the imagined problem here is that oppressed peoples worsen or endanger the lives of "good," "upstanding," and "virtuous" people, which, in turn, rationalizes ordinary violence against them. I will discuss this pillar in much more detail in a later chapter when I describe how practices of *victim-blaming* relate to ordinary trauma and systems of oppression.

Pillar 4: Compulsory Sacrifice for Human Betterment

Finally, in being labelled as constant threats to humanity, dehumanized people are expected to sacrifice themselves for or devote themselves to the bettering of human life. In this sense, disadvantaged people are eternally punished for crimes that systems of power frame them for, and their sentences are carried out in the service of advantaged peoples and institutions who are, more often than not, actually at fault. Various forms of medical abuse, prolonged servitude, worsened life chances, and other harms place disadvantaged people in a position where their quality of life is reduced that other people's might be improved. I need only think of the Tuskegee Syphilis Study, in which hundreds of impoverished Black men from Alabama were infected with and not treated for Syphilis, even after the development of Penicillin, so that researchers could better understand the progression of the disease. Medical abuses against people of colour, such as the Tuskegee Syphilis Experiment, have been and remain normal, just with a less explicit racialization, and they also impact poor people, people with disabilities, immigrants, women, and others.

The expectation to better the lives of regarded-as-more-fully human people also extends to the narratives surrounding disadvantaged people, so that even the stories told about them benefit people in power. Even stories that seem to applaud and celebrate oppressed people frequently work against their interests and often have relatively little to do with them at all. For example, supercrip narratives appear to applaud disabled people for "overcoming" their disabilities to accomplish some exploit they were not expected to be capable of. These feats range from climbing a mountain to driving a car to getting a date. Ultimately, these narratives reinforce the harmful associations between disability and weakness, for in these narratives, achieving anything while disabled is story-worthy because disabled people are expected to be incapable of doing almost everything (Clare 1999). Indeed, the purpose of such narratives has to do with the *enabled* world. "Inspiration porn," as other disability theorists or activists have called it, refers to enabled people's consumption of this kind of media in order to feel better about themselves. In addition to obscuring the structural realities of ableism, it allows able-bodied people to feel good about themselves, to believe they can overcome obstacles, and to pursue the lives they want to have.

The belief that disadvantaged people are responsible for the betterment of more fully human subjects also contains within it the premise that oppressed peoples actually exist for the advantaged, that in their dehumanization, they stop having a will entirely separate from and equal to other peoples. As I explain more in the chapter about trauma and social advantage, systems of power seek instil in their beneficiaries an understanding that the world and the less-than-fully human things within it exist, at least in part, for their use, consumption, and pleasure. Part of the reason why disadvantaged people are expected to improve the lives of others is because they are not totally seen as having a life all their own. Sure, they may have their own desires, dreams, or passions, but ultimately systems of power promote a narrative that disadvantaged people's lives matter not inherently, but because they are bound to the advantaged people around them. In an oppressive social order, oppressed lives are seen to matter less or stop mattering altogether when they no longer benefit advantaged people or, worse, start to actively work against the systems and structures on which the privileges of advantaged people are founded.

This is the narrative advanced by systems of power, and this narrative is the explanation for why disadvantaged peoples have to repeatedly assert the value of their lives, that their lives "matter." This narrative is also an explanation for why statements that "all lives matter" can never be anything more than the deliberate obfuscation of power and the injustice it creates. While I do not deny that all lives matter, the inherent value of advantaged people's lives does not regularly get brought into question. We do not spend hours debating whether cisgender people deserve access to affirming and life-enhancing care; or if White people should have to survive racial profiling, over-policing and incarceration; or if it would be too dangerous for White U.S. citizens to build lives free from poverty and political violence through immigration. So long as systems of oppression exist and are justified on the basis that some people are less-fully human than others, lives will be seen to matter or not matter in different ways. In reality, this devaluation of life is the source and consequence of all ordinary trauma, for it determines who can benefit from oppression and whose suffering can be normalized in the process.

Political Metonymy: An Extension of Dehumanization

Processes of dehumanization carry throughout the lives of oppressed people, often through not only daily microaggressions, such as misgendering and racial insensitivity, but also more severe forms of violence and traumatic harm, such as sexual assault, deportation, or incarceration. Since systems of power are always interlocking, intersectionality plays an enormous role in determining which people get regarded as fully human, by whom, and under what conditions. Paulina Abustan and A.G. Rud (2016: 17), echoing multiple other intersectionality theorists, write: "it is impossible to analyze multiple identities, experiences, and struggles separately when identities, experiences, and struggles are interwoven and connected." As we consider the complex relationships between ordinary trauma, systems of oppression, and processes of dehumanization, remembering the intersectionality not only of individual identities but also of axes of power is crucial for moving towards equity and social justice. Dehumanization takes on many different forms, but it is always repetitive, jagged, and compounding, and it impacts people differently in different moments and contexts.

There is no value in creating hierarchies of oppression, which is not what I intend to do here, but it is important to understand that individuals confront dehumanization unevenly relative to other people and at different moments during their lives. For example, we can recognize that escalating border violence within Trump's America makes immigrants more vulnerable to dehumanization than people accepted as citizens and that the harm (Brown) immigrants are experiencing today is at a different level of severity than it has been previously or may be in the future. Similarly, the relative severity of dehumanization depends upon the totality of individuals' identities and social locations. The ordinary traumatic events that an immigrant is subjected to, for instance, are likely to change based on their race, class, gender, ability, and sexuality, among other things.

However, there are also moments when the discursive construction of people as less-than-fully human operates through the denial that they have any other identities whatsoever – that the dehumanized part of their identity overshadows or erases other aspects of who they are. Dehumanization, in this sense, can also be the process of denying the complexity of life by presenting a group of people as if they are "all the same" (monolithic), lacking the supposed individuality of regarded-as-fully human people. Considering (Brown) immigrants, the denial of difference might take the form of reducing people to the fact of their border crossing (e.g. referring to them as "illegals"). In this case, immigrants aren't people with families or unique identities: they are reduced to nothing more than criminals who don't belong here, violations of the law that can disrupt order and make citizens – the people who are seen to belong here – less safe. Regardless of their own personalities, values, or actions, the rhetoric of illegality marks all Brown immigrants as outsiders and dangerous others.

Dehumanization through reduction is easy to find in the anti-immigrant rhetoric of the Trump administration because it rationalizes and spreads White supremacist violence necessary to their conservative power base. In May of 2018, Trump made the following statement: "You wouldn't believe how bad these people are. These are not people. These are animals." Made without reference to any other identities or characteristics than their position as immigrants, this tweet carried enough force to further dehumanize – to *animalize* – an entire group based on one facet of who they are and what they are assumed to have done. In a later declaration, Trump argued he was just referring to MS-13 gang members, yet the context of his statement suggests otherwise as does his administration's growing history of anti-immigration rhetoric and platforms. Indeed, the lack of specificity that allows for overgeneralization is significant to the function and reproduction of White supremacy: it promotes stereotypical thinking and erases complexity or individuality; further, it blurs distinctions between the "good" and "bad" people within a group, which means that all members become more suspect – more readily criminalizable.

Another way to think about dehumanization through reduction is as a *political metonymy*. Metonymy is a rhetorical manoeuvre in which a part of something stands in for the whole (e.g. "crown" in the place of "monarchy"). Even if Trump was referring just to gang members and not all Brown immigrants when he called them animals, the rhetorical context intentionally created the possibility for listeners to interpret his meaning to be all immigrants. Furthermore, in tying his anti-immigrant sentiment to gangs, he deepens the imagined association between Brown immigrants and all the things assumed to come from gangs, including drugs, violence, and other social problems. When used to advance political aims, metonymic moves like this do not just use the part to call to mind the whole, but they transform the whole in the process. Conflating immigration with gangs or immigrants with "bad hombres" does a lot to alter the social landscape surrounding border crossing: for people exposed to this rhetoric, the part (i.e. gangs and bad hombres) is meant to *become* the whole, to the point where mentioning immigration evokes images of its undesirable parts. Indeed, this reductive dehumanization makes such associations all but impossible to ignore.

And it is precisely because the part, in its limited, overly simplistic representation, becomes the whole that ordinary trauma against the entire oppressed group can be rationalized based on dehumanization of specific members. Agents of Immigration and Customs Enforcement (ICE), for instance, are given license to surveil, harass, and exert power over any immigrants whose profile too closely resembles the imagined features of a terrorist or "illegal alien" – a visage that just so happens to include most people with particular skin colours, languages, or geographic origins. Cruel practices of detainment, deportation, and incarceration, including deporting people to hostile countries like El Salvador and imprisoning them in the equivalent of modern-day concentration camps, are made possible by political metonymy. Regardless of what crimes they have committed – if any at all – Brown immigrants are automatically set up to be perceived as dangerous, guilty, and deserving of harsh, even inhumane punishment.

When part comes to stand in for the whole, so too do all of those things which are associated with it. In political metonymy, the part always has negative associations already in place, so people engaging in this practice are actually attempting to transfer these associations to the whole rather than create entirely new meanings. This strategy is effective because it allows them to use an association that already exists and that has likely been continually reinforced through socialization. Just as it is easier to build where the foundation has already been laid, so too does it take much less effort to convince people to accept an extension of something which they already believe to be true. In terms of dehumanizing immigrants, transferring the hatred, fear, and anxiety surrounding gangs or bad hombres to immigrants in general makes it much easier to turn public opinion against people crossing borders. In this sense, political metonymy could be seen as another example of the notion of transference that I wrote about in Chapter 1 – another pathway through which ordinary trauma can pass between oppressed people.

Furthermore, political metonymy makes it much more difficult to convince people of immigrants' humanity because they are now weighed down simultaneously by the presumed immorality of their border crossing and their manufactured connection with other things that are viewed as threatening to the safety and security of the "American" way of life. In this way, systems of oppression can continually recycle their logics while minimizing excess labour costs – in a very neoliberal capitalist sense, systems of oppression build and extend such associations to keep themselves efficient and productive while minimizing effort. Accordingly, political metonymy is one example of how Sara Ahmed's description of privilege as an "energy-saving device" (2013) also encapsulates the systems and structures from which privilege emerges. Indeed, through recycling or regenerating harmful *controlling images* like the "bad hombre," oppressive systems create more surplus from a smaller investment. Black feminist theorist Patricia Hill Collins (1990) defines controlling images as cultural productions that are meant to convince people that oppression is normal and natural, that oppressed people bring harm onto themselves. Political metonymy as a practice of spreading controlling images outward to more members of a group allows for the broader naturalization of oppression and ordinary traumatic harm.

Even as they refuse the complexity of people's lives, dehumanization through reduction and metonymy are not about ignoring other sites of difference (e.g. focusing just on immigrants' nationality). Rather, political metonymy is about causing people to assume other aspects of an oppressed group's behaviours/values can be represented by a subset of its most vilifiable members. Associating immigrants with bad hombres and gang members encourages us to believe that they will share the behaviours and values of uneducated, Brown men threatening American civility with violence and lawlessness. Terrorists also are assumed to be gendered, racialized, and sexualized in specific ways, such that Arab or Middle Eastern men are readily assumed to be guilty of terrorism even when they have done nothing wrong. Thus, to reduce social groups to monolithic representations is not to deny that they have other identities and social positions, but rather to spread controlling images that enter peoples' minds whenever that group or category is brought up.

Over time, thinking about other images or representations comes to require an active effort; to move beyond the ones prescribed by systems of power takes energy and intention. These images become involuntary and, to a certain degree, *compulsory*: people subjected to them have little power not to think about them (even if they do so critically), and there are internal and external consequences to resisting them. For example, speaking in favour of immigrants and naming the controlling image of bad hombres can lead to social ostracization and anger or political violence from those who have internalized this image. Similarly, unlearning anti-immigrant sentiments for non-immigrants entails processing difficult emotions that we have been conditioned to experience. Controlling images produce contexts of fear and a felt need for power and control among advantaged people, which justifies the presence of explicit and implicit state power. Controlling images like the terrorist, the bad hombre, and the predatory man in a dress conjure negative affective responses even when no actual danger of harm is present. These elicited responses coerce people into *complicity* with dominance and even galvanize them into oppressive action.

These controlling images also produce ordinary trauma against people whom they represent as threatening dehumanized others: as individuals come to fear a particular group of people because of what has been associated with them, members of that group become containers of cultural panic and anxiety that require greater regulation and/or removal. Practically, this means that oppressed people disproportionately encounter potentially traumatic situations. For example, border agents are significantly more likely to stop and request documents from people who resemble the stereotypical immigrant, just as the police are more likely to stop, search, arrest, charge, and assault people of colour (Alexander 2010). The problem is not that people of colour and immigrants are more likely to be in violation of laws, but instead that the social positions that they have been assigned to evoke a particular kind of affective response from the people around them. In being associated with criminalized controlling images, they are also associated with emotions that make advantaged people uncomfortable.

Furthermore, these controlling images become more concrete as people come into contact with and respond to them, meaning that negative affective responses like anger and fear can easily grow beyond control. If border agents disproportionately request documentation from people that look like Brown immigrants, or police disproportionately stop and search people of colour, then of course immigrants and people of colour are going to be found guilty more so than others. That's just what happens when the state targets people through racial profiling. Similarly, if we disproportionately ask people in bathing suits if they are going to the beach/pool, we will likely get a high number that say yes. There is a kind of *confirmation bias* at play when people act based on controlling images: we are conditioned to expect people to align to a specific image, so we treat them like that image and require them to repeatedly account for themselves, and in turn we find "evidence" to support the belief in that image.

The problem here is that most of us do not have the inclination, time, and energy to think in terms of proportionality because sheer numbers seem to tell enough of the story: seeing the frequency of guilt among immigrants or people of colour, regardless of context, is enough for many people to hold on to their prejudice and justify their feelings toward members of those groups. Confirmation bias is dangerous because people want to believe they are correct, so they look for ways to confirm their knowledge and avoid facts that challenge their worldview. For many people who are resistant to other perspectives, it does not matter if police targeted specific groups of people or if research shows that members of that group are no more likely to commit crime than the members of other groups; all that matters is that the police or ICE found x number of *them* were guilty and that *their* number is greater. Indeed, undocumented immigrants are actually much *less likely* to commit serious/violent crimes despite Trumpish rhetoric depicting them as dangerous. The notion of confirmation bias, through which power teaches people to pursue stories or data that confirm oppressive ideologies, reveals one of the most prescient dangers of uncontextualized and unevidenced data: namely, that it can create the illusion of a whole story while, like metonymy, only describing a part.

And it is not just that people seek out information to confirm what they already believe to be true: in the context of an inequitable and unjust society, oppressive misinformation is made readily available to them. For instance, the FBI as well as other governmental organizations have a long history of vilifying and criminalizing oppressed people, especially those engaged in activism against state violence. I think about how Angela

Davis and other people involved in anti-racist work were publicly branded enemies of the state in the same way that activists today, particularly those organizing and advocating against the genocide of Palestinians, get classified as terrorists. This kind of branding allows the state to surveil, regulate, and contain resistance in social movements by associating anti-oppression and anti-violence work with criminality. Consequently, the confirmation bias that derives from over-policing oppressed communities becomes a rationale for further state violence, thereby forming one of the core cycles of oppressive systems.

As a result of this harmful association, other activists doing similar kinds of work come to be seen as always already suspect. For instance, how readily are peaceful protesters portrayed as rebels/rioters when they speak against dominant groups, institutions, and governments? And, how frequently is this image manufactured by the police or military escalating protests through state violence, such as when the National Guard was deployed to silence and quell anti-ICE protests in California? The heightened presence of police and soldiers turned what was a lawful organized protest into a situation where people had to protect themselves from gas and guns while simultaneously being depicted as violent insurgents in need of regulation. Metonymy, in this instance, transfers the affective responses associated with "criminals" to activists opposing state violence. Much of the time, the only way for protesters/activists to maintain a "positive" public image is to align themselves with the state – the same state that abuses, violates, discards, and murders people like them every day. Metonymy, in this way, can yield what Marilyn Frye (1983) termed a "double-bind": either activists align themselves with oppressive institutions/governments by working within the legitimated spaces of social change or they become subjected to other forms of surveillance and discipline.

Negative affective responses towards members of dehumanized social groups are so deeply ingrained that people who seek to overcome conditioned feelings of hatred or fear or disgust can spend a lifetime broadening their perspective and still struggle. It is possible to question whether people are actually trying to overcome their prejudices or whether they are merely putting on a performance, but the fact remains that how individuals feel about difference and the people who are different from them is much like a habit: hard to break after years of practice. People often say that "feelings are fleeting," but this is not the case when feelings are guided and cultivated by systems of power. Of course, this recognition does not excuse the violent or otherwise harmful actions of advantaged people, but it does make clear that the process of social transformation never comes easily. People committed to improving their world (or even just their communities) have to accept that social change comes much too slowly and goes away much too easily, especially where oppressive systems corrupt our emotions and perceptions.

Even when someone does manage to "overcome" feelings of prejudice, histories of hatred and society's ongoing injustice can easily lure them back if they do not remain vigilant. This is part of what White anti-racist activist Chris Crass (cited in Russo 2016) defines as the "gravitational pull" of White supremacy and other systems of power. For when we strive to move in the direction of social justice, through the humanizing practices of liberation (Freire 2000 [1970]), we are inevitably met with a counterforce pulling us back towards normativity and dominance. That counterforce can feel comfortable or easy because dominance is a path of least resistance for those socialized into it. It is also the result of oppressive social moods, which I now turn to.

Social Mood and The Climates of Oppressive Feeling

Perhaps, a useful distinction to make here is that between *affect* and *mood*. Whereas affect refers to emotional states as they change between one moment and the next, mood is more lasting and can carry over longer periods of time. If we think about affect like a single coloured tile, then mood is the broader mosaic formed from many individual tiles. Over time, as tiles are added to this mosaic – as we experience different emotions across our interactions with other people – a mosaic emerges to tell a story of how our feelings towards particular groups of people are ordered/governed. Under systems of oppression, our affective responses are not random but conditioned and contextualized. The fear, anxiety, and anger as well as other negative emotions directed at oppressed people like (Brown) immigrants are not natural, for they come from the historical and ongoing impacts of White supremacy and capitalism. The mood of White supremacy is a violent shade of red or maybe a blinding and blaring shade of white.

Mood limits the affective responses most readily available to people by adding, subtracting, and re-arranging tiles so that we are more likely to feel some emotions while having a harder time feeling other emotions. My mother is an artist – she painted the cover art of this book – and one of her artistic mediums is to paint a canvas with a chaotic mixture of colours, cut the canvas apart into roughly shaped squares or tiles, and reassemble those tiles into a different piece of artwork that tells a more complicated story. The meaning and power of this medium come from the careful arrangement of the tiles – the creation of order from seeming chaos or disorder. The creation of social mood is a similar practice: Whereas the violence and harm of oppression tear the canvas apart, systems impose rigid order by influencing how we can reassemble its pieces and the meaning we can make from them. Our emotions, represented by the canvas tiles, are conditioned and ordered into a mosaic that portrays humans turned against one another.

Systems of power register at the level of mood to condition people to view social groups and categories of people in ordered ways both positive and negative. Thus, even though mood is often thought of as an internal state, it is also socially produced and shaped by distributions of power. The climate of police violence against people of colour, for instance, is partially the consequence of a racist social mood that makes it easier for officers to view people of colour as threatening, to feel negative emotions in their presence. The same is true for White people whose first instinct upon seeing a person of colour in "their neighbourhood" is to call the police, regardless of what the person was actually doing there. Racist moods can generate all sorts of feelings, ranging from anger ("How dare that person be here!"), to confusion ("What is that person doing here?), to fear ("What is that person going to do to me now that they are here?"), and so on. The mosaic moods fostered inside of us become exceedingly complex due to the influence of systems of power.

Another metaphor commonly used to distinguish between affect and mood is the difference between a daily forecast and larger patterns of weather. Affect might refer to the rains or sun shining down one day while mood is more like the changing of seasons or even the slow and steady pace of climate change. The metaphor of weather is apt since it captures sensations of oppression as well: reflecting on a quotation from Audre Lorde (1984: 160) – "In order to withstand the weather, we had to become stone" – Sara Ahmed (2013) asserts that "[s]ocial forms of oppression can be experienced as weather. They press and pound against the surface of a body; a body can surface or survive by hardening." We brace ourselves against situations and experiences that we know will elicit challenging affective responses, and over time, we can *harden* ourselves from the repetition of that bracing, of living with our muscles tensed and our shield raised. If mood too is like the weather, then the cultivated mood of an unjust society can be the lived reality behind the "pressing and pounding" of oppression, the reality through which oppresses people "become stone."

The exacting weather of oppression is, in part, the bellowing wind and withering sun of a *bad* social mood. Yet, recalling Ta-Nehisi Coates' statement that "race is the child of racism, not the father" (2015: 7), I want to emphasize how often bad moods come afterward. Importantly, the systems and structures put into place to dehumanize and oppress people exist to justify harm – they become necessary in response to harms *already committed* and once in place, they perpetuate harms into the *future* by classifying people and giving meanings to specific, typically arbitrary differences. Social moods are one of the tools that advantaged people can use to relieve the moral weight of harm already committed, ordinary trauma already inflicted. In this sense, social moods are revisionary: they are imposed to revise how we remember or analyse events from the past. For example, we can identify and critique much of the rhetoric European settlers used to rationalize the displacement, dispossession, and disappearance of Indigenous peoples in the Americas. However, it is important to remember just how much of that rhetoric was applied after the fact. Indeed, efforts to represent Indigenous people as "merciless Indian savages" were introduced to revise the narrative of European colonization away from genocide and land theft into the more acceptable vision of Manifest Destiny.

Systems of oppression traumatize and warp the mood of society against everyone assumed to threaten their political order. Long-term negative affect towards a social group or category as a product of a socially crafted moods has long-term ramifications for the people targeted by it. For instance, writing about the ordinary experience of sexual and state violence against Latinas at the United States–Mexico border, Ana Clarissa Rojas Durazo (2010: 80) laments:

> We are made through violence. Violence does not escape us; it is predictable and expected . . . Violence is the quotidian order of things, arranged institutionally in ties that bind: the school, prison, home, courtroom, and emergency room. We survive violent welfare policies, militarization and feminicide at the border, police and border patrol brutality and violation, dissolution of our families by child protective services, war, criminalizing drug laws, and much more.

Violence as the "quotidian order of things" is a good way of describing how trauma becomes ordinary. It is straightforward enough to imagine how a negative social mood contributes to this violence: a combination of fear, hatred, longing, and entitlement experienced within a border culture intent on maintaining the separation of *us* versus *them* produces a social context in which traumatic harm becomes not only common but also "predictable and expected."

The mood underlying ordinary trauma could also be thought of as the "mood" of response – that is ordinary trauma occurs when we are not in the mood to respond to violence or when the prevailing mood makes us *want to not* respond to/ignore violence. The mood of oppression is one of passivity and complicit bystanders. When Gloria Anzaldúa (1987) refers to borders as "heridas abiertas" (open wounds), she is, in part, describing the negative social mood of the border culture and how it contributes to normalized harm against bodies seen as existing on the wrong side of the border. The social mood of White supremacy reinforces the hostility of the border culture by marking *them* as bodies to fear and contain – as bodies deserving of violence because they threaten *us* with violence.

Mood as a tool of oppression also works to limit the presence of oppressed people in spaces that are socially valued to the point of becoming a pattern. Everyday experiences of removal/denial of access can be as simple as being turned down for a job because of something other than your qualifications, being treated differently than other patrons of a business because you are regarded as different from normal; or not be welcomed into a space because of your access needs. Often, people acting based on social mood inflected by systems of power are unaware of their doing so, though not always. For instance, sociological studies have found that identical résumés received different rates of response based solely on how strongly the name across its top was associated with particular racial groups. Résumés having "Whiter" sounding names in these studies received more frequent callbacks and were significantly more likely to receive interviews and job offers despite not containing any other differences in information. Most likely, the employers making decisions about which résumés to accept were operating from a place of internalized racial preference and possible animus (Bertrand and Mullainathan 2003).

One way to interpret this bias is as an effect of racist social mood that associates people of colour with negative affective response. Even if the people responding to these résumés were entirely unaware of their racial biases, they most certainly underwent an affective shift upon reading the coded name that caused them to evaluate the application differently than they would have otherwise. Perhaps they began to perceive the imagined applicant as less-than-fully human and therefore less worthy of a positive response. Perhaps their decision-making process stopped being about "How can I say 'yes' to this applicant?" and instead started to be about "Has this applicant done enough to prove themselves?" Since these résumés were identical, there is no argument for logic or rationality, and the most likely explanation is the evoking of racist beliefs and/or affective responses.

If affect is defined as changing and mood as more long-term, then the dominant frameworks surrounding trauma have certainly more often associated traumatic experiences with affect, especially considering their assumed extraordinariness. Even if the effects of trauma stretch across time, most conversations surrounding traumatic harm revolve around the underlying assumption that harm tends to be instantaneous, in both its onset and resolution – with the notable exception of complex trauma, which is recognized as being chronic and prolonged (Herman 1992; van der Kolk 2005). As I noted in Chapter 1, people tend to think of "shock trauma" (Bell 2017) – "a single, overwhelming incident that's larger that our ability to cope." While this description may work in some situations, it is not universal, especially relative to systems of oppression.

Ordinary trauma is more akin to mood given that it is iterative and often anticipated. Like rain in the spring and snowfall during the winter, an oppressive social mood gives rise to ordered, patterned experiences of trauma. While not predictable in the same way as a meteorologist might predict rain or snow, ordinary trauma has the tendency to manifest again and again in accordance with the mood of society. In this sense, mood can be a predisposition that calls forth violent futures where trauma becomes (and remains) too familiar. This is the sensation of walking on eggshells: while individual traumatic events are too unpredictable to prepare for, people who experience ordinary trauma tend to develop the ability to read and respond to mood in ways that allow for self-preservation. Oppressed people must develop this ability because it is crucial to their survival. They can smell the rain before the cloud appears, so to speak. In the following chapter, I will describe these cultivated feelings as a form of *presumptive trauma* like but distinct from *trauma hypervigilance*. Presumptive trauma encapsulates the way people become conditioned to anticipate trauma in the future and how this conditioning, in turn, supports complicity in and conformity to the existing social and political order.

As oppressed people learn to sense the moods around them (e.g. sense the fear or hostility repeatedly directed at them), many also assume responsibility for their own safety and well-being. Burdened with the knowledge of future trauma, people made vulnerable by systems of oppression find methods of protecting themselves through developing expansive understandings of the advantaged people and violent social institutions around them. W. E. B. Du Bois (2008 [1903]) coined the term *double consciousness* to describe how people belonging to oppressed social groups are forced to familiarize themselves with the worldviews of their more privileged counterparts if they are to survive. Du Bois first used the term to refer to the experience of Black people living in a racist society, but since then it has been taken up by many other social groups as a tool to describe their confrontations with systemic inequality and injustice. In some ways, coming to possess double consciousness can be traumatizing in itself, but great harm can also come from the realization of being in near perpetual danger, surrounded by other people that may very well be filled with anger, hatred, or disgust for the social positions that an individual is assigned to. These people can include members of our own families or communities and even people whom we are supposed to turn to for support and guidance, such as doctors, therapists, and spiritual leaders.

The inverse of double consciousness most often familiar to advantaged people is not just a "single consciousness" but *ignorance*, which Susanne Luhmann (1998: 149) defines as "an opposition to knowing." Much of the time, dominance works to prevent advantaged peoples from recognizing the ordinary traumatic conditions imposed on oppressed others as well as the true extent of their own privilege. Ignorance is not accidental; it is socially produced and politically maintained. Writing to White people, Ijeoma Oluo (2017) asserts: "[y]our survival has never depended on your knowledge of white culture. In fact, it's required your ignorance." Oluo goes on to write:

> No, I do not know everything. I do not cover every angle all the time. Sometimes, I'm flat-out wrong. But here's the thing: I do know white culture. I know white culture better than most white people know white culture.

> I know white culture, white history, white politics. . . . Why do I know white culture so well? Because I'm a black woman. And while I, and just about any person of color who has spent their lives in a white supremacist society, know enough about white culture to write a book or two on whiteness and option the bestseller movie rights, y'all know almost nothing about us and even less about yourselves.

Ignorance is a necessary part of oppression for it allows advantaged people to preserve their *innocence* – to pretend or convince themselves that the harms they cause are unintentional, unimportant, and/or underserving of accountability and remorse. Felman (1987: 79) further maintains that ignorance "is not a passive state of absence, a simple lack of information: it is an active dynamic of negation, an active refusal of information." To *accomplish* ignorance, and it is something accomplished through intentional actions, demands attention to what is known and deliberately not known. Accordingly, Deborah Britzman (1995: 154) asserts: "the relationship between knowledge and ignorance is neither oppositional nor binary. Rather, they *mutually implicate* each other, structuring and enforcing particular forms of knowledge and forms of ignorance" (emphasis added). Knowledge and ignorance are woven together, especially through systems of power, for the behaviours of advantaged people are predicated on a refusal to know the ordinary trauma of the oppressed.

Advantaged people are repeatedly conditioned and choose to know other things in place of suffering: profit in place of exploitation; expansion or development in place of environmental destruction and racism; national security in place of "transnational solidarity" (Davis 2015) or accountability across borders; to name just a few. The mood of oppression is founded on ignorance, for to generate negative feelings toward oppressed people, the advantaged must remain ignorant of the possibilities for other emotions. Ignorant of the fact that immigration makes a country stronger. Ignorant of the fact that racial diversity can be a source of joy and creation. Ignorant of the fact that making space for different body types/access needs leads to better, more integrated communities. Ignorant of the fact that supporting queer and trans people's identities and expressions leads to more honesty, safety, and connection. Ignorant of the fact that reproductive autonomy and reproductive justice are vital to healthy families and relationships. These and other areas of ignorance uphold oppressive social moods and prevent us from genuinely connecting with one another. It is only by overcoming ignorance that we can liberate ourselves and the people around us, for ignorance undermines love and authentic humanity.

Note

1 Many writers have started to use the phrase more-than-human world to push back against this pervasive devaluation of the natural relative to the human. I also use this phrase in many contexts, but I've decided not do so here because I want to identify how systems of power rely on the devaluation of the natural world in order to produce inequality and injustice. The privileges granted to humans are contingent upon their separation from and domination of nature, and the idea of a "more-than-human world," in the moment I write this text, masks existing power relations.

References

Abustan, Paulina and Rud, A. G. "Allies of Intersectionalities." In *Queer Studies in Education*, edited by N. Rodriguez. New York: Palgrave Macmillan, 2016.

Aggeler, Madeline. "Terry Crews: Men Don't See Women As 'All the Way Human.'" *The Cut*. https://www.thecut.com/2018/04/terry-crews-women-of-the-world-summit-cult-of-masculinity.html (published October 1, 2018).

Ahmed, Sara. "Feeling Depleted." *FeministKilljoys*. https://feministkilljoys.com/2013/11/17/feeling-depleted/ (published November 17, 2013).

Alexander, Michelle. *The New Jim Crow: Mass Incarceration in the Age of Colorblindness*. New York: The New Press, 2010.

Anzaldúa, Gloria. *Borderlands | La Frontera*. San Francisco: Aunt Lute Book Company, 1987.

Asian Communities for Reproductive Justice (ACJR). *A New Vision for Advancing Our Movement for Reproductive Health, Reproductive Rights and Reproductive Justice*. Oakland, CA: Asian Communities for Reproductive Justice, 2005.

Bell, Andrea, "Love and Connection: How Trauma Can Bring Us Closer Together." *Good Therapy*. https://www.goodtherapy.org/blog/love-connection-how-trauma-can-bring-us-closer-together-0905174 (published September 5, 2017).

Berila, Beth. *Integrating Mindfulness into Anti-Oppression Pedagogy: Social Justice in Higher Education*. New York: Routledge, 2015.

Berne, Patricia, Lewis, Jamal, Milbern, Stacey, Shanks, Malcolm, Vaid-Menon, Alok and Wong, Alice. "'Beauty Always Recognizes Itself': A Roundtable on Sins Invalid." *WSQ: Women's Studies Quarterly* 46, no. 1/2 (2018): 241–250.

Bertrand, Marianne and Mullainathan, Sendhil. "Are Emily and Greg More Employable Than Lakisha and Jamal? A Field Experiment on Labor Market Discrimination." *National Bureau of Economic Research* (2003).

Britzman, Deborah. "Is There a Queer Pedagogy? Or, Stop Reading Straight." *Educational Theory* 45, no. 2 (1995): 151–165.

brown, adrienne maree. *Pleasure Activism: The Politics of Feeling Good*. Chico: AK Press, 2019.

Bullard, Robert. "Confronting Environmental Racism in the 21st Century." *Race, Poverty, and the Environment* 10, no. 1 (2003): 49–52.

Carrillo Rowe, Aimee. *Power Lines: On the Subject of Feminist Alliances*. Durham: Duke University Press, 2008.

Child, Brenda. *Boarding School Seasons: American Indian Families, 1900–1940*. Lincoln: University of Nebraska Press, 1999.

Clare, Eli. *Exile and Pride: Disability, Queerness, and the Liberation*. Durham: Duke University Press, 1999.

Coates, Ta-Nehisi. *Between the World and Me*. One World, 2015.

Collins, Patricia Hill. *Black Feminist Thought: Knowledge, Consciousness, and the Politics of Empowerment*. New York: Routledge, 1990.

Connor, David. J. "Social Justice in Education for Students with Disabilities." In *The SAGE Handbook of Special Education*, edited by Lani Florian, 111–128. Thousand Oaks: Sage Publications, 2014.

Daring, Christa. "'Sex Workers Want Rights, Not Rescue': An interview with Christa Daring on the International Day to End Violence against

Sex Workers." *Poz.com*. https://www.poz.com/blog/sex-workers-want-rights-rescue (published December 17, 2018).

Davis, Angela. *Freedom Is a Constant Struggle: Ferguson, Palestine, and the Foundations of a Movement*. Chicago: Haymarket Books, 2015.

Du Bois, W. E. B. *The Souls of Black Folk*. Edited by Brent Hayes Edwards. Oxford: Oxford University Press, 2008 [1903].

Durazo, Ana Clarissa Rojas. "In Our Hands: Community Accountability as Pedagogical Strategy." *Social Justice* 37, no. 4 (2010): 76–100.

Felman, Shoshana. *Jacques Lacan and the Adventure of Insight: Psychoanalysis in Contemporary Culture*. Cambridge: Harvard University Press, 1987.

Freire, Paulo. *Pedagogy of the Oppressed*. New York: Bloomsbury, 2000 [1970].

Frye, Marilyn. *The Politics of Reality: Essays in Feminist Theory*. Trumansburg, New York: Crossing Press, 1983.

Gould, Janice. "The Problem of Being 'Indian': One Mixed-Blood's Dilemma." In *De/Colonizing the Subject: The Politics of Gender in Women's Autobiography*, edited by Sidonie Smith and Julia Watson, 81–87. Minneapolis: University of Minnesota Press, 1992.

Herman, Judith Lewis. *Trauma and Recovery*. New York: Basic Books, 1992.

hooks, bell. *All about Love: New Visions*. New York: William Morrow, 2000.

Kandaswamy, Priya. "Innocent Victims and Brave New Laws: State Protection and the Battered Women's Movement." In *Nobody Passes: Rejecting the Rules of Gender and Conformity*, edited by Matt Sycamore, 83–94. Emeryville: Seal Press, 2006.

LaDuke, Winona. *All Our Relations: Native Struggles for Land Rights and Life*. Boston: South End Press, 1999.

LaDuke, Winona. *The Winona LaDuke Chronicles: Stories from the Front Lines in the Battle for Environmental Justice*. Halifax and Winnipeg: Fernwood Publishing, 2017.

Lambert, Craig. "Trails of Tears, and Hope." *Harvard Magazine*. https://harvardmagazine.com/2008/03/trails-of-tears-and-hope (published March–April 2008).

Leo, Debra. "Being an Addict and Working the Streets on Skid Row." In *Keetsahnak: Our Missing and Murdered Indigenous Sisters*, edited by Kim Anderson, Maria Campbell, and Christi Belcourt, 4–8. Alberta: The University of Alberta Press, 2018.

Levins Morales, Aurora. *Medicine Stories: History, Culture and the Politics of Integrity*. Cambridge: South End Press, 1998.

Lewis, Johnye, Hoover, Joseph and MacKenzie, Debra. "Mining and Environmental Health Disparities in Native American Communities." *Ethics and Policy* 4 (2017): 130–141.

Lloyd, Genevieve. "The Man of Reason." In *Feminist Theory: A Philosophical Anthology*, edited by Ann Cudd and Robin Andreasen. Oxford, UK; Blackwell Pub., 2005.

Lorde, Audre. *Sister Outsider: Essays and Speeches*. New York: Ten Speed Press, 1984.

Luhmann, Susanne. "Queering/Querying Pedagogy? Or, Pedagogy Is a Pretty Queer Thing." In *Queer Theory in Education*, edited by William Pinar, 141–156. Mahwah, NJ: Lawrence Erlbaum Associates, 1998.

Mingus, Mia. "Forced Intimacy: An Ableist Norm." *Leaving Evidence*. https://leavingevidence.wordpress.com/2017/08/06/forced-intimacy-an-ableist-norm/ (published August 6, 2017).

Miranda, Deborah. *Bad Indians: A Tribal Memoir*. Berkeley: Heyday, 2013.

Moen, Calvin Rey and DeWolfe, Kaz. "Introduction." In *Much Madness: A Survivor's Guide to Extreme States and Self-Advocacy for Young Adults*, edited by Calvin Rey Moen and Kaz DeWolfe, 5–12. Brattleboro, VT: The Hive Mutual Support Network, 2019.

National Coalition against Domestic Violence [NCADV]. "Why Do Victims Stay?" https://ncadv.org/why-do-victims-stay (published November 4, 2018).

Oluo, Ijeoma. "White People: I Don't Want You to Understand Me Better, I Want You to Understand Yourselves." *Medium*. https://medium.com/the-establishment/white-people-i-dont-want-you-to-understand-me-better-i-want-you-to-understand-yourselves-a6fbedd42ddf (published February 7, 2017).

Pascoe, C. J. *Dude, You're a Fag: Masculinity and Sexuality in High School*. Berkeley: University of California Press, 2007.

Price, Margaret. "Cripping Revolution: A Crazed Essay." Plenary. *Society for Disability Studies*. San Jose, CA. June 18, 2011.

Roberts, Dorothy E. *Killing the Black Body: Race, Reproduction, and the Meaning of Liberty*. Random House, 1997.

Russell, C. and Semenko, K. (2016). "We Take 'Cow' as a Compliment: Fattening Humane, Environmental, and Social Justice Education." In *The Fat Pedagogy Reader: Challenging Weight-based Oppression through Critical Education*, edited by E. Cameron and C. Russell, 211–220. New York, NY: Peter Lang.

Russo, Ann. "Brokenheartedness and Accountability." *Journal of Lesbian Studies* 21, no. 3 (2016): 289–305.
Simpson, Leanne Betasamosake. *As We Have Always Done: Indigenous Freedom Through Radical Resistance*. Minneapolis: University of Minnesota Press, 2017.
Smith, Andrea. *Conquest: Sexual Violence and American Indian Genocide*. New York City: South End Press, 2005.
Smith, Andrea. "Heteropatriarchy and the Three Pillars of White Supremacy." In *Color of Violence: The Incite! Anthology*, edited by Incite! Women of Color against Violence, 66–73. Durham: Duke University Press, 2006.
Spade, Dean. *Normal Life: Administrative Violence, Critical Trans Politics, and the Limits of Law*. Durham: Duke University Press, 2011.
Stryker, Susan. "My Words to Victor Frankenstein Above the Village of Chamounix: Performing Transgender Rage." *GLQ* 1, no. 3 (1994): 237–254.
Subramaniam, Banu. *Ghost Stories for Darwin: The Science of Variation and the Politics of Diversity*. Chicago: University of Illinois Press, 2014.
Tal, Kali. *Worlds of Hurt: Reading the Literatures of Trauma*. New York: Cambridge University Press, 1996.
van der Kolk, Bessel. "Developmental Trauma Disorder: Towards a Rational Diagnosis for Children with Complex Trauma Histories." *Psychiatric Annals* 33, no. 5 (2005): 401–408.
Women of All Red Nations (W.A.R.N.). "Radiation: 'Dangerous to Pine Ridge Women' WARN Study Says." *Akwesane News*, 2017. Accessed August 17, 2025. https://www.oocities.org/lakotastudentalliance/warnstudy_radiation.pdf
Young, Iris Marion. *Justice and the Politics of Difference*. Princeton: Princeton University Press, 2011.

3

Historical and Presumptive Trauma: Ordinary Trauma in the Past, Present, and Future

Ordinary Historical Trauma: Living Histories of Oppression

An individual's age partly determines the forms of trauma they are vulnerable to, but trauma also exceeds the lifespan of individual people, especially for individuals who inherit histories of political violence and struggle. As I discuss ordinary trauma as an outcome of systems of oppression, I want to recognize that much of my thinking has been informed by discussions of *Historical trauma,* which is a framework that intentionally extends, at least partly, beyond the individual into consideration of the harms that families, communities, and social groups have experienced across time and space. The Substance Abuse and Mental Health Services Administration (SAMHSA) (2015) define historical trauma as "the cumulative emotional and psychological wounding, as a result of *group* traumatic experiences, which is transmitted across generations within a community." According to this definition, historical trauma is a term that captures the complex intersections of the personal, the social, and the historical. This term provides an opportunity to think

DOI: 10.4324/9781003716198-3

about trauma as being both intergenerational and transmitted through social contact, family structures, and diverse modes of kinship. Trauma as heritage and inheritance recognizes that traumatic experiences can reach far beyond the individual or groups that directly experienced them.

Trauma, in this sense, can be haunting: it lives on even when people who suffered it first-hand disappear, and it lingers in the relational spaces connecting people. Goodkind et al. (2012: 1023): "What is important about [the concepts of historical trauma and healing] is that they are *collective* and multilayered, rather than solely centered on the individual. This is different from the typical Eurocentric perspective on illness and treatment." The concept of historical trauma offers a valuable tool for thinking more holistically about traumatic harm, in terms of both expanding beyond individual harmed peoples and moving past individual moments of harm. Additionally, historical trauma helps to ground harm within the social and historical contexts in which it occurred, thereby offering an explanation for how and why that harm occurred as well as the importance of social in additional to individual approaches to healing.

Something that can be difficult to comprehend and that systems of oppression seek to deny is the ways in which historically violent governments, institutions, and peoples continue to impact oppressed people's lives in the present. Traumatic historical events may come to an end, but the ramifications of them continue for generations afterward and may never entirely go away. The present and future exist in a perpetual dialogue with the past, and each carries a capacity to transform the others. Educator AnaLouise Keating (2004: 99) aptly teaches that "many of us have been trained to regard history . . . as a linear timeline that clearly separates the present from the past and 'us' from 'them'." Historical trauma offers a space in which to understand how our ancestors and the people who came before us shape who we are in the present and could become in the future. It also creates space for healing and accountability. Keating goes on to write:

> Locating the past in a time entirely before ourselves, we separate ourselves from historical injustices and so cannot

> recognize that the land theft, human bondage, and other forms of conquest which began in the past continue to inform the present. In short, the linear perspective erects boundaries that deny accountability.

These erected boundaries also deny the presence of harms carried forward across time and space along the currents of history. In other words, the imagined separation of past, present, and future denies the need to be accountable for past harms because it hides how historical violence continues to impact people living today – how they, like haunting ghosts, have what Ann Cvetkovich (2012: 135) describes as "vivid afterlives." One particularly frightening thing about historical trauma is that we are creating and transmitting it *right now* – the trauma our descendants inherit from us and subsequently pass down to their descendants is churning in this present moment, which is, in itself, a culmination of moments past. How we live today will story the memory of future people, both with tales of how we struggled against systems of oppression and reminders of where we were complicit. Accordingly, we hold an incredible power to interrupt intergenerational and historical trauma by resisting current inequities and injustices and taking ownership of lingering harms from the past. Becoming *good ancestors*, to use the words of Daniel Heath Justice (2018), demands nothing less of us.

Michelle Sotero (2006: 99) notes that there is much evidence to support the idea that "PTSD can be genetically transmitted to secondary and subsequent generations." People that have experienced historical and intergenerational trauma carry forward past harms in our bodies and minds, both in a metaphorical sense and in an embodied, chemical, biological sense. The concept of historical trauma comes partly from people attempting to communicate how the violence of the Holocaust affected the children and other relatives of its survivors, who may have been born after World War II ended but nevertheless witnessed its horrors through their family members. These children's experiences of trauma were largely vicarious, felt through the lingering memories and embodied reactions of other people which they then internalized. In terms of ordinary trauma, we could think about this harmful internalization as an example of transference, through which the many damages of systems of oppression travel between oppressed people to reach beyond those most directly impacted. In addition, the notion that trauma can be transmitted across generations also has interesting implications for thinking about the transference of ordinary trauma between oppressed peoples.

However, it is vital to recognize that because historical trauma is most often a manifestation of systemic oppression, it is rarely just a remnant of the past. While many sources claim the Holocaust only lasted a little over a decade, the world felt its impacts for many decades prior to and following it, even still to this day. The people targeted by the Nazi regime (most notably Jewish people but also queer/trans folks, disabled people, immigrants, and people of colour) may never fully recover from the world-shattering trauma of over 6 million murders, and the violence against these groups did not magically end with the Allied defeat of the Axis powers. Anti-Semitism fuelled the Holocaust, and it did not disappear in the wake of World War II, as is evident from the resurgence of neo-Nazi and White supremacist groups around the world today. As with ordinary trauma – and historical trauma is quite ordinary – the same struggles, perhaps in different forms, continue to play out, such that the possibility of returning to the past remains ever present. As I describe more below, ordinary historical trauma tends to be cyclical, and intentionally so.

One of the greatest outcomes of historical trauma is the loss of identities, connections, and knowledges, which speaks to the way that historical trauma follows the four consequences of dehumanization. Traumatic group histories are oftentimes defined not only by an effort to remove and/or dominate members of oppressed group but also by the assault on their ways of being in the world and relating to one another. For example, the colonization of Indigenous peoples in North America did not just involve removal, murder, and the occupation of stolen lands. White colonizers also actively sought to eliminate the ways of knowing and modes of kinship common to Indigenous peoples through forced introduction to European norms and belief systems. Christian Missions and federal boarding schools, which were both to a large extent forced upon Indigenous families and communities, existed for this nefarious purpose. Leo (2018: 5) relates the nightmare of residential schools:

> Residential schools were a terrible nightmare. White people were in charge of the school and their main purpose was to 'beat the Indian out of us'. It was a means of controlling Native people and trying to subordinate us into White society. Young native people were ripped from their homes, beaten when we spoke our languages, and denied the right to our history, our culture, and the safety and wisdom of our families.

Indigenous children were stolen from their families by force or coercion to be "educated" in boarding schools, where they were punished for speaking the languages of their parents or practicing non-Christian religions/spiritualities. White colonizers overseeing these schools cut the children's hair (which often carried significant cultural meaning), stripped away their clothing, and gave them new, Anglicized names, all in an effort to break their connections to the tribes or nations they came from.

Stormy Ogden (2006) goes so far as to compare abuse within the boarding school system to abuse within the U.S. prison system, arguing that rely on both dehumanization and violence. Comparing boarding/residential schools to carceral sites exposes how they acted as tools of punishment, containment, and reformation designed to "civilize" and assimilate a group which Thomas Jefferson described in the Declaration of Independence as "merciless Indian savages." Gould (1994: 32) further describes the outcomes of settler violence for Indigenous peoples in the California area: "With the rapid demise and assimilation of California natives, we lost much of our culture, our ways of being in the world, our ways of apprehending reality." Part of this historical trauma materialized in the form of Indigenous people being forced into boarding schools where they "learned terrible things about ourselves: that our people were lazy and stupid, that we were brought into the missions like sheep, and that ultimately many of us were ungrateful for the gift of civilization the

Catholic fathers brought us" (33). Similar rhetoric was used to justify the enslavement of Africans during this period.

The assault on people's ways of knowing the world and relating to one another is an effective strategy for gaining control over them and containing resistance. Organizing against systems of oppression is much more challenging when people are divided from one another and less able to build communities. At the same time, the erasure of knowledge can have dangerous implications for a group's identity as well as their survival. How people perceive the world is a vital component of how we understand ourselves and others. When European colonizers interfered with the transmission of Indigenous ways of knowing from one generation to the next through such things as boarding schools, they were simultaneously interfering with how Indigenous children came to *see* themselves in relation to other people like and different to them. Indoctrinating European norms and belief systems messed with the modes of kinship common to Indigenous tribes/nations and, in doing so, isolated Indigenous children from their families and communities. Even when Indigenous children were allowed to return from the boarding schools, significant barriers existed to reunification because colonizers forced Indigenous children to speak a different language, both literally and metaphorically.

These histories demonstrate that historical trauma, as a temporal manifestation of ordinary trauma, can come from never being able to go back to the way things were before – that is that trauma can emerge as a result of forced separation from the past, from the theft of traditions and traditional knowledges, from the loss of connection to languages, ancestral lands, and belief systems (Gould 1994). Simpson (2017: 5) further explains that the harms of residential schools and other tools of historical trauma carry forward into modern-day institutions: "We live with the ongoing trauma of the Indian Act, residential schools, day schools, sanatoriums, child welfare, and now an education system that refuses to acknowledge our culture, our knowledge, our histories, and experience." This refusal of cultural recognition within current education systems is a continuation of historical colonial education systems that villainized, demonized, and dehumanized Indigenous peoples to the point where their cultures became seen as antithetical to the norms and belief systems of European settlers.

Before advancing forward, I want to briefly acknowledge here that at the same time as settler colonialism dehumanized/oppressed Indigenous people by undermining their sovereignty, violating their cultures, and refusing to accept their ways of knowing, European settlers were also appropriating traditions and knowledge from Indigenous groups to form the core tenets of the U.S. government. Speaking about racist language in the Declaration of Independence, Donald Grinde Jr. (cited in Shapiro and Grinde 2021) addresses this paradox:

> Well, obviously, the rhetoric in clause 27 about the merciless savages is derogatory and not a good thing. But there's a paradox here – that during this debate in June – May and June of 1776, the members of the Continental Congress invite 21 Iroquois chiefs to Independence Hall, and they are there during the debate over the Declaration of Independence.

Indeed, Indigenous people were welcomed as crucial advisors by the founding fathers of the United States even as derogatory rhetoric against them was used to establish a shared enemy as the basis for a more unified American identity. This paradox is interesting because it shows how the stolen humanity of oppressed peoples gets recycled into the dominance of advantaged people. Indeed, while Indigenous knowledge and culture were important parts of building an American civilization, the same society made active efforts to portray Indigenous people as uncivilized, as savages in need of European enlightenment, morality, and wisdom. European settlers by and large would not have survived migration into the Americas without the aid of Indigenous peoples, but dominant narratives continue to portray Indigenous people through a lens of barbarism and backwards cultures.

In addition to separation, isolation, and the displacement of group identification, the theft/eradication of culture/knowledge threatens the survival of oppressed peoples in other ways as well. To continue forward with the discussion of settler colonialism in North America, the continual removal and dislocation of Indigenous tribes and nations was not just about taking land away from them for settlers to occupy, but it also resulted in the disruption of important practices and traditions connected to survival and well-being. Indigenous tribes and nations were most often connected to certain land bases which determined much of their way of life as well as their ways of knowing the world. Relocating them to different lands through forced and coerced removal meant that Indigenous people were oftentimes made to abandon their traditions and cultural knowledge, both because the new environments tended to be greatly different and out of a need for their own survival. Different environments meant that different resources were available/not available, and displaced Indigenous people oftentimes lacked familiarity with the local plants, animals, and other aspects of their new environments. The resources used in cultural traditions, such as for basket-weaving, may no longer have been readily accessible. Particularly detrimental was separation from healing resources, such as medicinal plants. In addition to the tremendous and terrible loss of life from relocation (e.g. at least 4000 people died on the Trail of Tears), the trauma of removal was about the loss of land and land-based knowledge.

Again, however, while I am writing about past events, it is important to understand historical and intergenerational trauma as continuing into the present and future. Historical trauma as I have been describing manifests in the present and future because the loss of life, kinship, ways of knowing, and much more continue to affect people alive today and will affect people who have yet to be born. Furthermore, historical trauma does not operate solely through what has been lost or, more accurately, what has been stolen away; historical trauma also shows up in the present by way of harmful practices and living conditions that systems of power have introduced into the lives of oppressed peoples as a means to perpetuate themselves. I think here of the health and longevity of oppressed people and, specifically, of the life-shortening disparities and the living conditions they are exposed to. Much of the time, health disparities among oppressed peoples are the outcomes of historical inequity and injustice rather than any biological or intrinsic characteristics having to do with them.

For example, alcoholism and alcohol misuse are overly common among Indigenous peoples and represent one of their leading causes of death. The harm alcohol has done to Indigenous communities is one direct consequence of settler colonialism: settlers weaponized alcohol against Indigenous people in an attempt to coercively secure access to labour and resources, including land and knowledge. Furthermore, illnesses that disproportionately impact Indigenous people, such as diabetes, can be attributed largely to the inadequate kinds of food available to people living on reservations, many of which are impoverished and isolated. By reframing health disparities as sociopolitical rather than personal or biological, we can understand, in the words of Sousan Abadian (cited in Lambert 2008), that "social and economic conditions we are seeing [among Indigenous people in the US today] – the violence, suicide, addictions, endemic poverty, alcoholism – are to a large extent the *symptoms* of trauma" rather than an evidence of deficiencies or deficits among Indigenous people.

Even beyond the weaponizing of harmful substances and the disparities in health outcomes, ordinary historical trauma distributed by systems of power impacts the health of oppressed people through the ongoing need to cope with the stresses of past, present, and future harm. The weight of dehumanization and ordinary traumatic harm turns stress into a powerful and compelling force in oppressed people's lives that often compels us to seek relief. Common stress relievers, such as smoking and drinking (colloquially referred to as "self-medicating"), can help people to cope with oppression, but at the cost of becoming more likely to develop various sorts of illness; even as they may temporarily relieve suffering, they tend to return it with compound interest. Reflecting on the realities of drug use in this society, Wendell Berry (2003) writes:

> People use drugs, legal and illegal, because their lives are intolerably painful or dull. They hate their work and find no rest in their leisure. They are estranged from their families and their neighbors. It should tell us something that

> in healthy societies, drug use is celebrative, carnival, and occasional, whereas among us it is lonely, shameful, and addictive. We need drugs, apparently, because we have lost each other.

The misuse of substances can be especially potent under systems of oppression that create higher levels of social stratification, stronger barriers to genuine human connection across difference, and more rigid expectations for how people should relate to one another. I would add here that pain is also unevenly distributed, and that how people come into contact with drugs as well as how they are punished or not punished for using them is determined largely by the social positions we have occupy. Unequal access to medical and psychological care also increases the likelihood for many oppressed groups to use illegal drugs.

In addition to Indigenous peoples, I think here also about the ways in which queer and trans folks have been pushed into spaces where drugs and alcohol are readily available, such as bars or on the streets (Stanley 2011). For many, it can be difficult to find safe and welcoming communities outside of these spaces, which means that making connections to other queer and trans folks can require drinking or using other drugs. Additionally, I think about how this manifestation of historical trauma through substance use becomes a tool of contemporary violence against oppressed peoples through things like the so-called War on Drugs. Gabor Maté (2009) aptly explains that "[t]here is no war on drugs, because you can't wage war on inanimate objects. There's only a war on drug *addicts*. Which means we are warring on the most abused and vulnerable segments of society." Again, I find it necessary to sharpen this claim a bit because there is only a war against certain drug users, particularly people of colour, queer and trans folks, and sex workers, but I believe the underlying assertion remains true.

In addition to ongoing violence and unresolved social issues, like substance misuse, history, and historical trauma manifest in the present through practices of forgetting and ignoring. A lot of the time, sources of historical trauma do not actually give way to justice or disappear; rather, they just assume new or more insidious forms that are harder to recognize and resist. For example, anti-racist theorists and prison abolitionists like Smith (2006), Gossett (2011), Davis (2015), and Stanley (2011) argue that White supremacy continued to claim ownership and control over racialized bodies following the formal end of plantation slavery through the establishment of the prison industrial complex. People in prison, who are disproportionately from oppressed social groups, are expected to work for little to no wages, with fewer safety restrictions, and with minimal control over their labour. Profits and other benefits of this work typically go to more advantaged people and corporations, especially with the rise of for profit prisons that exist purely to extract surplus value from workers with fewer rights and reduced oversight. In many ways, incarceration is a form of modern-day slavery propagated by White supremacy and capitalism.

However, whereas the enslavement of Black people on plantations is now widely recognized as immoral, the exploitation of criminalized and imprisoned people is justified through racist carceral logics that mark them as deserving of harm. The imagined lack of "innocence" for criminalized people, whether or not they actually committed any crimes and regardless of if their actions merit the punishment they receive, becomes the basis for denying them access to social resources/supports and even basic rights or protections. The escalating violence against immigrant communities of colour, for example, depends on the criminalizing rhetoric of "illegals" – and the political metonymy that constructs them as gang members and violent criminals – to justify the terror of militarized ICE raids and the truly deplorable conditions of confinement in places like "Alligator Alcatraz" or El Salvador. Indeed, White supremacy has adapted following the abolition of formal plantation slavery and come to impose new forms of ordinary trauma through carceral institutions and practices that are more easily defended from resistance.

And the people subjected to them once again have to demonstrate their suffering in order to "earn" the favour of advantaged people. Methods of dehumanization, such as criminalization, create an image of oppressed people as always having to account for themselves, as always already deserving of punishments that become their ordinary trauma, unless they can show themselves to be different enough from other oppressed people. Things like "respectability politics," for instance, are rooted in an effort to conform to dominant cultural norms for the purpose of advancing socially. The goal here is to claim that particular oppressed people are deserving of greater privileges and acceptance to advantaged social positions because they are more similar to advantaged people than dehumanized others. As another example, the concept of "homonormativity" names the ways in which particular gays and lesbians (White, enabled, middle to upper-class, etc.) align themselves with dominant groups in an attempt to access the privileges that advantaged heterosexual couples experience (Duggan 2003; Stryker 2008).

Such efforts to align with advantaged groups and the norms established by systems of power often result in the furthering of ordinary historical trauma both for the people attempting to align with dominance and for other oppressed people like them whose experiences of harm become further normalized and entrenched in the social order. For instance, in the example of homonormativity, gay and lesbians may feel the need to sacrifice parts of their identities, their communities, and their desires to fit in with dominant society. Furthermore, in differentiating themselves from other people who share their identities and similar experiences, they cast those othered people as lesser than and typically more deserving of oppressive harm. In turn, this process of alignment reproduces the same systems of oppression they were trying to escape in the first place.

In this way, ordinary historical trauma tends to follow a cyclical path which keeps oppressed people in a perpetual state of crisis and traumatization. As depicted in Figure 3.1, it begins with the initial development of trauma through institutions, processes, policies, and/or acts of social/political violence. The development of this trauma is a direct outcome of systems of oppression that distribute harm towards specific groups of people who are perceived in some way as being less-than-fully human. In becoming traumatized, the impacted individuals, families, and communities come to experience increased health inequity in the form of worsened health disparities and reduced life chances. As a result of this inequity, oppressed people have a greater likelihood of suffering further oppressive violence or harm, such as incarceration or revictimization. In a state of heightened

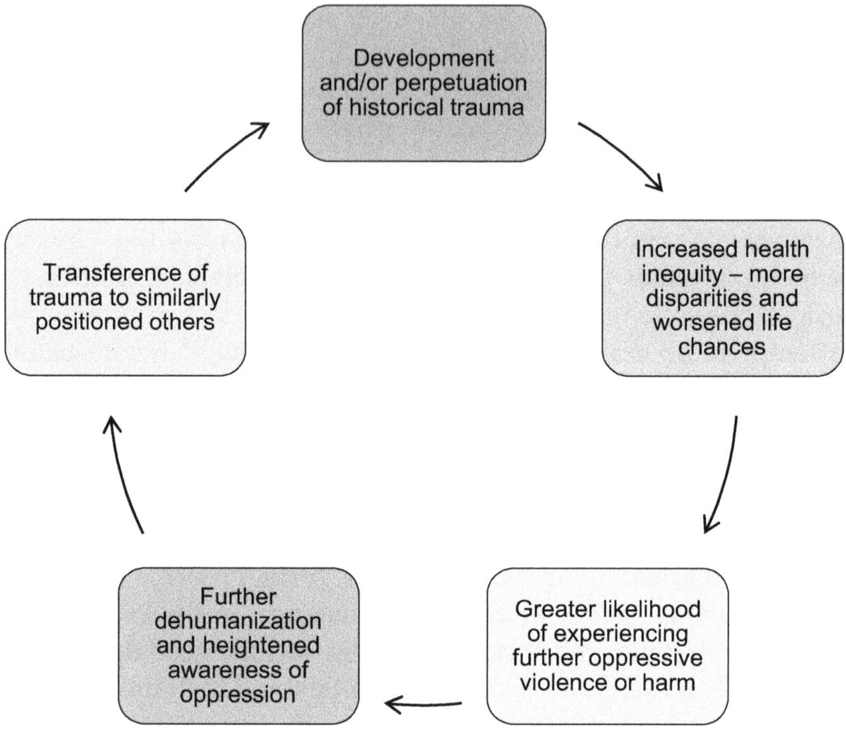

FIGURE 3.1 The cycle of ordinary historical trauma.

vulnerability, people may be subjected to further dehumanization, and they may internalize a sense of their own oppression. Such awareness can be demoralizing, leading to feelings like isolation, hopelessness, and despair, but it can also be a catalyst for resistance or community building which I discuss more later. Finally, through this awareness, transference takes place as the trauma is spread to similarly positioned people (e.g. in the way families raise their children or communities protect themselves), which starts the cycle over again.

Ordinary Presumptive Trauma: Anticipating Future Harm

The theory of ordinary historical trauma is a valuable tool for thinking about how legacies of socially situated political violence/

traumatic harm manifest among people whose relatives or ancestors have been subjected to oppressive social institutions and practices. Historical trauma is an outcome of systems of oppression that make violence, discrimination, or other harms directed at oppressed peoples appear necessary, permissible, and/or unremarkable. However, this term can also be somewhat misleading given that, most of the time, what gets counted as "historical" trauma is not just a matter of the past. Even if certain forms of harm come to be regarded as immoral (e.g. plantation slavery), the systems underlying them tend to remain in place and devise new methods for reproducing themselves as I described earlier (e.g. the exploitation of criminalized/incarcerated people). As Dom Chatterjee (2017) aptly explains, "When trauma is tied to systemic oppression such as racism, leaving it in the past can be and often is impossible."

As AnaLouise Keating (2004) reminded us earlier, for historical trauma to be useful, we have to move beyond a simple linear view of past, present, and future because this view prevents us from recognizing how historical harms manifest in the present, and it stops us from taking accountability. Ordinary trauma can never be purely historical if oppressed people continue to be targets of structured hatred and violence. In this sense, historical trauma is hardly ever just an act of pointing out the consequences of past abuse for it also acts as living proof that harm is still impacting oppressed people alive today. History matters because it establishes the present and shapes the future, and so too does historical trauma matter in part because it impacts how systems of oppression operate in the present and extend themselves into the future. In other words, there is no clear, linear distinction between past, present, and future; history is continuous, repetitious, cyclical, and interconnected.

Given that the systems of oppression underlying ordinary historical trauma rarely disappear, individuals who inherit the trauma of their relatives and ancestors are hardly in a position to assume that their futures will be liberated from threats of violence or social injustice. To the contrary, oppressed peoples frequently learn to anticipate how the past might repeat itself; we learn/are instructed to prepare ourselves for the cyclical resurgence of traumatic events which we have been exposed to, witnessed, and/or experienced ourselves. Prentis Hemphill (2017) explains:

> Our current systems promise complex, compounded and nearly constant trauma for Black people and ensure that we have little resources, space, time or energy to heal and little agency to protect ourselves and our loved ones from facing the same.

Similar statements can be made for queer/trans folks, disabled people, women, immigrants, and other people of colour, though of course the unique ways that these systems work across our differences matter. Thus, even where we can point to specific manifestations of trauma that are "over" or "in the past," the harms of oppression are not done, and the potential for future trauma remains profoundly present, both as a matter of fact and in people's thought patterns. For instance, Patricia Williams (1992: 154) writes:

> The individual unifying cultural memory of black people is the helplessness of living under slavery or in its shadow. I grew up living in the past: the future, some versions of which had only the vaguest possibility of happening, was treated with the respect of what already happened, seen through the prismatic lenses of what had already occurred.

Accordingly, oppressed people living with ordinary historical trauma find it necessary, much of the time, to protect ourselves and people like us any way we can. However, the protection we are able to provide is usually limited by our circumstances, so we make the best choices we can to keep our loved ones, families, and communities as safe, alive, and connected as possible. As a reminder, Mimi Khúc (2024) teaches us that everyone living under oppression experiences varied levels of structured unwellness, and so we must make difficult decisions about how to respond to and care about one another while grappling with the uneven weight people carry from their ordinary trauma. Sometimes, the choices we make are the lesser of two evils because there is no "good" option available to us when grappling with oppressive systems; sometimes, survival is the only option.

For instance, children born into oppressed social groups, much of the time, are exposed to historical trauma not by accident, but in order to warn them about things they will more than likely face as they grow up. Parents may teach girls about sexual violence to warn them away from who they perceive to be dangerous boys/men; parents of colour may teach children to avoid police and ICE agents out of fear of violence; queer and trans elders may warn younger queer and trans folks about the importance of being cautious and alert in public spaces that have histories of heteronormative violence. This intentional exposure to trauma, while often a source of harm and suffering for children who are made familiar with the injustices aimed at people like them, anticipates and attempts to prepare them for the harms of a predictably traumatic future. It is an open acknowledgement of the understandable and logical distrust felt toward governments, social institutions, and advantaged peoples. It is also an example of the intentional transference of that distrust onto future generations and an act of readying children for a life filled with unwanted, unwarranted struggle. This type of ordinary traumatic transference is a tool for survival, though regrettably so.

The transference of ordinary historical trauma from relatives and communities to children is one example of what I will call *presumptive trauma*, which most directly impacts oppressed people who learn to continually bear the burden of looming structural violence. Presumptive trauma is another component of how ordinary trauma moves across time. It is the inverse of ordinary historical trauma, yet also its firstborn child: whereas historical trauma emerges because of unresolved harms that occurred in the past, presumptive trauma is always found in the future, where it conjures up dreadful visions about the possibilities of violence or harm lurking around every corner. "Presumptive" means assumed in the absence of contradictory information, so presumptive trauma, as I define it, refers to a profound belief that traumatic experiences are only ever a few steps away, that any social interaction could easily result in violence, rejection, the loss of connection, and/or something else that is just as undesirable. Presumptive in this context might also refer to the traumatizing realization that other people may not see our humanity reflected in their eyes and that they may act toward us accordingly. In other words, the presumption of our own systemic dehumanization, the knowledge of our own ongoing structured oppression.

This kind of anticipated trauma serves a protective function for oppressed people that keeps crisis mode in neutral but prepared to ignite at the flip of a switch; it's like keeping the engine running because you might need to escape at any moment or obsessively reaching into your pockets to make sure you haven't lost the ID that gives you permission to be where are. Peter Levine (2010: xiii) says that "[t]rauma is not a disease, but rather a human experience rooted in survival instincts," and presumptive trauma is a way of recognizing that oppressed people are conditioned to remain in survival mode – that our survival instincts are constantly primed. The idea of presumptive trauma both agrees with and also complicates Bessel van der Kolk's wisdom: "[t]rauma causes people to remain stuck interpreting the present in light of the past" (2015). Though this claim may be true of trauma in general, it acquires a unique meaning in the contexts of ordinary presumptive trauma. For while particular events may come to an end, the social conditions in which those past events occurred remain largely the same, and systems and structures of power work to ensure that the past will most certainly occur again. In other words, because ordinary trauma is both structured and normalized, interpreting the present in light of the past is a *logical* and *rational* thing to do.

Presumptive trauma is somewhat similar to but distinct from trauma *hypervigilance*, which Lily Hope Lucario (2022) describes as

> the continual need to work people out in order to protect oneself from further harm or reduce the harm coming. Hypervigilance becomes a natural part of the survivor's subconscious needs and therefore continues even when the harm and abuse have ceased. Hypervigilance is about far more than assessing the physical environment. Often

> when enduring prolonged abuse, the victim learns to assess & anticipate all . . . moods, actions, words, behaviors, facial expressions, tone of voice, etc. in order to stay safe.

Hypervigilance is the consequence of prolonged or severe exposure to traumatic harm that emerges in response to learned fear about people's intentions, motivations, and capacities for violence. In acting from a state of hypervigilance, harmed people are attempting to shield themselves from some potential harm which they imagine to be present, even when it is not. This self-protection may take the forms of people-pleasing, deference, or other conditioned behaviours; it can involve limiting time in public spaces and carefully monitoring how to be in public (e.g. always sitting against a wall or near an exit). Presumptive trauma leads to many of the same habits, but its defining feature is that the things traumatized people feel the need to vigilantly protect themselves against are *normalized* under the existing social and political order – that is traumatic and harmful experiences which systems of power make ordinary and mundane. Presumptive trauma is, for this reason, a rational response to anticipated events that are *likely* to reoccur because systems of power have been made them so. Presumptive trauma emerges from the understanding that harm and suffering will most likely continue in the future because they have been made routine and unexceptional.

Consequently, presumptive trauma could be thought of as a kind of priming in which people reasonably prepare for future encounters with already experienced kinds of traumatic harm. Because ordinary trauma is frequently transferred between oppressed people, presumptive trauma can affect those who have been directly harmed as well as those who have in some way witnessed or been exposed to the trauma of other people. Most of the time, presumptive trauma is built from an awareness of multiple traumatic harms that have occurred over time across social interactions. Relating the experience of racial trauma, Monica Williams (2015) explains:

> We are surrounded by constant reminders that race-related danger can occur at any time, anywhere, to anyone. . . .

> Over the centuries the black community has developed a cultural knowledge of these sorts of horrific events, which then primes us for traumatization when we hear about yet another act of violence.

Priming is preparation; to be primed is to be ready, to free oneself of doubt or surprise because harmful things are *no longer* surprising, but expected.

I may feel strong emotions, but I am never surprised when I read about yet another murdered or assaulted trans person or yet another queer person who has been evicted from their home or yet another disabled person denied access to healthcare and struggling to get their basic needs met. As a member of these oppressed groups, regardless of whether I have personally experienced the same harms, I live with a knowledge of how frequently these things happen within ableist, queerphobic, and transphobic societies, and I live with the knowledge of how easily some of those stories could have been about me or my loved ones. The understanding that people experience ordinary traumatic harm because of identities/social positions that we share is harrowing and terrifying; in identifying with them, I both mourn for their suffering and internalize fear of how easily that suffering could become my own. Presumptive trauma often means holding truths beyond comprehension, truths that just weigh too much; it is the over exhaustion of awareness, the red spot in your eyes after looking directly into a too bright light.

Judith Herman (1992) writes that "[a]fter a traumatic experience, the human system of self-preservation seems to go onto permanent alert, as if the danger might return at any moment." Many medicalized and pathologized approaches to healing from trauma focus on strategies to unmake this state of impending crisis, of trauma hypervigilance, so that people can return or go back to their lives before the trauma occurred. Much of the time, this approach is about integrating the traumatic experience, about helping people learn to accept and understand what happened so that they can move on. But, as I mentioned earlier, ordinary trauma is not a matter of experiences that we struggle to integrate, but rather a matter of experiences that society integrates too readily because it was built to integrate them; experiences that we are expected to accept with minimal resistance. As an extension of ordinary trauma, addressing presumptive trauma requires dis-integration through social change. For if we do not seek to change society away from structural oppression, then oppressed people cannot reasonably be expected to unlearn presumptive trauma.

***

Presumptive trauma negatively affects people who spend a lifetime holding it in their bodies, minds, and spirits. As with historical trauma, the well-being of oppressed people diminishes when presumptive trauma influences our decision-making processes and the conditions of our lives. Feeling so close to traumatic events all the time and constantly approaching social interactions across difference with an excess of caution can generate a detrimental level of anxiety that may push disadvantaged people into isolation from others, at times even others from their own social groups. As said before, this anticipation of harm can lead to dangerous practices of self-harm and stress relief, such as smoking and drinking. It can also burn out a body much more efficiently, creating aches and pains faster and slowing bodily regeneration, as with the steadily deteriorating spine of an overused book at the local library. Presumptive trauma can make it harder to develop authentic connections to and be vulnerable with other people, which can cause many oppressed people to have smaller support systems, or none at all. Furthermore, it increases the difficulty of reaching out, pursuing desires, and asking for fair treatment and recognition.

Ordinary presumptive trauma lives in a context of broken connections, missing connections, and harmful misconnections. Presumptive trauma manifests where we are conditioned and instructed to believe particular things about our relationships in the future: that people will refuse to care about us because of who we are or what we look like; that we will be subjected to hatred and violence because other people regard us as less-than-fully human beings; that there will be no space made for us where other people gather, leaving us isolated; and so on. Presumptive trauma emerges when the moment of traumatic experience or a series of such moments fracture across time and space such that our core perception of other people and of the relationships we might form with them cause us to recall/relive the pain we felt before and to prepare ourselves to experience that pain all over again.

As one example of the trauma of White supremacy, Ruby Smith Díaz (cited in Samaran 2019: 83) names the need for people of colour to recover from "growing up in an environment where they were told that the color of their skin was ugly or unattractive and that they would never be loved because of the color of their skin." Such a sentiment is not random or reducible to any single racist person; rather, the devaluation of people of colour, especially dark-skinned people of colour, and the denial of their beauty is grounded in the logics of White supremacy. Moreover, it is likely that love was withheld from them because of the colour of their skin, given how often White people are conditioned to view non-Whiteness as threatening, unattractive, and undesirable. The internalization of beliefs like this one exemplifies how ordinary trauma can manifest as the presumption of lost relationships or the withholding of care. Indeed, learning to hold a belief that skin colour is a barrier to other people loving you can morph into the belief that love is for other people, that women of colour are less deserving of care or affection, and, therefore, that they should not expect relationships to be kind. Each of these beliefs, in turn, increases the likelihood of relational violence and the barriers to forming genuine, uplifting connections to other people.

In discussing her experiences with violence/trauma as a woman of colour, Sara Ahmed (2017) writes about the ways that bodies learn to respond when they perceive crises. She develops the argument that violence and trauma create muscle memories: experiencing these things over the course of our lives causes us to carry our bodies in more rigid, controlled ways that feel more protected or comfortable in hostile spaces. Presumptive trauma, as an experience of being perpetually prepared for crisis, generates an embodied response as well: to live in the anticipation of trauma is to act as if future crisis is inevitable and to proceed accordingly. This conditioned response, the muscle memories or trauma, are not only part of surviving oppression, but they are also a way that oppression wears us down over time by gradually weakening our health and well-being. Living in crisis/being ever on alert for the next crisis yields long-term mental and physical health inequities, and it also leads to missed opportunities for personal and relational growth.

I spoke to a friend of mine who crosses to the other side of the road whenever she is walking alone and sees a man approaching her. As if part of how her body is programmed, this action feels almost involuntary to her because she is not always aware that she is doing it. Without even thinking, her body moves into the learned rhythm of self-preservation that her muscles have memorized. Jameela Jamil (2019) similarly recounts:

> I once said no thank you to a man when I was 19 and didn't have an excuse . . . and he punched me in the face. After that whether or not I have a boyfriend, I say I do. Being a woman is truly, constantly scary. It's like existing on thin ice.

For me, even though I am not always consciously evaluating the people around me, within a few moments of meeting them, I have made a decision about whether or not I am willing to express myself around them, and I reposition my body and conversation style to reflect this internal decision. Whereas as my friend acts in anticipation of gender violence, I aim to protect myself against ableism and queer- and transphobia by masking my identities from people who have not shown to me that they are trustworthy. This is presumptive trauma in action: the experience of my subconscious mind recalling past harm in order to prevent it from happening again or at least to limit its impacts. Presumptive trauma is reflected in how oppressed people carry our bodies in different situations, contexts, and relationships.

It's quite draining, being always vigilant and primed across social interactions or encounters. Sometimes it's physically exhausting, such as when oppressed people move out of our way to distance ourselves from unknown, threatening others. It is also spiritually and psychically draining to repeatedly navigate what feels like hostile or treacherous situations. And it is also emotionally draining in terms of damaged or lost relationships. Jillian Carter Ford (2016: 36) explains that the experience of oppression and presumptive trauma is one of energy lost:

> A consequence of inequity is energy lost. The measure of energy consumed in preparation for the possibility of being ignored, hyper-seen, unwillingly looped into a conversation, or touched is significant. These and other microaggressions happen so frequently in white heteronormative spaces that cost consideration can become automatic. Whether automatic or conscious, accumulation of constant concerns draws on the finite amount of energy that we have as humans.

Presumptive trauma is a form of cost consideration in that it centres around an anticipation of microaggressions and other more severe sorts of ordinary traumatic harm resulting in lost energy. Whenever I think about going into spaces where I will be continually misgendered or grouped together with "other men," I immediately feel drained. Sometimes, my partner and I choose not to use accessibility devices because we dread having to suffer through another round of the "oh, bless your heart" pity and endure the not-so-secret stares of judgement as people passing by. Making a decision not to use accessibility devices, such as a wheelchair or cane, can then cause us greater physical pain, which consumes even more of our energy. This account of oppression and presumptive trauma as energy lost is the inverse to Ahmed's description of social privilege as "an energy-saving device" (2013), and it helps to clarify the conservation of energy rule: privilege reduces energy expenditure for advantaged people as oppression increases energy use for disadvantaged others.

Bearing in mind that ordinary presumptive trauma can only exist alongside systems of power that make violence and harm against particular groups of people appear both expected and unremarkable, it is important to recognize that oppressed people aren't acting irrationally or excessively when we live our lives always ready for the next assault – when we "remain stuck interpreting the present in light of the past" to remember van der Kolk's words. Presumptive trauma is a level-headed and understandable response when people have struggled just to survive and live good lives, and any suggestion to the contrary that challenges the cultivated sense of presumptive trauma among oppressed peoples is most likely grounded in the same systems that make trauma ordinary in their lives to being with. A harsh reality of presumptive trauma is that there always seems to be evidence to justify their initial presumption and any associated responses. Even if no harm actually occurs, and even if the other person, people, or institutions had no intention of causing harm, presumptive trauma ultimately stays logical because of the frequency with which that is not the case as well as the potential severity of harm.

I can infer that my friend who automatically crosses the street whenever she is walking by a man might decide to do the same even if she knew beyond a doubt that no harm would come to her, just as I would still selectively choose to mask or not mask around other people based on my impressions of them. Our emotions are not illogical: they have a purpose and meaning, and they emerge from critical thinking as we attempt to make sense of the world around us. The stakes in instances of presumptive trauma are both the actual safety of the people involved and their internal sense of security. Intimately knowing the trauma of oppression makes vulnerability a difficult space to occupy even when surrounded by other people who are deserving of our trust. So even if an all-knowing deity or oracle were to come into my life to tell me which people I should trust or which would cause me suffering, I'm doubtful that I would willingly become any more vulnerable than I am today because trauma redefines exposure into something overwhelmingly horrible and menacing. My closest friends and family, people whom I have shared myself with, can only catch slivers of my true self because even with them I am preparing an internal barricade. Similarly, you could introduce the heteropatriarchy to its feminist Ragnarök and my friend would still cross the street at that first sight of some strange man. Call it a bad habit, but moving beyond such things is near impossible when they have become so deeply ingrained in our sense of self as to become *unnoticeable*.

This point is crucial: acting from presumptive trauma is not always conscious or intentional; oftentimes, presumptive trauma leads to automatic behaviours and choices which we do not knowingly do/make. Remember, presumptive trauma is rooted in our survival instincts, and when we are actively surviving oppression, deliberate thoughts can come too slowly or it can be too difficult to confront head on. In this sense, the ordinariness of trauma takes it beyond questioning or doubt to a place of habit. The trauma we presume will happen in the future is a precursor to our habituated and presumed behaviours and ways of existing in the world. Our bodies and minds come to learn how they should function in the absence of evidence to the contrary. The "muscle memory" of survival creates an internal path of least resistance that normalizes protective behaviours while also forming barriers to behaviours that feel vulnerable or dangerous. Over time, such ingrained muscle memories alter the connective tissue of our relationships, enabling them to move and grow in some ways while restricting them in others. These paths of least resistance we tend to follow come to determine, in part, the trajectories of our lives as well as our families, communities, and kinship networks.

Presumptive trauma is a learned response of oppressed people seeking to protect ourselves from harm, but more advantaged people oftentimes misinterpret this defensive response as a slight against their character. When disadvantaged people speak out against presumptive trauma or call for a world liberated from systems of oppression or even just do things to keep ourselves safe, advantaged people frequently react as if they are personally at fault for every single abuse or violation. The illustrative hashtag "not all men" exemplifies how advantaged people negatively respond to critiques of toxic masculinity by making it about them. Pointing out the state of fear that many women experience when surrounded by men and asking men to be more aware of their actions somehow gets twisted into a movement to celebrate "good" men. Women expressing their fears and asking men to stop making them afraid cause men to feel personally *attacked*.

The conversation shifts from one about male dominance and gender-based violence to one about supporting and uplifting men. In doing so, the system of male dominance is protected.

I wonder what sort of a man would feel the need to shift the conversation away from gender-based violence and oppression other than one who is afraid of or opposed to thinking about such things? To say "not all men" is actually, it seems to me, a betrayal of an anxiety that the utterer is, in fact, one of the men that women fear. For if they were certain that women meant other men, then they would not feel the need to defend themselves or people like them. This anxiety is one example of how the fragility of advantaged people (discussed more in the following chapter) becomes exhausting for disadvantaged people who have to navigate not only their ordinary trauma but also the ego and emotions of people in power. I also maintain that such anxieties and fragility are intentionally cultivated in advantaged people in order to reproduce oppressive systems: when men feel anxious about critically naming male dominance, about acknowledging their privilege, they are more likely to silence resistance and oppose changes to the social order.

In these ways, the "not all men" movement reveals another aspect of historical trauma and presumptive trauma: instead of being about "good" men's need to disassociate from "bad" men that are doing masculinity "wrong," this phrase actually emanates from a deep fear that their own past and future actions will come under fire, that they are in fact guilty of doing the very things women are speaking out against. Historical trauma for advantaged people has to do with internalizing the harms past generations have caused to other people and coming to terms with the inheritance of this legacy. Presumptive trauma for advantaged people refers to the knowledge that this legacy is not over. The phrase "not all men" attempts to prevent the realization and acceptance that men, as a group, have historically subjugated, exploited, and violated women; the men who use this phrase seek to deny their willing participation in the masculine tradition of violence. In this sense, "not all men" is a discursive resource that men can employ to avoid reckoning with the pillars of their power, an act of resistance to the acknowledgment that their power is grounded in the domination of other people, regardless of how "good" they are. Men that use this phrase are in fact afraid that it does apply to them and that women are refusing to put up with mistreatment any longer.

Interestingly, historical and presumptive trauma for advantaged people might be thought of as a deep anxiety about being called into accountability for past, present, and future harm – that is a fear of being made to account for their place in history. This anxiety is one of the things that I explore in more detail in the following chapter.

References

Ahmed, Sara. "Feeling Depleted." *FeministKilljoys*. https://feministkilljoys.com/2013/11/17/feeling-depleted/ (published November 17, 2013).

Ahmed, Sara. *Living a Feminist Life*. Durham: Duke University Press, 2017.

Barlow, Jameta Nicole. "Resorting Optimal Black Mental Health and Reversing Intergenerational Trauma in an Era of Black Lives Matter." *Biography* 41, no. 4 (2018): 895–908.

Berry, Wendell. *The Art of the Commonplace: The Agrarian Essays*. Washington, DC: Counterpoint, 2003.

Chatterjee, Dom. "Mental Health is Different for People of Color in These 3 Ways." *Restforresistance.com*. https://restforresistance.com/zine/mental-health-is-different-for-people-of-color (published April 29, 2017).

Cvetkovich, Ann. "Depression Is Ordinary: Public Feelings and Saidiya Hartman's Lose Your Mother." *Feminist Theory* 13, no. 2 (2012): 131–146.

Davis, Angela. *Freedom is a Constant Struggle: Ferguson, Palestine, and the Foundations of a Movement*. Chicago: Haymarket Books, 2015.

Duggan, Lisa. *The Twilight of Equality? Neoliberalism, Cultural Politics, and the Attack on Democracy*. Beacon Press, 2003.

Ford, Jillian Carter. "'I'm Feelin' It': Embodied Spiritual Activism as a Vehicle for Queer Black Liberation." In *Yoga, The Body, and Embodied Social Change*, edited by Beth Berila, Melanie Klein, and Chelsea Jackson Roberts, 29–40. Lanham: Lexington Books, 2016.

Goodkind, Jessica, Meredith, Hess Julia, Gorman, Beverely, and Parker, Danielle. "'We're Still in a Struggle': Diné Resilience, Survival, Historical Trauma, and Healing." *Qualitative Health Research* 22, no. 8 (2012): 1019–1036.

Gossett, Che. "Abolitionist Imaginings: A Conversation with Bo Brown, Reina Gossett, and Dylan Rodriguez." In *Captive Genders: Trans Embodiment and the Prison Industrial Complex*, edited by Eric Stanley and Nat Smith, 357–376. Oakland: AK Press, 2011.

Gould, Janice. "Disobedience (in Language) in Texts by Lesbian Native Americans." *Ariel* 25.1 (1994): 32–44.

Hemphill, Prentis. "Healing Justice Is How We Can Sustain Black Lives." *Huffington Post*. https://www.huffpost.com/entry/healing-justice_b_5899e8ade4b0c1284f282ffe (published February 7, 2017).

Herman, Judith Lewis. *Trauma and Recovery*. New York: Basic Books, 1992.

Jamil, Jameela. (@jameelajamil). "I Once Said No Thank You to Man When I Was 19 and Didn't Have an Excuse . . . and He Punched Me in the Face: After That Whether or Not I Have a Boyfriend, I Say I Do: Being a Woman is Truly, Constantly Scary: It's Like Existing on Thin Ice." X, March 24, 2019.

Justice, Daniel Heath. *Why Indigenous Literatures Matter: Indigenous Studies Series*. Waterloo, ON, Canada: Wilfrid Laurier University Press, 2018.

Keating, AnaLouise. "'Making New Connections': Transformational Multiculturalism in the Classroom." *Pedagogy* 4, no. 1 (2004): 93–117.

Khúc, Mimi. *dear elia: Letters from the Asian American Abyss*. Durham: Duke University Press, 2024.

Lambert, Craig. "Trails of Tears, and Hope." *Harvard Magazine*. https://harvardmagazine.com/2008/03/trails-of-tears-and-hope (March–April 2008).

Leo, Debra. "Being an Addict and Working the Streets on Skid Row." In *Keetsahnak: Our Missing and Murdered Indigenous Sisters*, edited by Kim Anderson, Maria Campbell, and Christi Belcourt, 4–8. Alberta: The University of Alberta Press, 2018.

Levine, Peter. *In An Unspoken Voice: How the Body Releases Trauma and Restores Goodness*. Berkeley, CA: North Atlantic Books, 2010.

Lucario, Lily Hope. "Hypervigilance Is the Continual Need . . ." *Facebook*. Hypervigilance is the continual need to . . .—CPTSD Foundation | Facebook (published June 8, 2022).

Maté, Gabor. *In the Realm of Hungry Ghosts: Close Encounters with Addiction*. Random House Canada, 2009.

Ogden, Stormy. "Pomo Woman, Ex-Prisoner, Speaks Out." In *Color of Violence: The Incite! Anthology*, edited by Incite! Women of Color against Violence, 164–169. Durham: Duke University Press, 2006.

Samaran, Nora. *Turn This World Inside Out: The Emergence of Nurturance Culture*. Chico: AK Press, 2019.

Shapiro, Ari and Grinde, Donald Jr. "Examining a Racist Passage in The Declaration of Independence." *NPR*. https://www.npr.org/2021/07/02/1012680822/examining-a-racist-passage-in-the-declaration-of-independence (published July 2, 2021).

Simpson, Leanne Betasamosake. *As We Have Always Done: Indigenous Freedom Through Radical Resistance*. Minneapolis: University of Minnesota Press, 2017.

Smith, Andrea. "Heteropatriarchy and the Three Pillars of White Supremacy." In *Color of Violence: The Incite! Anthology*, edited by Incite! Women of Color against Violence, 66–73. Durham: Duke University Press, 2006.

Sotero, Michelle M. "A Conceptual Model of Historical Trauma: Implications for Public Health Practice and Research." *Journal of Health Disparities Research and Practice* 1, no. 1 (2006): 93–108.

Stanley, Eric. "Introduction: Fugitive Flesh: Gender Self-Determination, Queer Abolition, and Trans Resistance" In *Captive Genders: Trans Embodiment and the Prison Industrial Complex*, edited by Eric Stanley and Nat Smith, 1–13. Oakland: AK Press, 2011.

Stryker, Susan. "Transgender History, Homonormativity, and Disciplinarity." *Radical History Review* 100 (2008): 145–157.

Substance Abuse and Mental Health Services Administration (SAMHSA). "Types of Trauma and Violence." *Samhsa.gov*. https://www.samhsa.gov/trauma-violence/types (published 2015).

van der Kolk, Bessel. *The Body Keeps the Score*. Penguin Books, 2015.

Williams, Monica. "The Link between Racism and PTSD: A Psychologist Explains Race-based Stress and Trauma in Black Americans." *Psychology Today* (2015). https://www.psychologytoday.com/us/blog/culturally-speaking/201509/the-link-between-racism-and-ptsd (published September 6, 2015).

Williams, Patricia. *The Alchemy of Race and Rights*. Cambridge: Harvard University Press, 1992.

4

Victim-Blaming and Fragility: How Systems Distribute Harm and Accountability

Victim-Blaming as a Process of Normalizing Oppressive Harm

Systems of oppression generate ordinary trauma through ongoing structural violence whilst simultaneously portraying harmed people as the cause of the violence perpetrated against them. Victim-blaming occurs when people advantaged by systems of oppression deny their accountability/fault by instead transferring it to oppressed people whom they have harmed. Victim-blaming becomes necessary when advantaged people do things that are regarded as immoral or "bad" and as a result make systems of oppression more vulnerable to resistance. Through various dehumanizing tactics, such as associating harmed people with deviant and suspicious behaviours, advantaged people aim to re-establish themselves as morally upright and worthy of their systemic power while also portraying disadvantaged others as somehow deserving of harm. Sonya Renee Taylor (2018: 11), for example, writes:

> Living in a female body, a black body, an aging body, a fat body, a body with mental illness, is to awaken daily to

DOI: 10.4324/9781003716198-4

> a planet that expects a certain set of apologies to already live on our tongues. There is a level of 'not enough' or 'too much' sewn into these strands of difference.

It is within the constructed spaces of "not enough" and "too much" that victim-blaming lies, and these always already present expectations of apology contribute to a hostile culture in which oppressed people are perpetually needing to justify, explain, or account for ourselves. Importantly, I want to make it clear that victim-blaming is not primarily about harmed people – we are just the convenient receptacle for other people's immorality. No, victim-blaming is primarily about preserving the social order and the many systems of power that give it shape. Victim-blaming is yet another example of how the well-being of advantaged people depends on the never-ending traumatization of oppressed others. It is a tool that advantaged people and social institutions utilize to fulfil their desires when social norms and codes of morality deny them access. It forgives harmful behaviours by defining social conditions in which those behaviours supposedly become acceptable or even reasonable.

At its core, practices of victim-blaming are about rearticulating structural violence and harm as punishment, such that instead of being a perpetrator of violence, the harm-doer becomes an innocent dealer of natural consequences, while the harmed person becomes somebody who "got what they deserved." Victim-blaming, in this sense, functions through the carceral logics of *guilt* and *innocence*, which serve as political determinants of who can be justifiably harmed versus who deserves justice and social resources, respectively (Kandaswamy 2006). Prentis Hemphill (2019) offers a vital critique of innocence and guilt:

> Innocence is a concept that protects some people from becoming the banished and perpetually guilty, the Black. Innocence is the always afforded benefit of the doubt, the far reaching extension of humanity. At its' worst, the insistence on innocence becomes the barrier to true humanity itself and to real reflection, growth and maturity.

Those who are not perceived as innocent, who are defined as guilty until proven otherwise, become marked as both as sources of danger/harm and as deserving of violence and harm. Carceral logics like these underpin the traumatocracy through which certain experiences of trauma are made socially legible while others are denied recognition and validation (Carter 2019). Whether or not harmed people can be reasonably blamed for the violence committed against them, according to the logics of systems of oppression, mediates perceptions about the legitimacy of their trauma. Those who can be blamed are deemed less deserving of care, support, and justice within problematic narratives of dominance.

Carceral logics of guilt and innocence carry extensive racial histories, reaching back at least to the settler colonization of the Americas, and they have been embedded into practices of Black enslavement, Indigenous genocide, land occupation, theft, and more (Hemphill 2019). Victim-blaming is an effective weapon against oppressed peoples because of how systems of power normatively distribute perceptions of guilt and innocence, so that particular people (e.g. people of colour, queer and trans folks, impoverished people, disabled people) are presumed to be guilty while others are more readily accepted as innocent. Through legitimized processes of othering – like criminalization, medicalization, and pathologization – oppressed people are marked with an aura of suspiciousness which leads to fear, distrust, and animosity and hatred. This aura emerges from and contributes to negative social moods that underlie various forms of violence as discussed in the previous chapter. Victim-blaming appeals to this aura as a means to establish harmed people as guilty of social transgression and harm-doers as therefore not guilty of a punishable offense. Accordingly, victim-blaming undermines the innocence of harmed peoples in order to undermine the guilt of people who cause harm.

For example, advocates and activists organizing against gendered violence are exceedingly familiar with the realities of victim-blaming, and we spend a great deal of our time convincing people that victims/survivors are not responsible for the violence another person commits against them. Feminist-led, anti-violence efforts during the past several decades have done much to make sexual and domestic violence legible as widespread social issues in need of a social response. Many advocates and activists have worked to build an image of victims/survivors as innocent people harmed by violent perpetrators. While this appeal to innocence has been incredibly helpful in gaining support from the public and greater recognition within the traumatocracy, it has also resulted in a situation where the gains of the mainstream anti-violence movement are less accessible to people who cannot align themselves with socially constructed understandings of innocence (Kandaswamy 2006). Transwomen and women of colour, for instance, belong to social groups that are often perceived as deviant or immoral in some way – who, to recall Sonya Renee Taylor's words from above, "awaken daily to a planet that expects a certain set of apologies to already live on our tongues."

Thus, even as this image of innocence advances a strong message about the immorality of sexual and domestic violence, so too does it permit harm doers to refuse accountability by claiming that people they harm are less-than-fully innocent and, consequently, deserving of the harms they were subjected to. In these situations, victim-blaming has relatively little to do with challenging the immorality of sexual and domestic violence and has more to do with portraying harmed people as unworthy of social support because of their histories of guilt or deviance. When the immorality of harm is predicated on the innocence of harmed people, it inevitably leaves oppressed peoples susceptible to ordinary violence and abuse, especially where violence and abuse are represented as upholding the social order. Indeed, power sets the stage for oppressed people to be seen as anything other than innocent and, because we live in a carceral state, for the less-than-innocent to be abused and violated through acts of punishment.

Consequently, given that victim-blaming does not necessarily challenge what society views as immoral, its primary purpose is to mark specific bodies and minds as inherently abusable and violable, such as how settler colonialism marked Indigenous women in the Americas as inherently "rape-able" (Smith 2005).

Victim-blaming is a declaration that oppressed people bring violence upon themselves by existing in the wrong times, places, and/or manners, that they are the cause of their own trauma, and that the path to restoration or safety is to correct themselves rather than harm doers. Through this logic, victim-blaming acts as an insidious distortion of facts in which histories of perceived deviance from innocence get twisted into suitable stand-ins for consent or justifiable reasons to disregard boundaries. Again, victim-blaming tactics often are not about claiming that violence is not immoral, but to the contrary, these tactics protect perpetrators by claiming that what happened was not actually what it appears to be of if it was, it was somehow acceptable or deserved.

Through victim-blaming, harm-doers can transform their guilt into a misunderstanding (i.e. they cannot be held accountable because they did not mean to cause harm) or into a matter of doing what was good and right (i.e. they were somehow upholding morality or protecting other people). Such appeals allow harm doers to establish an emotional connection to other people, especially to socially advantaged people who may feel a need to deny accountability for their own behaviours and who have a vested interest in maintaining systems of oppression. Harmed people on the other hand become seen as guilty of leading harm doers on, of failing to communicate their boundaries effectively, of "secretly wanting it," of being suspicious or threatening, of endangering others. As harmed people become seen as guilty of these and/or other offenses, they start to be perceived as less innocent and, therefore, as less deserving of support and kindness. Accordingly, victim-blaming is dependent on the presumption that legitimate harm, requests for support, and calls for justice should be reserved for innocents and that the guilty or, at least those imagined to be guilty, should not receive access to these things. In this way, victim-blaming functions as a form of *denial* that lets people off the hook for caring about harmed people or, worse, causes them to show up in support of harm doers.

Through problematic appeals to innocence and guilt, victim-blaming gets connected to the privatization and depoliticization of trauma (Naples 2003) that I discussed in Chapter 1 – that is the reduction of normative, social forms of trauma to individual, deviant people. Specifically, Carter (2019: 28) argues: "We're taught that the problem of trauma lays in the individual. It is up to [traumatized people] to overcome our hardships and become a fully realized person." Practices of victim-blaming rely on this individualized conception of trauma and extend it to refuse accountability: not only are harmed individuals responsible for our own healing from trauma, but we are also expected to handle it on our own because victim-blaming makes it seem as if we are responsible for the very things we are healing from. Part of the reason why people are so frequently opposed to things like universal healthcare is that neoliberal discourses of personal responsibility coupled with the privatization and depoliticization of trauma lead to a belief that people would be getting more than they deserve.

However, when we recognize trauma as a social, political, historical outcome of oppression, and when we accept that victim-blaming is a falsification of reality rooted in logics of power, then we can begin to understand our unfilled responsibilities to each other and start to figure out strategies for collective care. Paulina Helm-Hernandez (2013) expresses the danger of this individual perspective:

> All too often the ways we have dealt with our trauma has defaulted to individual approaches, which can lead to a particular lack of accountability about our behavior with each other. A lot of people are willing to acknowledge that our responses are rooted in trauma, but we're not talking about how we're willing to transform that.

Moving beyond victim-blaming and the oppressive systems supporting it is a necessary part of transforming this individual response towards accountability. Yet, I feel a need to ask why victim-blaming and individualization are so appealing to so many people. Why do so many of us, including oppressed people, so readily accept this individual perspective when it is so detrimental to our well-being and freedom?

***

Victim-blaming is a traumatizing inquisition: when victim-blaming occurs, harmed people's every last action comes under scrutiny, and they must justify themselves to other people in a way that is rarely expected of more advantaged folks. This expectation can be traumatizing both because it requires the harmed person to reveal some of the most intimate aspects of themselves to all too often unforgiving audiences and because it is all too easily internalized as a truth: even as victim-blaming leaves people naked and vulnerable, at the same time, it can fill them up with a deep sense of self-doubt which strips away their self-confidence and resolve. Internalized victim-blaming swiftly morphs into a betrayal of the self: if people start to blame themselves for their own suffering, then they may find themselves walking down a path of self-hatred that is difficult to leave, all the while questioning how and why they could so harm themselves. For some, internalized victim-blaming leads to future encounters with abuse and/or violation as they come to see themselves as undeserving of a life without these things. For others, internalized victim-blaming turns into self-harm – mental, emotional, and physical acts of violence against their own bodies/minds. In this sense, victim-blaming can extend ordinary trauma by convincing harmed people that they *should* be harmed, that they do not deserve access to resources or support, and that they are exaggerating or making up what the harm doer did to them.

Victim-blaming causes immense harm to oppressed peoples, but it also reaches far beyond them to affect any and all who witness it. Bearing witness to victim-blaming for many people ultimately reminds them that their continued existence or safety is dependent on appeasing systems of power and the advantaged people around them. Yet, it is also about denying their own vulnerability as well as calming fears that the safety provided by conformity is imaginary. Victim-blaming shifts attention away from ordinary trauma in the lives of oppressed peoples and towards the need for "rehabilitation" (i.e. re-education about looking/acting/being in line with normativity). Coming into direct contact with systems of oppression can be frightening, even dangerous, for oppressed people for many different reasons, so when traumatic events against people like them occur, the paths of least resistance, the path of immediate survival, is oftentimes to find an explanation that goes beyond their similarities to the harmed person.

In other words, victim-blaming allows oppressed people to identify some other causal factor for the traumatic harm that they do not share with the harmed person/people. Without this alternative explanation, they would have to accept the harsh reality that the traumatic harm could have just as easily happened to them or to other people they relate to and care about. For many people, victim-blaming can be a *method* for surviving oppressive social conditions and for coping with the ever-present realities of structural violence through disassociation – that is, by developing an understanding of the harmed person as deviant in some other way, targeted for some other reason. Identifying with harmed people means coming to terms with the realization that the sources of connection are simultaneously the sources of abuse and violation against them. For example, if I identify myself with another disabled person who is harmed by ableist violence (e.g. denied reasonable medical care, denied access to a public space), then I also have to accept that I might experience violence because of my disabilities. This realization leaves many people feeling overly helpless and afraid, so they turn to victim-blaming to regain even a small sense of security.

However, for oppressed people, victim-blaming can only ever offer temporary relief because in denying shared vulnerability, spiritual harm materializes and generates a lingering internal wound. This internal wound emerges because even individuals that buy into victim-blaming know down in their cores that the length of someone's dress, or the presence of alcohol, or previous sexual encounters, or whatever else is never truly the cause of harmful acts. Indeed, victim-blaming is a sheer sheet people throw over their heads to hide from the knowledge of their complicity in and vulnerability to systems of oppression. Victim-blaming continues to be a viable strategy to undercut and invalidate harmed people's efforts to hold perpetrators accountable solely because people choose not to reckon with that which they already know. Like a false idol, people empower victim-blaming and the harm doers who rely on it through a misguided faith and fear of what would happen if we stopped believing in it. For oppressed folks, victim-blaming can be an adherence to silence through which people cling to a longing for safety, but, as Audre Lorde (1984: 41) teaches us, silence will not protect us; it suffocates us and keeps us from one another.

Perpetrators of harm as well carry the knowledge that victim-blaming is a grand illusion, yet they propagate it because it preserves their advantage while simultaneously obfuscating the pillars of power. As with a puppet-master performing before an audience of people wanting to believe his show, systems of oppression work most effectively when advantaged people are not forced to acknowledge injustice and the harms they inflict on other people. Victim-blaming is the key to transforming inner turmoil over the abuse, violation, and exploitation of oppressed people into something they can live with. Through victim-blaming, advantaged people can cause harm while continuing to believe in their own goodness; they can preserve their spiritual well-being and an image of themselves as good, morally upright people.

For example, the genocide of Indigenous peoples all over the world, including those in North America, has been justified through constructed images of them as "savages" and the threat they supposedly pose for more "civilized" (i.e. White colonizing) people (Smith 2005). While I believe that many settlers did and do feel the weight of our actions, the thefts of land, labour, and life are made reasonable through dehumanizing and otherwise assaulting the character of harmed Indigenous peoples. Even though I firmly believe that all people feel the effects of their violence, they manage to live with themselves afterwards by developing a repository of victim-blaming narratives to "settle" their disquieted hearts, minds, and spirits. I recall Ta-Nehisi Coates' assertion that "race is the child of racism, not the father" (2015: 7) because this quote captures how harm-making systems produce the tools for their own justification: whether talking about slavery, colonization, incarceration, or militarism, White supremacy fabricates a fictional narrative of race to justify harm and violence against racialized peoples so that White people can avoid difficult feelings that get in the way of dominance.

The need to explain, rationalize, and come to terms with acts of violence committed against other people is precisely why victim-blaming has more to do with perpetrators of harm than harmed peoples. In benefitting from injustice and inequity, in choosing to abuse and violate oppressed others, advantaged people run a risk of seeing the monster within themselves, of catching a glimpse of what they have become and why so many other people fear or despise them. If humans are truly in a never-ending pursuit of authentic connection with one another, as I believe we are, then harm doers have sabotaged this pursuit in the name of *power over* (i.e. dominance) rather than *power with* other people (Albrecht and Brewer 1990). Without meaningful opportunities to build authentic connections with other people, what remains to make advantaged people fully human? From my perspective, claiming power over another person is dehumanizing on a spiritual level. Oppression may give advantaged people social recognition/privilege, but it wounds the spirit in a profound lasting way. Bearing this spiritual wound is painful and creates the need for advantaged people to dislocate it elsewhere, often onto dehumanized, oppressed others by constructing narratives that make their dominance seem unavoidable and even desirable.

It is important here to draw out a distinction between humanity under systems of power and *authentic humanity*. As I have been describing up to this point, humanity through systems of oppression is a ceaseless competition for dominance in which people seek to be recognized as fully human in order to gain access to resources that can improve the quality of their lives. It is grounded in injustice and an inequitable distribution of life chances, and individuals are expected to put themselves and people like them first. This distorted version of humanity is easily stolen away by discourses and violent practices that associate disadvantaged people with the less-than-human world, most often animals and/or deviants. Conversely, authentic humanity derives from tapping into sources of unification that empower us to come together in a shared pursuit of life and radical love. We attain authentic humanity by rooting our own well-being in the nurturance of others (without neglecting self-care, of course).

There is little room for injustice or inequity because the suffering of other people reverberates through the human spirit that binds us together. Under authentic humanity, traumatized connections to other people cause us pain and fill us with an honest desire for reunification through healing. Authentic humanity isn't compatible with systems of oppression which endorse dominance, division, and competition. To the contrary, authentic humanity is in many ways synonymous with the disability justice principle of *interdependence*: a concept that describes how things exist in togetherness, how they are connected to and depend on one another (Mingus 2017; Sins Invalid 2016).

My articulation of authentic humanity is connected to Paulo Freire's description of authentic liberation as "the process of humanization" (2000 [1970]: 79). He goes on to write that:

> The pursuit of full humanity, however, cannot be carried out in isolation or individualism, but only in fellowship and solidarity; therefore, it cannot unfold in antagonistic relations between oppressors and oppressed. No one can be authentically human while he prevents others from being so. Attempting *to be more* human, individualistically, leads to *having more*, egotistically, a form of dehumanization.
> (85–6)

The pursuit of authentic humanity is the pursuit of collective liberation, of resistance against interlocking systems of oppression that separate people from genuine connection, dialogue, and love across difference. In humanizing ourselves through a practice of humanizing those around us, especially oppressed peoples who have been systemically marked as less-than-fully human, we achieve a more just world in which structural violence is abolished and our shared capacity for loving one another is more-fully realized. For practices of humanization to be liberating, however, they must be varied and holistic, including relational, institutional, and structural components. Otherwise, we are addressing the symptoms of oppression, not the systems that produce harm.

Victim-blaming is one way that advantaged people seek to escape feelings of guilt over their failure to pursue authentic human connections and, as a result, their own full humanization: attributing their failure to dehumanized others allows advantaged people to avoid losing the internal sense of their own humanity in the wake of causing traumatic harm to the oppressed. Consequently, the true utility of victim-blaming for advantaged people comes partially from the preservation of their dominance, but ultimately more so from the illusion of their in-tact connection to the unifying human spirit connecting all people. As the social construction of humanity under systems of power comes into conflict with authentic humanity, which exists apart from injustice, discrimination, and competition, victim-blaming emerges as the tool of reconciliation that empowers advantaged people to profit from oppression without grasping what they sacrifice in the process. Violence, injustice, trauma – victim-blaming makes it so that these things do not disrupt advantaged people's belief in their own authentic humanity because the harmed person is made to be less-than-fully human. The immorality, deviance, savagery, or other dehumanizing attribute of the harmed person supposedly made authentic human connection impossible; thus, the harmed person, and not the harm doers, produced the separation between people and damned themselves. Accordingly, they become subject to discipline and punishment, while the advantaged person who caused harm is freed from any need for accountability.

When harmed people try to hold harmed doers accountable, systems of oppression pick up on and exploit people's longing for authentic humanity by framing oppressed folk as divisive, selfish, and harmful or dangerous to other people. Accordingly, systems of power rely upon victim-blaming both to characterize harmed peoples as overreacting to violence committed against them and also to make it seem as if they are making things worse by refusing to "let it go" and seek reconciliation and connection. Victim-blaming asserts that perhaps harmed people did experience harm at the hands of another person, perhaps not, but that ultimately what happened was their fault and that by acting out against harm doers, they are preventing both people from realizing authentic humanity. This shift in accountability happens because victim-blaming relocates the moment(s) of injustice from the act of violence, discrimination, or other harm to the unfair slander against the so-called perpetrator's character and to other immoralities on the part of the harmed person. Again, we can see how the guilt directed onto the harmed person becomes a rationale for their suffering and the key to undermining calls for justice and accountability.

Consider the routine murder of Black people, particularly Black men, by police in the United States that has been taking place for as long as there have been police in the United States. Victim-blaming lies at the heart of police work, and it most often manifests under a guise of "justifiable uses of force." White police officers can so frequently get away with the murder of Black people because they are able to use the fatal logics of the police state to rationalize their violence while dehumanizing and vilifying their targets. Lawyers portray Black victims/survivors as terrifying monsters, as vicious animals, as drug dealers, as gang members, and as rapists. Highly publicized murders over the past several years are meant to leave viewers with a sense that Black people are always to blame for their own destruction – that they are never innocent and always inherently guilty. Janaya Future Khan (2020) says:

> Much of the construction of whiteness relies on the notion of inherent innocence and, in order for there to be innocence, there must be that which is not. Black people are never considered truly innocent. The widely held belief that black people 'deserve it' is so pervasive that it doesn't ever need to be said. It is embodied in every person who suggests that Trayvon Martin shouldn't have been wearing that hoodie; that Rekia Boyd shouldn't have been outside her house; that Michael Brown shouldn't have talked back; that Aiyana Stanley-Jones shouldn't have been sleeping in her bed; that Tamir Rice shouldn't have been playing in the park; that Sandra Bland shouldn't have been driving her car. This hideously loaded conclusion is something that black children become aware of as soon as the outside world becomes aware of them.

Somehow unsurprisingly, this victim-blaming logic does not look that different from what it was a hundred years ago or two hundred. The Ku Klux Klan founded itself on the same logics that the police state openly relies upon today, and Black people are lynched all the same. It is important to remember that modern-day police evolved from "slave patrols" whose main task was to locate and capture enslaved people fleeing from plantations.

Victim-blaming, in these cases, looks like an assertion that the police officer firing a gun was not actually the moment of immorality, but that the murdered Black people were somehow in the wrong, often for doing *nothing* more than existing. Yet, this is not a coincidence: police and prisons as they exist today are modern expressions of White supremacy that developed in response to the "abolition" of slavery (Smith 2006). The carceral logics of the police state dehumanize and shorten Black lives precisely because they carry forward from an economic and political system that refused to see Black people as anything more than 3/5 of a person. Additionally, this example speaks to the way that victim-blaming entwines with presumptive and historical trauma: not only can Black people/other people of colour reasonably be afraid of the police because of the ordinariness of violence against people of colour throughout the history of America, but they can also presume that White supremacy will in some way blame them for the violence they anticipate. Presumptive trauma, therefore, is the lived experience of anticipating future harm as well as the knowledge of needing to account for oneself when that harm eventually occurs.

Near identical practice of victim-blaming pervade the debates over Trump's containment of undocumented immigrants and the separation of families from their loved ones. Throughout his first term, hundreds of children were abused, neglected, and trapped in cages. Whether released or not, these children and their families have experienced far too great a trauma to ever justify. Many children no longer recognize their parents; some families may never regain the sense of wholeness that was taken from them. Throughout his second term, the creation of detention centres that eerily resemble concentration camps as well as the deportation of immigrants to nearly untraceable and unregulated prisons in El Salvador and elsewhere are traumatic beyond my imagining. Rampant, militarized ICE raids despite mass protests show the lengths his conservative, fascist regime is willing to go to in promoting White supremacy. People across the country are terrified and angry.

Yet, even in the face of such blatant hatred and structural violence, people have the audacity to blame immigrants because they did not enter the country through the proper channels or have their legal documents perfectly in order. They ignore the fact that many undocumented immigrants cross the border because their lives have already been imperilled – parents often make the decision to enter this country precisely because they want to keep their children safe and provide them with the things they need to lead joyous, worthwhile lives. But even if people are not seeking refuge or fleeing from poverty, victim-blaming still makes completely no sense because the response is so disproportionate. Undocumented immigration is only a misdemeanour – a low-level offence being elevated to the state of a national emergency. It's like saying it's ok to hold an assault rifle to somebody's head and separate them from their children just because they crossed some imagined line. Even worse, the person holding the gun made them cross the line in the first place by exploiting, stealing, and impoverishing the other side.

One of the most dangerous aspects of victim-blaming is that it often does not lie but distorts the facts and ignores the historical contexts in which violence unfolds. If police just go off of past records, they are certainly justified in overpolicing people of colour. The disproportionate arrest rate of people of colour seems to "prove" that they are indeed more likely to be violent or dangerous criminals. But doing that only makes sense if people ignore the role racism has historically played in shaping these arrest rates – yes, people of colour are disproportionately "criminals," but they are also disproportionately targeted at every level of involvement with police, from stopping and searching all the way up to arresting, charging, and incarcerating (Alexander 2010). In addition, victim-blaming typically focuses only on isolated moments of harm instead of all the events leading up to it and the contexts surrounding it. When parents are blamed for the harm enacted against their children following criminalized acts of border crossing, the White supremacist settler colonial histories of the borderland disappear as do imperial histories of the United States that have contributed to severe economic and social disparities which make border crossing so prevalent. People forget that the line dividing the United States from Mexico was formed just a few hundred years ago and literally ripped families apart. And we also refuse to recognize just how much of the violence in Central and South America is the product of the U.S. government influencing politics and distributing weaponry to keep countries in a near constant state of warfare. Much of the violence, poverty, homelessness, and hunger impacting these countries is a direct consequence of exploitative U.S. domestic and international economic policies.

Victim-blaming is only capable of looking at one event at a time, and these broader histories of struggle are intentionally removed from the narrative. Advantaged people and oppressive social institutions benefit from victim-blaming's singular focus in that it allows them to deny accountability for taking part in legacies of violence and discrimination. Supposedly, those histories no longer matter, and the bystanders who witness victim-blaming are most often not knowledgeable about such things or unwilling/unable to consider them. Part of the issue here has to do with the way people tend to think about our relationship to time: as I wrote in the section about historical trauma, people often underestimate the power past events have in shaping the present and future, and we too often consider violence and discrimination to be relics of the past even when they are, in fact, ongoing. It is hard for many people to fathom how greatly the actions of our ancestors affect us still, but things like the transatlantic slave trade, the genocide of Indigenous peoples, and legally enforced racial segregation were so historically momentous that their effects are still felt. Activists calling for reparations or the decolonization of Indigenous lands are not doing so out of greed, but because communities of colour and Indigenous communities are still grappling with these histories of struggle. This ongoing impact of historical trauma is why it is so vital, in the words of Aurora Levins Morales (1998), to *restore* the historical context.

Doing so can counteract victim-blaming by helping people understand how harm manifests in the present moment and to respond to that harm from a situated awareness of the past.

***

Systems of oppression rely on victim-blaming to mask harmful actions in the present as well as those which extend across time. Oppressed people are often held responsible for trauma that occurs in a single moment as well as trauma that gives shape to the general conditions of our lives. Whether trauma is isolated or a continuation of harmful historical experiences, oppressed people are never freed from the expectation to account for ourselves and "prove" our trauma is legitimate. Furthermore, victim-blaming, while most easily identifiable at the micro, individual level, also affects entire communities of people that are collectively portrayed as acting against their own interests. Community-level issues are typically caused by injustice and inequitable access to resources, but systems of oppression continue to craft narratives in which members of a community bring about their own suffering. These narratives portray community decisions, values, and practices as the primary source of harm but tend to leave out or disregard broader forces and explanations that come from outside of the community.

The Moynihan Report is one glaring example of what victim-blaming looks like at the macro level. Daniel Patrick Moynihan conducted research for and wrote the report while serving as Assistant Secretary of Labor under Lyndon B. Johnson. In it, he maintains that the poverty of Black people is primarily an effect of the structure of Black families and, especially, the rise in Black, single-mother households. According to the report, as interpreted by psychologist William Ryan, the primary cause of Black poverty was the actions of poor Black people rather than broader socio-structural arrangements of the country. As a consequence, even though the Moynihan report somewhat acknowledges the effects of racism and slavery, it manages to blame poor Black people for poverty while removing accountability from Whites. Policing and incarceration, racist educational institutions, discrimination in housing and workplace – Moynihan characterizes all of these external, structural explanations as less significant to the rates of poverty among Black people. Accordingly, the best method for lessening poverty among Black people is presented as internal rather than external: Black people must change themselves if they want to better their lives and communities. Such problematic sentiments and negative beliefs continue to resonate today, and they have become even more prevalent and pronounced through the conservative Trump administration.

And here is where we come upon the aspect of victim-blaming that is so distinctly American: believing itself to be a nation founded on freedom, liberty, and justice, the all American ideal of success through hard work promotes a belief that failure is personal, resulting from poor work ethic, lack of dedication, over-consumption, and so on. In order for people to believe in their ability to "pull themselves up by their bootstraps," they must also believe that we live in a meritocracy – a society in which people earn success through what they can accomplish and not just who they are. Within a meritocracy, individuals' social locations are malleable and never deterministic; the people who have the hardest lives are most often the ones who have not worked hard enough to acquire the luxuries enjoyed by others. However, we do not live in a meritocracy – regardless of how hard people work or what their abilities are, where individuals are born, how they are categorized, and their relationships with other people are immensely more predictive of the condition of their lives. Most people never leave the social locations they were born into, and those who do most often move downward. The "American Dream" is a hallucination shared by millions; the "American Dream" is a stock story used to normalize and preserve existing power relations, particularly in relation to race, class, ability, and nationality, and it "is one of the most deeply held tenets of American life" (Bell 2010: 37).

The preservation of the American dream is another example that reveals how victim-blaming centres around the needs of advantaged people, for by defining the conditions of oppressed people's lives as an outcome of their own choices, it reaffirms the narrative that advantaged people earned their privileges. According to the American Dream, inequity and injustice are secondary concerns to the work people invest into their own lives; inequity and injustice may be a part of life, but they are surmountable obstacles for all people who are willing to put in the work.

Advantaged people love to tell stories about their *humble beginnings* because it places them on equal footing with oppressed people and masks the escalators and elevators that moved them up in the world: they proclaim that they worked hard to become successful and so can anybody else. This narrative about the possibilities of a better future through hard work hides the roadblocks that systems of oppression produce to maintain social order and dominance. When oppressed people stumble upon these roadblocks, they are told that the way is open, that they just have to keep going, but they usually cannot make it through. All of the detours lead in circles, or lead to "brick walls" (Ahmed 2013), so that oppressed people wind up back where they started, watching as others drive down a road closed to them. And then they are blamed for getting lost; they are told that other people found the way, even other people like them, so what is the problem? The United States is a nation founded on victim-blaming and injustice repackaged as freedom, democracy, and merit.

Realizing the deception of the American Dream is a traumatic moment because it entails the loss of an imagined future where life is not so hard or tiresome. Like so many other moments in oppressed people's lives, this moment is one where the oppression and dehumanization of them and people like them becomes apparent, and they are told to feel shameful and bad for it. Poverty is malignant ordinary trauma because it denies life and also because it eats at the souls of impoverished people who have to witness other families going to a grocery store and leaving with bags full of food, or other people chasing dreams of a college education, or other parents who never struggle to secure basic needs for their children, and so many other things which they want but may never be able to claim for themselves. Coming to terms with the great hallucination of the American dream can result in presumptive trauma for people who let go of their hopes for the future and accept that hardship they have been experiencing are likely to follow them throughout their lives. Indeed, once people come to this realization, they may begin to doubt the sense of their own security and abandon their dreams. Or, if the planets miraculously align, they may begin to dream of a different world – a world liberated from White supremacist, heteropatriarchal, ableist, capitalism.

At the same time as poor people are shamed/degraded for living in poverty, so too are they repeatedly fed narratives about the people who "made it" – the ones who managed to climb their way to a higher social position and escape poverty. Here is an interesting and important facet of victim-blaming that people less frequently discuss: while it is common to see victim-blaming in the form of assault on the humanity of harmed people, victim-blaming also looks like celebrations of other people moving out of a disadvantaged position to one of social and material privilege. Such celebrations seem positive enough, and for many people they offer hope for a better future. However, the spreading of these narratives can serve a much more nefarious purpose in line with oppressive systems: in celebrating the achievement of one or a few oppressed people, they simultaneously send a message that people who have not also been as successful could have tried harder, done better. In showing the possibility of moving up to a better social position, they downplay the importance of social/structural barriers to economic mobility and return the conversation to accusatory questions and the invalidation of ordinary trauma. Success stories say, "If these people were able to make it, why can't you do the same?"

Moreover, celebratory narratives are oftentimes attempts by advantaged people to deceive oppressed people into working against their own best interest and communities. What Marx would call a "false consciousness," these narratives contribute to an illusion through which oppressed people come to support social arrangements that only ever benefit other people. The fabricated belief in social mobility that is not realized for the majority of people who hold it causes people to act as if they are already members of the advantaged class. Josiah Bartlet (Martin Sheen), president on political drama *The West Wing*, said it well: "It doesn't matter if most voters don't benefit. They all believe that someday they will. That's the problem with the American Dream: it makes everyone concerned for the day they're going to be rich" (2001). Advantaged people use false consciousness to expand their own power by appealing to oppressed people's desire to live in a different social location and the belief that someday they might. Advantaged people feign as if they were not actively trying to deceive, cheat, and steal from oppressed people.

I want to conclude this section by recognizing that victim-blaming is, ultimately, about social division and that its highest purpose is to undermine accountability, solidarity, and coalition building. When we blame people for violence or traumatic harms against them, we inevitably align ourselves with power and the sources of suffering. Coming back into togetherness with one another and moving toward our authentic humanity and collective liberation means that we can no longer pretend that violence is sometimes ok – that it can be excused because of some arbitrary transgression by the harmed person. Nora Samaran (2019: 10) writes:

> [W]e have to work together to see beyond our current social conditioning and ways of treating each other. This change is not about being 'good people' in an individualistic sense. It is about strengthening our understanding of our position within these massive systems of power and oppression that structure social existence, so that we can better recognize systemic harm occurring, even though it is typically masked. We need to work to become better able to recognize it and then become able to say no to it.

And we must figure out how to do so without blaming the people experiencing and surviving oppressive harm. What does it mean to truly come together? How do we practice genuinely caring for each other by working to dismantle oppressive systems around us? Accountability is not victim-blaming; it is actively siding with people who have been harmed and collectively working to prevent such harm from happening again. We need to learn to choose each other even when it is difficult or exhausting, for until we do, ordinary trauma will keep on happening and multiplying and things will remain ever the same.

Fragility as an Outcome of Refusing Accountability

Under systems of oppression, people treated as fully human are elevated into of dominance by racism, sexism, classism, ableism, sanism, queerphobia, transphobia, and so on. These systems make it such that to be perceived as fully human is to exist in close proximity to the "mythical norm" of Whiteness, heterosexuality, cismaleness, wealth, Christianity, ability, etc. (Lorde 1984: 116). Where perceptions of humanity have been so thoroughly distorted by power, socially advantaged peoples often come to hold feelings of entitlement to the bodies and minds of oppressed others. In gaining recognition as properly developed and disciplined people within an established social order, individuals accepted as fully human are granted power to commit acts of ordinary trauma against those regarded as less-than-full human – acts like assaulting, policing, silencing, invalidating, and marginalizing.

Advantaged people are also, much of the time, enabled to participate in more extreme forms of violence/trauma, so long as they keep within loosely established parameters. Indeed, the regarded-as-fully human, while occasionally called out for their mistreatment of oppressed others, are allowed, expected even, to take part in varying levels of abuse and violation that uphold the social order. In fact, recognition as fully human subjects is depends on the active dehumanization and oppression of other people, both because humanity is defined against these other people and because they must refuse the other from within themselves through continuous denial and rejection. Think, for example, how often toxic hegemonic masculinity demands that men publicly disassociate themselves from femininity or homosexuality as a part of their performance of gender (Connell 1995; Pascoe 2007). Or, how routinely enabled people feel pressure to "prove" their difference from disabled folks as if they too will not one day become impaired – after all, people can only ever be temporarily able-bodied.

To make trauma into an extraordinary human experience while still maintaining inequity and injustice, systems of oppression must displace the majority of traumatic harm onto the less-than-fully human other, so that people in advantaged social positions become less familiar with the sensations and experiences of suffering. Janaya Future Khan (2020) says: "Privilege isn't about what you've gone through; It's about what you haven't had to go through," which is another method of articulating Sara Ahmed's description of privilege as an "energy-saving device" (2013). Yet I feel the need to ask: What is gained from expending energy, and what is lost from not expending our energy? Is not going through difficult things an important part of learning how to respond to the trauma in our lives? And, if advantaged people get into a habit of displacing violence/trauma onto oppressed people, how does that impact their capacity to process pain and suffering into acceptance and growth?

In a previous chapter, I referenced Jillian Carter Ford's description of inequity as "energy lost" (2016: 36) to write about the concept of presumptive trauma as an experience of lost energy – energy expended in the preparation for harm. Yet, if privilege follows the opposite path, if it routinely conserves energy rather than expends it, then do advantaged people experience the *inverse* of presumptive trauma? Something akin to the constant shedding of concern? Is there an experience particular to advantaged people of existing in public spaces without the constant fear of violence or ordinary traumatic harm being imposed against them? Because of the routine displacement of traumatic harm onto oppressed peoples, advantaged people as a whole, I argue, come to have an underdeveloped capacity to handle ordinary traumatic events when they do occur. As a consequence of occupying dominant social positions, they become *fragile*.

Even though most advantaged people will experience trauma during their lifetimes, they are conditioned, by social systems, other people, and their own experiences of power, to believe that traumatic harm will be extraordinary, outside the range of their usual human experience. Whereas people harmed by systems of oppression will typically learn to accept trauma as a familiar presence in their lives, advantaged people will come to (subconsciously) rely on the invisible protections of their privilege. When those protections disappear or fail, the difficult-to-process experience of suffering feels unbearable, so advantaged people need to redirect it somewhere else because they lack the fortitude and endurance to hold it. I define this lack of learned resiliency as *fragility*: the inability to bear more and more due to histories of being expected to bear less (Ahmed 2017; DiAngelo 2018). As a reminder, Ahmed (2017) describes resilience as a conservative technique of governance:

> We can see how resilience is a technology of will, or even functions as a command: be willing to bear more; be stronger so you can bear more. We can understand too how resilience becomes a deeply conservative technique, one especially well-suited to governance: you encourage bodies to strengthen so they will not succumb to pressure; so they can keep taking it; so they can take more of it. Resilience is the requirement to take more pressure; such that the pressure can be gradually increased.

Fragility is the outcome of pushing resilience onto oppressed and dehumanized people: the end result of expecting others to bear the pressure for you, fragility emerges as vulnerability, as weakness, as the inability to take more pressure, and especially as a fear of losing control. Familiarity with ordinary trauma grants oppressed people the knowledge and experience to fortify ourselves against presumed traumatic events to the best of our ability (i.e. to become resilient), but as advantaged people become unaccustomed to such things, or at least come to believe that trauma is infrequent/unlikely – extraordinary – they fail to prepare themselves for things which might happen in the future; they drop their guard. In interpreting trauma this way, advantaged people leave themselves susceptible, and, as I explain momentarily, their experience of harm often results in greater ordinary traumatic acts being committed against oppressed people seen to be the source of their suffering.

As a metaphor, think about the hygiene hypothesis, which claims that exposure to infectious agents during childhood is necessary for the proper development of the immune system. As the spaces surrounding children are stripped of infectious agents (e.g. by cleaning products that eliminate 99.9% of bacteria) and as children are increasingly moved to more "hygienic" locations, their immune systems become less prepared to respond to infectious agents that they do encounter. The rise in allergies over the past several decades, for instance, might be an unintended consequence of stopping children from "getting dirty" (Clough 2010). Trauma could be seen to work in a similar way: people experiencing ordinary trauma tend to be more prepared or primed for traumatic events – they build up more resilient "immune systems" – whereas more advantaged people tend to be less ready. As trauma becomes extraordinary for advantaged peoples, as they become less familiar with the sensations and knowledge of traumatic experience, their capacities to make sense of and work through trauma atrophies. Thus, even as systems of oppression both privilege and protect advantaged peoples, so too do they leave them vulnerable and fragile, at times incapable of handling situations that are even slightly discomforting.

Robin DiAngelo (2018) describes this development as a lack of "stamina" cultivated through an ordinary lack of effort and separation from most causes of discomfort. The experience of social and material privilege is, in many ways, an experience not of stamina depletion but of stamina deterioration; a skill shrunk through a lack of use. A reversal of Ahmed's description of surviving oppression as developing "muscle memories," a life of privilege is one that leads to muscle decay because the strength-building work is being done elsewhere. This muscle decay is an outcome of benefitting from inequity and injustice, and it reveals the urgency of naming fragility and working against it. Rumya Putcha (2018) states that "[i]t is important to remember that white fragility is white supremacy." In other words, a life experienced through the domination of others is the only one in which such fragility exists. The same is true among other sites of difference. For fragility can only be a tool for shutting conversations down that privileges the comfort of advantaged people over the trauma of the oppressed. But as Ijeoma Oluo (2017) asserts: "Our humanity is worth a little discomfort, it's actually worth a lot of discomfort."

Offering another interesting and informative metaphor, Ahmed (2013), drawing on the works of M. Léon Dumont and William James, likens institutional advantage to the relative ease of turning a lock that has been smoothed over time through frequent use:

> Another of Dumont's examples is the reduction over time of the force required to work a locking mechanism. The more you use a mechanism, the less effort is required; repetition smooths the passage of the key through the hole. James describes this reduction of force or effort as essential to the phenomenon of habituation. I would claim that the lessening of effort is essential to the phenomenon of privilege. If less effort is required to unlock the door for the key that fits the lock, so too less effort is required to pass through an institution for bodies that fit.

Like keyholes, social institutions and structures are made to accommodate and permit the bodies of particular advantaged people who "fit" – who are supposed to be there. Those who "misfit" (Garland-Thompson 2011), however, must invest more effort to pass through social institution, to pass around its "brick walls" (Ahmed 2017). This differential input requirement contributes to presences and absences within social institutions: it creates imbalances that benefit certain bodies and minds while keeping others farther behind or below. Yet, there is also a notable danger in this ease of access, for what happens when the friction disappears? When people grow used to passing through institutions and structures without obstruction? Do keys not grow more fragile or locks less secure the more they are turned? If we follow the metaphor of privilege as a lessening of effort, perhaps of gaining entry through doors left ajar/open, then we must take seriously the physical, mental, emotional, spiritual, and relational damages of privilege over time for advantaged peoples.

***

Systems of power leave advantaged people less-than-prepared to manage traumatic events that impact them and the people like them, and these systems also change which things get counted as trauma. When authentic humanity gets warped into competitions for dominance, the most traumatic events imaginable to the fully human centre around the collective action of oppressed others, though advantaged people may be unable to recognize or comprehend this deep fear within themselves. Since the conditions of advantaged people's lives are built from the exploitation and dehumanization of other people, this fear most often manifests as an anxiety that oppressed others will steal things from them, including material possessions, lands, safety, and even life itself. Having been raised to internalize the logics of domination advanced by systems of power, many advantaged people struggle to comprehend collective action from oppressed people as anything other than threatening to their position in a social order. Indeed, systems of oppression make it so that pursuit of social justice always appears to be a flipping of social hierarchy in which the disadvantaged will come to dominate, exploit, or abuse advantaged people in the same ways they have been mistreated. What advantaged people as a whole ultimately fear most deeply is not the other, but occupying the position of the other and being subjected to the ordinary trauma of that position.

Yet, fear of losing one's social position and the advantages it provides is just one part of this problem. The collective action of the oppressed conjures not only the threat of loss but also of the call to reclaim authentic humanity. Healing the tears in the human spirit is painful, for it requires advantaged people to recall the parts of themselves they left behind in the pursuit of their dominance. Collective action/resistance causes the open wounds marring the spirit of humanity to burn in remembrance of what we once were and what we may again become: whole. Being confronted by the realities of what is happening to other people – people whom we are fundamentally connected to on a spiritual level – is one of the first steps in recovering from the harm inflicted by systems of oppression, yet it is also a cause of profound suffering that advantaged people feel a strong impulse to avoid and put off. The promise of restoration through the collective action of oppressed people can produce wells of guilt that overwhelm advantaged people who must reckon with their oppressive treatment of others as well as the harm they inflicted upon themselves in process of claiming dominance (Freire 2000 [1970]).

In addition to the collective action or resistance of oppressed people, systems of oppression condition advantaged people to perceive the denial of privileges they were promised access to as traumatic. When advantaged people lose access to privileges or resources, especially to someone whom perceive as less-than-fully human, the issue once again becomes about imagined theft: having already claimed certain privileges for themselves, advantaged people are primed to lash out at other people grasping what they are conditioned to believe belongs to them. When another advantaged person claims that desired object or privilege, the most common responses are to (1) accept competition, (2) find a method of dehumanizing them, or (3) place blame on an already dehumanized group. Given that option three tends to be the path of least resistance under systems of power that aim to turn difference into discord, it is a common source of animosity between people from different social groups competing for social and material resources.

However, when advantaged people feel entitled to something and somebody whom they do not regard as fully human claims it and/or refuses access, violence in many terrible forms is the typical response. In these instances, there is no recognition of valid competition among equals because the other person is assumed to lack the qualifications needed to participate. On the contrary, oppressed people are disadvantaged from the very start as individuals from more privileged social locations make problematic assumptions about how someone they perceive as lesser could manage to secure something they feel entitled to. To maintain their feelings of superiority and avoid feelings of dissonance, advantaged people must construct a shallow narrative in which oppressed people secured that which does not belong to them, that which they do not deserve, through lying, cheating, stealing, or other dishonest means.

The astonishingly high number of people who believe in reverse racism or the dangers posed by affirmative action (Ansell

2013) are a testament to this biased worldview. For advantaged people as a group, the only logical explanation as to why a person of colour would be hired for a job before them, for instance, or gain admission to a prestigious university before a White applicant is that they cheated and stole and lied, or that the process was rigged against them. To truly accept any other explanation, advantaged people must admit that this other person is, in some way, superior to them, which clashes with everything they have been conditioned to know about themselves and the world around them. For instance, consider a poor, White, American worker talking about immigrants from Mexico "taking our jobs." Framing the issue of unemployment and economic insecurity in this way does a number of things that support systems of oppression and pit disadvantaged people against one another.

1. In focusing on imagined competition between poor Whites and Mexican immigrants, the American worker promotes racist beliefs while failing to account for corporations that underpay and devalue their employees to the point of job insecurity. Exploitative corporations are effectively removed from this conversation before it even starts.
2. Second, even though immigrants stealing Americans' jobs is a myth used to support violent anti-immigration policies and agencies like ICE, this worker manages to move attention away from the other White people that are likely the true competition. Other White Americans in this scenario are assumed to be just as entitled to employment by virtue of their citizenship status.
3. Third, the use of "our" makes a rhetorical gesture that defines immigrants as not part of the population of the United States, and in doing so, transforms this situation into a battle of *us* versus *them*, between the people that are seen to belong here and those who are not.

Thus, such a simple declaration does the work of establishing a (White) national population, protecting and even promoting capitalism, fuelling hatred/racial prejudice, and much more. This brief example illustrates what Amy Brandzel (2016: 4) argues about citizenship – namely, it works as "not only the central structure for reifying norms of whiteness, heterosexuality, consumerism, and settler colonialism within the United States" but also as a regulatory tool through which social "norms are brutally enforced against nonnormative bodies, practices, behaviors, and forms of affiliations through oppositional divide-and-conquer logics."

I want to note as well that the objects of desire for advantaged people are not just things like money and property; they might even view oppressed people themselves as existing for their benefit and/or possession. Through processes of dehumanization, advantaged people stop regarding others as autonomous, conscious beings existing in their own right. Through a lens of dominance, dehumanized others come to exist solely or primarily in relation to the needs and desires of advantaged people, as an extension of them rather than as unique individuals. Re-asserting their independence and refusing to be so diminished by power becomes a daily practice for oppressed people resisting systems of power. I think here of the speeches men commonly make to show their support for efforts to end gender-based violence in which the reasons for their caring have more to do with them than with the people impacted by sexual violence. In such speeches, violence against women starts to matter because the men have wives, daughters, nieces, and female friends. The issue of violence against women becomes urgent because of how it impacts advantaged people through their relationships to women. Consequently, it becomes needful for women to reiterate that their ordinary trauma matters *regardless* of men in their lives. They have to assert and continually defend their autonomy as more than just extensions of the men around them.

However, whenever oppressed people assert their independence, it often results in volatile responses from the advantaged people who feel entitled to their bodies and minds. Indeed, because advantaged people often fail to see oppressed others as existing on their own terms, assertions of independence are regularly redefined as refusals to deliver that which the fully human feel entitled to. Frequently, this redefinition comes in the form of a debt unpaid (e.g. when men expect sex after taking women on expensive date; Perry 2008). At other times, this redefining is a refusal to accept no as an answer (e.g. men assuming that women are playing "hard to get" and making multiple sexual advances, or the chanting from the Yale chapter of Delta Kappa Epsilon that went "No means yes, yes means anal"). Sometimes, assertions of independence result in physical confrontations or threats to the safety and/or well-being of the people making them. For example, one of the most perilous times for people involved in abusive relationships is when they attempt to escape from their abuser's power and control. The mere act of pursuing life independent of the abuser incites their rage and violence. When abusive people murder their intimate partners, it is commonly preceded by separation or by the harmed person's attempting to leave the relationship (Tjaden and Thoennes 2000).

Whatever their specific response to the oppressed other may be, the message sent is always one of ownership, entitlement, and dominance. Volatile responses from advantaged people are common because systems of power have put them in such a position that assertions of independence from oppressed others may seem to constitute their own form of trauma: not only are they being refused access to what systems of oppression have conditioned them to expect from others, but they are also being told that the desire and will of someone they view as a lesser being is of equal or even greater importance than their own. Through declarations of independence, oppressed peoples constitute a state of emergency for the advantaged in which the life they feel entitled to comes under fire. These declarations may cause them to perceive social catastrophe on the horizon that destabilizes their sense of security, tied both to a present that is not what they believed and to an imagined future that may never come to pass. The sense of looming catastrophe can mimic sensations of trauma and convince them of an urgent need to re-establish order. Thus, a state of emergency comes into being not only in relation to but also as the consequence of the *state of emergence* oppressed people claim for themselves (Bhabha 1986).

Declarations of independence from oppressed people are not inherently traumatic, but they become so through systems of power that leave advantaged peoples unsure of their position in a social landscape they cannot dominate. Coupled with their underdeveloped capacity to work through events they perceive as traumatic – their fragility, they oftentimes respond to declarations of independence in extreme and unpredictable ways. For example, men's gun violence, including mass shootings/school shootings, is frequently preceded by rejection or separation from women they have shown a sexual interest towards. In early 2018, Austin Rollins took a handgun into his Maryland high school and murdered Jaelynn Willey, a girl that he had recently been in a relationship with, before shooting himself in the head minutes later. Around that same time, across the country, Dimitrios Pagourtzis carried a shotgun to school and over the course of 30 minutes, murdered eight students and two teachers and injured many more. One of the first people Pagourtzis killed was Shana Fisher, a classmate he had been making aggressive sexual advances towards for months before she publicly rejected him in front of their classmates. His journals indicate he wanted to take his own life following the shooting.

While not all cases of men's gun violence revolve around women refusing them or that broke their hearts, the frequency with which these kinds of shootings occur suggests that existing constructions of masculinity leave many men vulnerable to and unprepared for interactions that do not go their way. Many social theorists and activists have taken up the term fragility, as I use it here, to describe how people occupying privileged social positions experience this kind of profound vulnerability to the judgements of others and the need to control their social interactions. In a context of ordinary trauma, the fragility of advantaged people accounts for the ways that systems of oppression make the privileges they create seem to be perpetually on the verge of vanishing, as if people benefitting from inequality and injustice are constantly in danger of losing their power. While this sense of impending loss is made up and illusionary – structural oppression is still firmly in place – it comes to be weaponized against oppressed others in ways I have been describing. Conquering this vulnerability entails asserting power over *them* and reclaiming superiority and difference.

***

Ahmed (2013) asserts: "If social privilege is like an energy saving device, no wonder that not to inherit privilege can be so trying. There is a politics to exhaustion. Feeling depleted can be a measure of just what we are up against." If a politics of exhaustion exists in which some of us come to feel depleted as an effect of how we are positioned under systems of oppression, then so too must there be people benefitting from feelings of depletion, people who become energized or freed to use excess energy. More immediate access with less energy expended is characteristic of privilege, but to know this experience of privilege over time and come to expect, even feel entitled to, such experience, greatly influences individuals' perceptions of the world, how they make sense of things and process new information, and how they form relationships. Fragility germinates through the experience of privilege as advantaged people come to be less capable of accepting and positively responding to refusals of their will; they cannot make sense of the denial of their desire/control, nor do they believe they should have to because the history of repeatedly and consistently getting their way leads them to believe that they *should* get their way without resistance, judgement, or complaint.

In the 2018 book, *White Fragility*, Robin DiAngelo uses the concept of fragility to consider the question of why it is so exhausting and challenging to speak with White people about racism. Fragility, for DiAngelo, comes from a failure to build-up what she terms "racial stamina": in being shielded from racial discomforts through ongoing segregation (physical and mental), White people come to have a hard time engaging in discussions about racism, both because of how infrequently they are made to do so and because White supremacy pressures people of colour to show deference and compassion to White people. Related to the underdeveloped capacity for managing ordinary trauma, fragility in this sense operates through an avoidance of situations that are discomforting, and it often results in adverse responses from the fragile group. Accordingly, the politics of exhaustion surrounding fragility are twofold: (1) the fatigue and depletion that oppressed people feel when interacting with fragile people; (2) the energy spent avoiding recognition of and accountability for oppressed people's suffering, which, in turn, leads to less and less stamina for listening across difference.

The underlying fear that leads to a loss of stamina and the emergence of fragility comes from an uncertainty of control: upon being faced with the discomfort brought about by oppressed people asserting their humanity, advantaged people risk becoming uncertain of themselves and their future; their hostile or negative responses are about regaining a feeling of certainty through eliminating sources of uncertainty. As I described earlier, this eliminating can be as extreme as murder, but more often, it comes from avoidance tactics, such as shutting down conversation whenever someone mentions racism in a room full of White people or ensuring that White people's feelings are always, always at the centre (Oluo 2017). When advantaged people set the terms of social change, limited stamina keeps the pace slow and manageable, sometimes even at a standstill. Oppressed people, then, have the added burden of surviving their ordinary traumatic experiences while attending to the emotional needs of advantaged people. This burden creates an additional level of exhaustion, especially given that failing to keep advantaged people emotionally regulated can result in everything from being yelled at, to being physically or sexually assaulted, to being incarcerated/deported, to being murdered.

Fragility is a concept that moves across sites of difference, but it does not function in exactly the same way for all oppressed peoples. Even though fragility is cultivated across difference through similar systems or practices, such as the avoidance of discomforting situations, it shows up differently relative to diverse systems of oppression. For example, men benefitting from sexism are not fragile in the same ways as White folks benefitting from racism, because gender oppression does not operate in the same way as racial oppression, nor are its effects identical. Furthermore, the adverse responses triggered for White people by the threat of feeling inferior to people of colour is not the same as that for men at the prospect of unruly and "nasty" women. Consequently, even though I use fragility to explore multiple privileged positions, it is crucial to recognize and understand the term's specific impact. Just as universal accounts of trauma inevitably leave out specific traumatic events/histories of harm (Cvetkovich 2003), so too do singular understandings of fragility lessen the term's usefulness for explaining the effects of power on the mentality of advantaged people. Fragility needs to be contextualized within interlocking systems of oppression. We need to be asking: How does fragility manifest differently through White supremacy, patriarchy, queerphobia, transphobia, and neoliberal capitalism? What aspects of these structures lead to fragility and in what ways?

Further, fragility is an intersectional construction: in addition to crossing sites of difference, fragility in relation to specific systems of power is dependent on individuals' multiple other identities and social locations. Since the advantages people receive from systems of power change based on the totality of how they are categorized/grouped (e.g. Black men and other men of colour do not benefit from sexism in the same way as White men), feelings of anxiety at the prospect of losing privilege or control over other people tend to produce particular and situated reactions. As individuals gain/lose access to social and material resources based upon their social positions, this sense of entitlement can fluctuate. For example, White men in general are socialized to believe that the world exists for them and oftentimes feel entitled to the bodies and minds of women in general. Men of colour, however, are often punished for showing any kind of sexual attraction towards White women, and over time, their feelings of entitlement might develop differently. Even though heteropatriarchy continues to teach men of colour that women are not "all the way human" (as Terry Crews said), the intersections of sexism and racism, mark some women as beyond their control, as "belonging" to someone else. And the entitlement of White men to women in general has historically been lethal both to women and to men of colour, from sexual/domestic violence to lynching and incarceration.

In order to protect themselves from advantaged people's fragility, oppressed peoples must remain aware of it at all times. Advantaged people, however, eagerly deny their vulnerability by way of identity construction, narrative control, or shows of strength and aggression. Privileged identity categories, such as Whiteness or masculinity, are built through rejections of weakness and things assumed to be weak. For example, fragile men actively differentiate themselves from women, whose femininity is constructed as weak and in need of protection by men (e.g. think about any of the "you _ like a girl" statements used as insults). Such efforts are about transferring fragility to other people, both to girls/women and to other men at whom the insult was aimed. Claiming the power to name someone else's weakness is an assertion of strength or superiority to that person: not only are they marked as weaker, but advantaged people are also able to mask their fragility through a claim to dominance. As oppressed identities or social positions come to be associated with weakness, fragility becomes affixed to them as well, rather than to advantaged identities and social positions (e.g. fragile men produce narratives of delicate women to re-establish their own strength).

This practice of rejecting weakness is central to the competition for humanity, in such a way that advantaged people guarantee they win by making sure that oppressed people only ever lose. The rejection of fragility is central to what C. J. Pascoe (2007) terms the "fag discourse," in which adolescent men and boys use homophobic insults against one another as a way of demonstrating their masculine strength and control. The use of gendered/sexualized insults against each other is all about performing – and compelling others to perform – gender as a metric of belonging to dominant social positions: by participating, boys and men assert that they are indeed masculine enough to evaluate and criticize the masculinity of others. Taking part in this culture is tied to anxiety about aligning with the ideal embodiment of "hegemonic masculinity" (Connell 1995) – a patriarchal gendered performance that normalizes violence against women and compels men into egotistical competitions with one another.

As I come to the end of this chapter, I want to propose that fragility is the inverse of collective resilience and our interdependence. Lucién Demaris (n.d.) maintains that: "What makes a community of individuals resilient is not self-mastery or will – it is the quality, strength, and inclusivity of our relational bonds." Interdependence, similarly, is accomplished through the recognition and cultivation of restorative and transformative connections. Fragility is the by-product of a society based in violence and competition where truly meaningful relationships are rare and difficult to come by. Fragility is the consequence of benefiting from structural oppression and desiring dominance to the point where the advantaged person knows, perhaps not consciously, that their social positions and privileges are built upon faulty foundation. Advantage breeds fragility because power breeds resistance, and the promise of change one day arriving threatens to topple the pillars of dominance upon which advantaged people have established themselves and their livelihood. Fragility is the felt need to bear less and less as others are made to bear more and more, but it evokes a deep-seated anxiety about what happens when that weight is redistributed. Becoming fragile means that power relations must be upheld because there is no certainty of survival in a world without it.

References

Ahmed, Sara. "Feeling Depleted." *FeministKilljoys*. https://feministkilljoys.com/2013/11/17/feeling-depleted/ (published November 17, 2013).

Ahmed, Sara. *Living a Feminist Life*. Durham: Duke University Press, 2017.

Albrecht, Lisa and Brewer, Rose. *Bridges of Power: Women's Multicultural Alliances*. Philadelphia: New Society Publishers, 1990.

Alexander, Michelle. *The New Jim Crow: Mass Incarceration in the Age of Colorblindness*. New York: The New Press, 2010.

Ansell, Amy. *Race and Ethnicity: The Key Concepts*. New York: Routledge, 2013.

Bell, Lee Anne. *Storytelling for Social Justice: Connecting Narrative and the Arts in Antiracist Teaching*. New York: Routledge, 2010.

Bhabha, Homi. *Forward to Black Skin, White Masks by Frantz Fanon, VII-X*. New York: Grove Press, 1986.

Brandzel, Amy. *Against Citizenship: The Violence of the Normative*. University of Illinois Press, 2016.

Carter, Angela. "Disabling Trauma: Toward a Crip Critique of Post-Traumatic Stress Disorder." Ph.D. Dissertation. University of Minnesota, 2019.

Clough, Sharyn. "Gender and the Hygiene Hypothesis." *Social Science and Medicine* (2010): 1–8.

Coates, Ta-Nehisi. *Between the World and Me*. One World, 2015.

Connell, R. W. *Masculinities*. Berkley: University of California Press, 1995.

Cvetkovich, Ann. *An Archive of Feelings: Trauma, Sexuality, and Lesbian Public Cultures*. Durham: Duke University Press, 2003.

Demaris, Lucién. "About Us—Relational Uprising." Accessed August 20, 2025. https://relationaluprising.org/mission (n.d.).

DiAngelo, Robin. *White Fragility: Why It's So Hard for White People to Talk About Racism*. Beacon Press, 2018.

Ford, Jillian Carter. "'I'm Feelin' It': Embodied Spiritual Activism as a Vehicle for Queer Black Liberation." In *Yoga, The Body, and Embodied Social Change*, edited by Beth Berila, Melanie Klein, and Chelsea Jackson Roberts, 29–40. Lanham: Lexington Books, 2016.

Freire, Paulo. *Pedagogy of the Oppressed.* New York: Bloomsbury, 2000 [1970].

Garland-Thompson, Rosemarie. "Misfits: A Feminist Materialist Disability Concept." *Hypatia* 26, no. 3 (2011): 591–609.

Helm-Hernandez, Paulina. "Interview." *Kindred Southern Healing Justice Collective*. http://www.healingcollectivetrauma.com/paulina-helm-hernandez.html (published February 2013).

Hemphill, Prentis. "Letting Go of Innocence." https://prentishemphill.com/selectwritings/2019/7/5/letting-go-of-innocence (published July 5, 2019).

Kandaswamy, Priya. "Innocent Victims and Brave New Laws: State Protection and the Battered Women's Movement." In *Nobody Passes: Rejecting the Rules of Gender and Conformity*, edited by Matt Sycamore, 83–94. Emeryville: Seal Press, 2006.

Khan, Janaya Future. "Janaya Future Khan's Guide To Understanding White Privilege." *British Vogue*. (published June 3, 2020).

Levins Morales, Aurora. *Medicine Stories: History, Culture and the Politics of Integrity*. Cambridge: South End Press, 1998.

Lorde, Audre. *Sister Outsider: Essays and Speeches.* New York: Ten Speed Press, 1984.

Mingus, Mia. "Forced Intimacy: An Ableist Norm." *Leaving Evidence*. https://leavingevidence.wordpress.com/2017/08/06/forced-intimacy-an-ableist-norm/ (published August 6, 2017).

Naples, Nancy. "Deconstructing and Locating Survivor Discourse: Dynamics of Narrative, Empowerment, and Resistance for Survivors of Child Sexual Abuse." *Signs* 28, no. 4 (2003): 1151–1185.

Oluo, Ijeoma. "White People: I Don't Want You to Understand Me Better, I Want You to Understand Yourselves." *Medium*. https://medium.com/the-establishment/white-people-i-dont-want-you-to-understand-me-better-i-want-you-to-understand-yourselves-a6fbedd42ddf (published February 7, 2017).

Pascoe, C. J. *Dude, You're a Fag: Masculinity and Sexuality in High School*. Berkeley: University of California Press, 2007.

Perry, Brad. "Hooking Up With Healthy Sexuality: The Lessons Boy Learn (and Don't Lean) about Sexuality, and Why a Sex-Positive Rape Prevention Paradigm Can Benefit Everyone Involved." In *Yes Means Yes! Visions of Female Sexual Power and a World without Rape*, edited by J. Freedman and J. Valenti, 193–208. Berkeley: Seal Press, 2008.

Putcha, Rumya. "The Trouble with Yoga: Why Yoga Studios are the New Country Club." *Texasobserver.org*. https://www.texasobserver.org/the-trouble-with-yoga/ (published November 29, 2018).

Samaran, Nora. *Turn This World Inside Out: The Emergence of Nurturance Culture*. Chico: AK Press, 2019.

Sins Invalid. "Skin, Tooth, and Bone. The Basis of Movement is Our People: A Disability Justice Primer." *Sins Invalid*, 2016.

Smith, Andrea. *Conquest: Sexual Violence and American Indian Genocide*. New York City: South End Press, 2005.

Smith, Andrea. "Heteropatriarchy and the Three Pillars of White Supremacy." In *Color of Violence: The Incite! Anthology*, edited by Incite! Women of Color against Violence, 66–73. Durham: Duke University Press, 2006.

Taylor, Sonya Renee. *The Body Is Not an Apology: The Power of Radical Self-love*. Oakland, CA: Berrett-Koehler Publishers, 2018.

Tjaden, Patricia and Thoennes, Nancy. *Extent, Nature, and Consequences of Intimate Partner Violence: Findings from the National Violence Against Women Survey*. Washington, DC: National Institute of Justice, 2000.

West Wing. "Ways and Means." October 24, 2001.

5

Experiential Illegibility: Tools for Denying and Invalidating Ordinary Trauma

Fatphobia and the Trauma of Not Being Seen

Fatphobia refers to the systematic fear and hatred directed at people regarded as fat and/or "obese." Fat bodies, mine included, transgress the hyper-normative expectations placed on individuals to conform to social constructions of thinness, which are thoroughly embedded in discourses of beauty, health, and ability. For many people, attaining a socially acceptable thin body is physically impossible without starving ourselves and removing some of our less necessary bones. *Fat shaming* happens when people are made to feel bad, guilty, gross, or otherwise shameful for not being thin, irrespective of whether or not we are living a so-called healthy lifestyle. Indeed, fat-shaming has relatively little to do with how individuals treat our bodies, and it is almost entirely the consequence of how much space they seem to take up, which is reflective of a deep, misguided assumption that body size is primarily the outcome of consumption. Terah Stewart (2018: 31) explains that

> Fatphobia is a function of a pervasive and broad thin-centric culture that places types of physical bodies in hierarchical terms, with fat being one of the worst kind of

DOI: 10.4324/9781003716198-5

> bodies a person could have. Like most forms of oppression (ableism, transphobia, racism, sexism, cissexism, homophobia, classism, etc.), fatphobia manifests in destructive ways that go beyond individual attitudes and beliefs. Fatphobia has wide-reaching systemic and structural implications for fat people that negatively affect mental health, physical health, career opportunities, and overall well-being.

In the fatphobic world, fat people are never seen as healthy because they *choose* to overeat, or *refuse* to exercise, or *brush off* the advice of dietary specialists and doctors. Weight and body size are presumed to be entirely in their control, and they are punished for supposedly losing control by way of gluttony. Fatness becomes an obvious marker of fat people's *failure* to value our own lives as well as an open invitation for critique from others. Stewart (2018: 31) goes on to write: "As someone who has had to navigate an oppressive system at multiple social identity levels, fatphobia still seems to be an acceptable form of bias."

Like other systems of oppression, fatphobia is deeply intersectional and impacts individuals differently based on their other identities or social locations. How people are disciplined for their body sizes, which body sizes they are permitted to occupy, and what privileges they are granted/denied access to as a result vary relative to other aspects of people's lives, even if certain experiences appear to be the same across difference. Emi Koyama (2004) maintains: "Contrary to the idea that fat oppression functions in some sort of socially accepted vacuum, anti-fat attitudes and systems have everything to do with racial and class politics, not just gender politics." Koyama continues:

> We need to pay attention to the many ways in which fat oppression is embedded not only in sexism, but also in racism, classism, heterosexism, ableism and other oppressions. Instead of merely arguing that fat is normal and healthy, we need to challenge the concepts of normalcy and health altogether, and question who is arbitrating these categories and who benefits.

For example, harmful beliefs about consumption are filtered through classism, to the point where fat people on welfare are propped up as a shining example of why "government handouts" have gone too far. Anti-social welfare platforms often point to poor people's assumed excessive consumption (e.g. bewildered conservatives talking about how much food people can get on food stamps). Fatphobia is also a deeply gendered, sexualized, racialized system: men are much more often allowed to be fat because hegemonic masculinity encourages the occupation of space, whereas women are urged more often to occupy less space – to make themselves smaller, for example, by losing weight. However, acceptance of fatness is often less accessible to men of colour and queer men. Similarly, weight and size are weaponized against trans people of all genders (e.g. to call their gender into question) and disabled folks (e.g. as a way to blame our impairments on our personal behaviors). Grasping the workings of fatphobia requires analysing each of the systems it interacts with to identify and rout out these shared meanings and entangled discourses.

Fatphobia is a source of ordinary trauma for many of us, yet it is also one of the most scoffed at and ignored systems of oppression that the non-fat world refuses to acknowledge. Much of the harm resulting from fatphobia is connected to the denial or invalidation of fat people's experiences of violence and injustice: because the negative experiences fat people face are normatively connected back to our weight, which we are told is supposed to be in our control, our worsened life chances and greater susceptibly to harm are most often attributed to our own failures to take care of ourselves rather than to the systematic assault on our existence. This problematic representation of fatness is rooted in a neoliberal understanding of health. As Kerrie Kauer (2016: 91) writes,

> The lack of one's health, or disease, is often blamed on the individual and their inability to obtain or maintain a healthy body by engaging in carefully prescribed exercise and fitness regimes. Such models of wellness and health reproduce classed, raced, gender, and sexed bodies that serve the consumer capitalist marketplace . . . while

> simultaneously pathologizing and demonizing transgressive corporality.

In other words, the neoliberal construction of fatness says that fat people lack discipline or control over our bodies and fail to engage with capitalist markets in appropriate or expected ways. This portrayal pulls attention from systems of oppression that devalue and denigrate fat bodies by defining fatness as a consequence of personal irresponsibility for which people should experience shame. Thus, not only is fatness considered a state of lessened humanity brought about by a shameful excess of consumption, but fat people are also held responsible for their own dehumanization and any resulting consequences. Like people oppressed by other systems of power, fat people tend to internalize this shame, which often leads to increased risk of harm from unsafe and/or unhealthy practices, such as eating disorders or fear about going to medical professionals. In some ways, fatphobic ideas about the "unhealthiness" of fat bodies become self-fulfilling prophesies because they prevent fat people from equitably accessing care and support readily available to the thin-bodied world.

Accordingly, fatphobia disguises the ordinary trauma fat people routinely experience in two central ways: first, it makes it seem like fat people, instead of broader systems of oppression, are responsible for our own struggles and that our lives would be better if we made different or "healthier" choices; second, it makes it more onerous for fat people to avoid and respond to ordinary traumatic events that could easily impact any person. We are denied the benefit of the doubt and forced to bear excessive levels of blame because other people and systems refuse their responsibilities to us; they deny our interdependence as well as our community. This kind of denial feels like being told the engine in your car is rotting because you fill it with bad gas and then careening down a hill because the mechanic forgot to check if your brakes were in good, working condition. Just as it makes no sense to blame all of a car's mechanical issues on the owners, nor does it make sense to blame fat people for all of our hardships or to assume that we do not have other hardships unrelated to weight or size. Yet, this narrative is a common tactic systems of oppression deploy to mask their presence.

The relationship between ordinary trauma and denial becomes quite clear when considering fatphobia. Fatphobia tends to operate invisibly by convincing thin-bodied people that harms fat people experience come from our own choices which cause us to not be healthy. At the same time, investments in fatphobic logics and the failure to recognize that fat people's lives may be more complex than our weights limit vital access to social support. Experiences that may be universal to all human beings are too often eclipsed by a tendency to attribute harm solely to fatness. Doctors, for example, routinely misdiagnose people because they assume that the reason for pain, or depression, or whatever else brought the patient into their office was caused by them being overweight. Fat people frequently live with serious undiagnosed medical conditions, like cancer or heart failure, for much longer than anyone should have to simply because doctors are not expecting to discover those things. For many fat people who confront this medical bias and discrimination, it seems like doctors forget about all ailments that cannot be cured by diet or exercise. Fat people die because medical professionals too often do not see us as anything other than fat people.

These instances of fatphobia among medical professionals are one example of what Rachel Fassler (cited in Joe Fassler 2015) refers to as "the trauma of not being seen," which is a sort of ordinary traumatic harm that can emerge when doctors, therapists, counsellors, and other medical professionals make decisions about how to treat someone based on assumptions about their identities/social positions. The trauma of not being seen is both a result of denial and a consequence of the invisiblization of oppressed people's experiences, both of which are socially, politically, and historically inflected. For Rachel Fassler, the trauma of not being seen was connected to a denial of the legitimacy of her pain bound up in misogynistic beliefs about women's tendencies to exaggerate and make up pain. Similarly, the lived experiences and needs of fat people are often buried under an assumption that losing weight or changing diets will solve all the problems; fat people are too often not seen as anything more than the weight and size of our bodies, especially those of us are also disabled, poor, or not White.

For me in thinking about ordinary trauma, "not being seen" holds a dual meaning: (1) literally not being seen by doctors as worthy of culturally competent, compassionate, or immediate care (e.g. being continually pushed back or repeatedly interrogated about our experiences); (2) not being "seen" as fully human because of those dehumanized and disadvantaged parts of ourselves, such as our genders, sizes, and disabilities – parts of ourselves which, because of how they have been constructed through systems of oppression, come to influence how others treat/refuse to treat us. Johanna Hedva (2016), writing in response to Fassler's article, writes that the trauma of not being seen is a deeply racialized phenomenon. Hedva explains that vulnerability and visibility are always racialized and mediated by systems of power:

> *The trauma of not being seen*. Again – who is allowed into the public sphere? Who is allowed to be visible? I don't mean to diminish Rachel's horrible experience – I myself once had to wait ten hours in an ER to be diagnosed with a burst ovarian cyst – I only wish to point out the presumptions upon which her horror relies: that our vulnerability should be seen and honored, and that we should all receive care, quickly and in a way that 'respects the autonomy of the patient', as the Four Principles of Biomedical Ethics puts it. Of course, these presumptions are what we all should have. But we must ask the question of who is allowed to have them. In whom does society substantiate such beliefs? And in whom does society enforce the opposite?

Indeed, the presumption of deservingness of access to such care is dependent on the racial dominance of Whiteness, which means the trauma of not being seen is both structured and experienced differently across racial categories. This difference exemplifies Angela Carter's assertion that the "social constructs of race, class, gender, sexuality, ability, and citizenship intertwine to inform *who* gets to claim trauma, what kinds of trauma are recognized, and what approaches of life and healing after trauma are viewed as appropriate" (2019: 4).

The trauma of not being seen also exemplifies what Calvin Rey Moen and Kaz DeWolfe (2019: 7) explain as *medical paternalism*, "which is when healthcare providers make decisions on our behalf, supposedly acting for our own good. This can shut us out of that decision-making process, and losing our ability to make our own decisions can be traumatic." Trauma is born from medical paternalism because it *infantilizes* people and, in doing so, strips away agency and autonomy; it tells us that someone else knows more about our bodies/minds and what they need than we do to the point where we should follow their direction without giving input. The normalcy of medical paternalism underlies and amplifies everything from the refusal to recognize people's pain to the involuntary institutionalization or forced medication of insane or Mad people (Mahan 2019). Paternalist tendencies contribute to ordinary trauma because they prioritize the knowledge of advantaged people, who often are also people causing harm, above the lived experience and knowledge of oppressed and harmed people; in other words, paternalism creates a *dependency* in which oppressed people have to perform our pain and suffering in a way that earns us recognition from those in power.

Furthermore, by interfering with our decision-making capacities, medical paternalism undercuts the control we have over our own healing processes and generates a pressure for us to "heal" according to what people in power decide is appropriate or desirable. This most often means changing – often "fixing"/"curing" – our bodies and minds so that they conform to normative modes of being. I will dig deeper into some of these ideas later on in this chapter, but for now I just want to name medical paternalism and the trauma of not being seen as one of the ways in which oppressed people are denied power and control over our own realities. I also want to note that, in the words of Sonya Renee Taylor (2018):

> There is no standard of health that is achievable for all bodies. Our belief that there should be anchors the

systemic oppression of ableism and reinforces the notion that people with illnesses and disabilities have defective bodies rather than different bodies.

Denial and Ignorance: Refusing to Recognize Systems of Oppression

When we name and resist systems of oppression, it is fairly easy to explain ordinary trauma as being about something more than a particular characteristic of some group of individuals; but when these systems are hidden or obscured or normalized, the denial of their existence becomes both accusation and judgement. To refuse the existence of systems of oppression is to make a claim that the people who experience ordinary trauma are either lying or at fault. It is not possible to deny the existence of an oppressive system without being complicit in it and harbouring hatred/prejudice towards the people it impacts. For doing so simultaneously denies one's participation in it – and therefore their need for accountability – and invalidates the experiences of people who have been harmed by it. Denial is a decision to take the side of the oppressor, to spread distrust for oppressed people, and to privilege the worldviews of dominance.

Trauma comes from this denial, both because it leads to further harm and because it entails a devaluation of oppressed people's perspectives and histories relative to more advantaged people. There is a reification of the belief that the wills and narratives of the advantaged are superior to or more compelling than those of the oppressed. Consequently, ordinary trauma both is produced through denial and can be an act of denial. And, denial is closely related to *ignorance*, which Susanne Luhmann (1998: 149) explains as "not the opposite to knowledge but an opposition to knowing." Denial is about taking the side of ignorance when ignorance is challenged, about refusing to know when the opportunity for knowing makes itself present. To deny people's lived experience is to refuse to know them *on their own terms* through their learned perceptions of the world.

Ordinary traumatic denial does not have to be an explicit or conspicuous practice of refusal. People do not have to be vocalizing or intentionally spreading denial for systems of power to benefit from it. In fact, denial breeds in silences, often reproducing itself through what is not said, what is not done, and what is persistently made unknown. If compassion and care have to do with showing up and making space for other people, then denial or ignorance are about withholding these things. It hurts when I hear people spewing fatphobic remarks, but it hurts even more when I watch other people walk by, minding their own business, doing absolutely nothing to counteract the public assault on fat people's existence. The same is true for other forms of violence or discrimination that I experience, like ableism or queer- and transphobia. Complicity does nothing to challenge the hatred or prejudice of other people; they only ever send a message that such feelings are excusable, understandable, and, worst of all, shared. Writing about abuse in intimate, heterosexual relationships, Lundy Bancroft (2003) explains:

> If you are aware of chronic or severe mistreatment and do not speak out against it, your silence communicates implicitly that you see nothing unacceptable taking place. Abusers interpret silence as approval, or at least as forgiveness. To abused women, meanwhile, the silence means that no one will help – just what her partner wants her to believe. Anyone who chooses to quietly look the other way therefore unwittingly becomes the abuser's ally.

Of course, there are valid reasons why someone might remain silent or not show up (e.g. to ensure their own safety or because of disabilities), but we live in a society where showing up for other people is too often the *exception*, not the rule. Not showing up becomes traumatic in its repetition because it leads people to stop reaching out, to choose isolation over healing relationships because nothing else seems possible. The trauma of not showing up builds on and deepens the trauma of not being seen when oppressed people come to realize that they struggle along without the support of a community.

Because systems of oppression encourage loneliness and complicity, denial as not showing up is normative. The resistance people have to showing up is also a consequence of living in a society that so rarely teaches us how to effectively manage or make sense of our own pain, let alone someone else's. Judith Herman (1992: 7) argues that siding with people who cause harm is easier than showing up for harmed people because the harm doer require little while the harmed person asks for what can seem like too much:

> It is morally impossible to remain neutral in this conflict. The bystander is forced to take sides. It is very tempting to take the side of the perpetrator. All the perpetrator asks is that the bystander do nothing. He appeals to the universal desire to see, hear, and speak no evil. The victim, on the contrary, asks the bystander to share the burden of pain. The victim demands action, engagement, and remembering.

Harm doers are empowered both if people support them and if people do nothing at all – a fact which is true at the individual, interpersonal, and systemic levels. Abusive relationships fester in the absence of active bystander response, and oppressive social conditions spread in the absence of sustained, collective resistance. When advantaged people fail to show up for oppressed people, especially those advantaged people who call themselves allies, they prioritize their own *comfort* over other people's safety and well-being. That is, they continue to deny the significance of oppressed people's ordinary trauma in relation to the easiness of their own lives. And that betrayal creates a profound and disturbing wound. Not showing up reveals how often appeals to allyship are actually "invitations to be [or appear to be] a good and generous person, rather than the necessary expressions of our interdependence" – that they are, therefore, "woefully unequal to the task of sparking concerted mass action on the scale we now urgently need" (Taylor and Hunt-Hendrix 2019).

Denial can be about not showing up, or it can also be about not caring enough to do anything. Among the most challenging barriers to dismantling systems of oppression is the denial that people's experiences of violence/discrimination are meaningful and worthy of rectification. Oppressive systems benefit as much from apathy and complicity as they do from more overt expressions of hatred. Statements like "calm down" and "you're overreacting" are part of a larger culture of silence in which perpetrators of harm are granted protections while harmed people are denied the right to speak out about their experiences and to demand to be treated better. It is also indicative of how the existing social order empowers advantaged peoples to deny the need for their accountability. Advantaged people too often have to be convinced to listen to – not just hear, but actually *comprehend* and *internalize* – things oppressed people are trying to communicate to them. Oppressive systems instil a belief in advantaged people that those whom they view as less-than-fully human are not as deserving of being heard and that they are less reliable narrators of past events (i.e. they can't be trusted anyway).

Accordingly, apathy for social issues does not just refer to a lack of care or attention; instead, apathy is a dangerous by-product that results from denying the worth of oppressed people's lives, experiences, and perspective. It is socially enforced and politically significant. As with ignorance, apathy is not just an absence of care but a learned and conditioned carelessness within a social/political order that codifies people as differently deserving of kindness, care, and love. For instance, reflect on how often a social issue that oppressed peoples have been organizing against does not receive attention until an advantaged person starts talking about it. Moreover, consider how often acts of raising awareness for social issues earn advantaged people praise, but results in harassment, disparagement, and criticism for people impacted by those issues. I have witnessed professors and scholars of colour go through a gauntlet of scrutiny after bringing up issues of race that White scholars are celebrated for naming. I have also seen this happen to disabled scholars, women scholars, and queer and trans scholars.

As a White, male-passing teacher, I have rarely been criticized for bringing up feminist issues, anti-racist issues, or global issues. As someone who is less marked by my identities, I get to raise those issues without being punished or singled out for doing so. The same is true of my publications: I get praised for attending to intersectionality, and forgiven for not doing so, in ways that other people are denied. My perspective about/attention to such things is valued because of my advantaged social positions. The denial of voice impacting oppressed people, in this way, often translates to a further privileging and social elevation of advantaged people who graciously express their ideas.

***

One of the many privileges systems of oppression bestowed on advantaged people is the deep-seated belief that the world, or at least a part of it, was made for them and other people like them. Similarly, advantaged people often internalize a mistaken belief that their experiences are normal, if not universal. The denial of other perspectives and experiences as well as the refusal to recognize ordinary trauma and the systems that produce it is partially the effect of this dominating belief. Acknowledging/validating other people's lived experiences requires advantaged people to accept that their lives are not the cornerstones of existence but rather that systems of oppression have indoctrinated them into believing this lie. Indeed, whereas oppressed people must expand their consciousness to incorporate their own worldviews as well as those of their oppressors – recall the notion of *double consciousness* used by W. E. B. Du Bois (2008 [1903]) –, advantaged people can more often move throughout their lives without developing a consciousness of power or its impact on oppressed people.

Once again, this lack of conscious awareness is a part of how privilege becomes an "energy-saving device" (Ahmed 2013) as a well a hermeneutic/interpretive device to make the world a simpler place. For advantaged people, the way they perceive the world is *unfragmented* by the complexity of a split consciousness, or at least it is meant to be so. Consequently, denial serves a particularly important function for advantaged peoples because it enables them to preserve their constructed innocence. Denying experiences and perspectives of oppressed others empowers advantaged people to continue believing in their own supremacy and their own innocence *at the same time* – to go on believing the world was made for them and that their experiences are universal while also denying their complicity in other people's suffering. In this way, ignorance serves to resolve any cognitive dissonance that can emerge through an awareness of oppression.

While not understanding other people's experiences is, in part, the result of not having those experiences, it is also true that systems of oppression and the advantaged people who profit from them actively foster ignorance to maintain dominance. I return to Susanne Luhmann's account of ignorance as "an opposition to knowing" (1998: 149): the process of maintaining and reproducing dominance involves ongoing suppression of knowledge and understanding because they carry the potential to expand consciousness beyond the mythologies of power (Levins Morales 1998). Developing an opposition to knowing is mandatory for preserving the innocence of advantaged people who must always be prepared to deny and refuse to accept the ordinary trauma of oppressed people. This opposition is a necessary part of reproducing power because it hinders oppressed people from gaining legitimacy as traumatized subjects – it keeps their experiences illegible and, therefore, unworthy of intervention or change from people in power.

Of course, the opposition to knowing is not always explicit or overt: often, it emerges through the segregation of differently identified and situated peoples as well as the diverse ways we codify knowledge as "general" or as belonging to/being for specific groups. For example, stories about heterosexual, White, middle to upper-class, enabled, etc., men are most often categorized as "general" stories to be enjoyed by a "general" audience. Deviations from this narrative trend usually result in categorization into alternative genres: stories about women become "women's literature," stories about queer and trans people fill a shelf or two titled "LGBTQ literature," and so on. These are not just stories by or about oppressed people; they are stories intended *for* and marketed *at* them, and advantaged people are excused from the need to engage with them. These stories become marked as an exception from the norm, as specific to someone who has not had a "normal human experience." In categorizing a story as "Black literature" or "Asian literature," the story becomes about Black and Asian peoples, but stories about or from people in the mythical norm remain undifferentiated and, therefore, seen as relevant to all of humanity. Indeed, White stories aren't coded as White stories, and neither are men's stories are not coded as men's stories; they tend to be categorized by their content rather than the social positions of their authors.

As another example, consider the fuss many enabled people make about accommodations in the classroom for disabled people. The majority of classrooms/other educational spaces are designed around the experiences and needs of enabled people, with "special education" being a notable exception. Ableism in education occurs not because teachers are inherently/intentionally prejudiced, though many certainly are, but rather because relatively few have actively developed a consciousness of disability oppression or a disability justice lens which would allow them to challenge ableist systems and structures. Over time, enabled students develop the subconscious belief that learning spaces are made for them, and they often feel confused, upset, or personally offended when other students criticize or seek to change the classes they are part of. Since advantaged people are conditioned to believe in the normalcy of their experiences, they struggle to understand how other students' needs aren't met when theirs are. As a result, enabled students can have a hard time recognizing accommodations, such as a different environment for tests or extra allowed absences, as essential to disabled students' equitable education and well-being. This same difficulty extends to teachers who are unwilling to make accommodations on the grounds that they disrupt the classroom and give an unfair advantage when, in fact, they do the opposite: address barriers to fair access to learning and equal participation.

As a product of entrenched beliefs in the universality of their experience, advantaged people have a difficult time coming to terms with the reality that other people may experience things differently during their lives or that their unique experiences and needs are significant facets of human experience. Experiences that diverge from advantaged peoples' understanding of the world are routinely ignored or belittled, treated like they have lesser value or importance. The need for classroom accommodations as I just discussed is one example. Menstruation and pregnancy are another. While they are readily accepted as gender specific,[1] at the same time, they are continually demeaned by advantaged people who downplay their significance. For example, people without uteruses devalue menstruation and pregnancy through claims that they are not as painful or important as people with uteruses "pretend" they are. Gender is a powerful determinant in whose feelings of pain are accepted and trusted and whose are doubted and questioned. The refusal to validate and believe women's pain is tied to medical paternalism that assumes women are weak and prone to exaggeration. Moreover, the "pink tax" on menstrual products – the fact that people who menstruate have to pay so much for a basic need – is really telling of how advantaged people see menstrual products as luxuries, not necessities.

Denial of significance also comes when advantaged people appropriate the experiences of oppressed people or make it seem as if there was some kind of equal partnership going on. Men love to assert that pregnancy is an equal partnership, that they contribute 50% just like their partners – they say, "We are pregnant." While pregnant people undoubtedly contribute the vast majority of substance, labour, energy, and time to reproduction, advantaged people diminish this involvement and substantiate their own, as if the sacrifice they are making is just as important/burdensome. The denial that the pregnant person is making a significantly heavier contribution empowers advantaged people to feel that they should have at least an equal say in whatever decisions the pregnant person makes. This belief is one of the reasons why many men feel so comfortable contributing to and even dominating discussions about abortion that have absolutely nothing to do with them. Furthermore, advantaged people make up their own narratives that bolster their contributions, making it seem as if they did more work than they actually did. For example, the narrative about male sperm valiantly fighting their way to the female's egg through treacherous obstacles like warriors through a battalion of enemies – that does not happen. In reality, it is actually the other person's body that chooses whether or not to direct the sperm towards the fertile egg, and the egg that decides whether or not to embrace the sperm.

And here we get back to the real reason why denial of oppressed people's experiences is so important to advantaged people: their power and control. When advantaged people, many of whom have little to no familiarity with ordinary trauma or the needs of people different to them, are over-represented in positions of power, oppressed people suffer. Without equity, diversity, inclusion, and access – let alone equity and social justice – oppressed people are placed in a difficult position where they have to continually assert the worth of their lives to an audience that regards them as less-fully human and that does not understand what they need. Advantaged people, even if they are well-meaning, do not share in the experiences of oppressed people and are therefore unreliable allies at best. The entrenched denial of other people's experiences and perspectives is hard for advantaged people to unlearn, which is why people familiar with ordinary trauma are always the best advocates for themselves, and among the greatest threats to systems of power. Keeping oppressed people on the outside in marginal or disadvantaged positions is essential to deferring accountability and ensuring that their needs are never entirely met. In other words, denying oppressed people access to positions of power is what enables advantaged people to continue denying the hard realities of inequity and injustice.

While I have many issues with Sheryl Sandberg's book *Lean In: Women, Work, and the Will to Lead* (2013: 3), she offers a great example of how denial of representation leads to denial of needs.[2] In the opening pages, she recounts an experience during her pregnancy in which she was running late for a meeting and had to get across the parking lot in a short amount of time. Unable to locate a space closer to her office, she had to park far away. She admits, "To this day, I'm embarrassed that I didn't realize that pregnant women needed reserved parking until I experienced my own aching feet." Even as a woman in a position of power, the needs of pregnant people eluded her consciousness until she became pregnant herself. As a result of the privilege of non-pregnancy, she came to view her own experiences as universal given that she had no experiences to the contrary and was able to remain unaware of the particular needs of pregnant people. I do not think that Sandberg intentionally overlooked the needs of her pregnant employees, but that is not the point to take home here. Rather, it was the lack of representation that allowed for this denial of equity.

This kind of equitable representation becomes important partly because oppressed people are the most knowledgeable about their own lived experience and needs and partly because denial also functions through devaluation of oppressed people's voice. Indeed, advantaged people often think of themselves as having the most important things to say – they have been conditioned to – so they do not listen to oppressed people as fully/actively. The rate at which men interrupt women and disregard their ideas only to claim them with confidence later on is demonstrative of this point. So even when oppressed people do express their needs or ask for change, it is questionable whether the advantaged people they are talking to will even be paying them attention. I return to Sandberg's example about the need to have reserved parking for pregnant people. She problematically attributes her lack of awareness to pregnant people's silence, their "not wanting to ask for special treatment" or lack of "confidence or seniority to demand that the problem be fixed" (3). Advantaged people make many such claims about the fault being with other people – this kind of victim-blaming logic reaches everything from pay inequity to sexual violence – but how much inequity and injustice come from them not listening to or not providing channels for communication? I would wager that Sandberg was not the first person to seek to address this problem. But even if she was, silence is enforced, it is bought through power and dominance. The silence she points is not just about a lack of confidence – it comes from advantaged people enforcing their power to maintain the status quo or the threat thereof.

Compulsory Survivorship: Creating the Good Survivor™

Through my participation in anti-violence movements as an advocate, activist, and educator, I have become increasingly aware of how often survivor narratives get twisted to accomplish specific political goals which may or may not align with what harmed people want and need. Survivor narratives have become their own disciplinary *genre* and as such frequently compel harmed people to account for themselves and their trauma in regulated and commodifiable ways. Having become a genre all their own – that is, a category of storytelling that follows an expected arc and draws on familiar tropes, survivor narratives have taken on recognizable forms and functions that govern how harmed people are expected to share their experiences and ask for support. In particular, harmed people tend to be rewarded when they contribute to *narratives of sameness* that align with logics of power or with dominant social movements advocating for their own interests. These narratives bolster an over simplistic understanding of what it means to be a Good Survivor ™ that can make harmed people vulnerable to power, either from oppressive systems or from other people seeking to appropriate their experience for various own political ends. Angela Carter (2019: 55) writes:

> Once traumatized, you're trapped in a narrative limbo; a discursive bind. . . . If you speak your traumas, your experience is turned into platitudes. If you want your story to be understood – to be heard – you must tell it in a typical narrative structure, despite the fact that nothing feels typical or structured about what you're going through or living with now. . . . These narrative frameworks turn trauma into a commodity, easy for others to consume – a spectacle for an audience to take in without having to truly bear witness to the atrocity at hand or having to face their own sociopolitical belief systems.

The normative, disciplinary structure of survivor narratives make trauma legible within logics of power and consumable by a society obsessed with the spectacle of suffering. Importantly, the genre of survivor narratives is one that deliberately fosters ignorance: they regulate what knowledges can be spoken, what truths can be named, and which people can be blamed for harm. Survivor narratives are intentionally *disempowering*, even if following them does grant harmed people access to various kinds of social support. They stifle resistance with the too often unfulfilled promise of acceptance/access to needed resources. They call to the deep longing for care that many survivors feel in a society seemingly devoid of love or compassion, yet even when we follow their instructions, they do not unmake suffering or heal injuries for the majority of us. Oftentimes, the opposite is true: they reproduce the very same systems that harmed us in the first place by preventing us from identifying the true source of our harm and pushing us to conform to truths that have never belonged to us.

Writing against the "psychiatric gaze," Jijian Voronka (2019: 16), for example, explains that:

> We make ourselves knowable and build ourselves through the stories that we weave of our past, present, and possible future. But we learn through practice that the value of these stories in the mental health marketplace is conditional. We are rewarded for, and are encouraged to become experts at, producing 'resilience and recovery narratives' that work to build larger framings of us as redeemable subjects. And so as storytellers, we learn to mediate our stories so that they fit within wider resiliency/recovery narratives.

Contorting our lived experience to fit within the genre of survivor narratives allows oppressed people to make ourselves into "redeemable subjects," but not everyone can fit in this genre because not everyone has survived in the *right* ways – for example, along the expected paths of resilience and recovery. Many of us take too long to heal, express the wrong needs, or fail at the performance in other ways. And some of us are never given the chance to be a part of these narratives to begin with because of assumptions about who we are and what we have (not) experienced. The structuring of survivor narratives is racialized, gendered, sexualized, classed, enabled, and otherwise exclusionary – for example, in the expectation that harmed people present themselves as innocent (Kandaswamy 2006). These narratives are set up to intentionally leave people out.

The normative genre of survivor narratives is one component of what I refer to as *compulsory survivorship*. This concept argues that ordinary representations of trauma tell individualized and oversimplified narratives about what is *supposed* to happen after a traumatic event has occurred, including how individuals are *supposed* to move out of "oppressive victimization" and in the direction of a more "liberated survival." It offers a critique of the ways that "victim" and "survivor" become value-laden and governable, rather than merely descriptive markers: victim becomes the categorization people are compelled to reject because it is imagined to inhabit the space of weakness, vulnerability, and/or ongoing suffering; survivor becomes the identity people are urged to pursue because it supposedly represents a space of strength or recovery that can only be attained by overcoming victimization (Arielle 2016). Consequently, how harmed people respond to ordinary traumatic experiences is not a neutral process, for according to the logics of power, there are recognizably positive and negative, good and bad, desirable and undesirable ways of surviving trauma (Coulter-Thomson 2016; Lowry 1993).

Politics of survival are especially present in instances of ordinary trauma where traumatizing events – as well as sources of harm – are contested and differently recognized across social positions and lived experiences. For example, how someone is expected to recover from an accidental house fire is different from how they would be expected to heal from child sexual abuse or police violence. This is because compulsory survivorship is an outcome of multiple systems of oppression that are embedded in dominant discourses of health, wellness, care, recovery, justice, spirituality, morality, and so on. At the core of compulsory survivorship are ableism and sanism, two interconnected systems of oppression that influence which minds and bodies are seen as disposable or violable and which are seen as valuable. Leah Lakshmi Piepzna-Samarasinha (2019) asserts that normative ideas about survival are rooted in an ableist politics of cure:

> The idea that survivorhood is a thing to fix, cure, or get over, and that a cure is not only possible and easy but is the only desirable option, is a foundational belief in mainstream ways of understanding survivorhood and survivors. And the idea of survivorhood as solely an unfortunate condition to cure is an idea with deep roots in ableism.

The representation of harmed people as needing to be "cured" or "fixed" punishes them for holding onto past experiences of harm and compels them to let go of their negative emotions and memories, both of which underlie calls for accountability from advantaged people and institutions or governments. Ultimately, compulsory survivorship is about refusing the need for accountability by regulating how harmed people are allowed to express pain and call for justice and social change. Talking specifically about rape culture, which is one of the places compulsory survivorship shows up most intensely, Piepzna-Samarasinha (2019) writes that:

> Rape culture creates many things to manage survivor knowledge and tamp it down. Sometimes, I call it the Survivor Industrial Complex: the web of institutions, practices, and beliefs that works to manage, contain, and offer resolution to survivors of sexual violence. . . . One of the biggest ways the Survivor Industrial Complex manages all those messy, powerful survivor emotions and truths is by deploying the idea of the good or fixed survivor. . . . In contrast, the bad survivor is the one who's still 'broken', still freaking out, still triggered, still grieving, *still remembering. Still making you remember*. . . . And often, as survivors, we don't want to be them, because being them means not being healed. It means that we've failed at surviving.

Framing good survivorship around forgetting and letting other people forget and associating remembrance with the "bad survivor" is an effective method of reducing the impact survivor knowledge has on social conditions and systems. In terms of ordinary trauma, compulsory survivorship promotes the silence and deference and fear necessary for the continuation of systemic and structural violence in the lives of oppressed people – it is one of the pervasive and internalized forces operating to keep traumatic experiences ordinary while also allowing advantaged people to keep on acting from their power. Bad survivors, the people who refuse or fail to survive and heal in the ways they are compelled to, become associated with difficult emotions, disruptions, and disorder. They are trouble-makers and rebels, but through a lens of good and bad survivorship, the threat they pose to social order is reduced and redirected into something wrong with them. Their efforts to name and resist social issues or oppression become pathologized, transformed from legitimate self-advocacy or speaking out into clear evidence that they need to be cured or fixed.

***

References to the "compulsory" abound across feminist, queer, disability, and other critical theory: Adrienne Rich (1980) proposed the concept of *compulsory heterosexuality*, a useful counterpart to the idea of heteronormativity that explains how patriarchy coerces and forces women into unequal relationships with men. Relatedly, asexual communities often discuss *compulsory sexuality*, that is, "a set of social attitudes, institutions and practices which hold and enforce the belief that everyone should have or want to have frequent sex (of a socially approved kind)" (Millbank 2012). Robert McRuer (2006) and Alison Kafer (2013) have written about compulsory able-bodiedness and compulsory able-mindedness, which are concepts that describe the coercive enactments of power through oppressive systems of ableism and sanism.

As part of this work, Kafer writes about *compulsory nostalgia* in which people with acquired disabilities are expected to long for some past version of themselves that has yet to become impaired. Mia Mingus (2017) also describes the expectation forced upon disabled people to expose ourselves – both physically and emotionally – to the enabled world in order to access the things we need to survive. Mingus refers to this mandatory exposure as a norm of "forced intimacy," but it carries the same weight and meaning as *compulsory intimacy* might. Nearly every axis of power can be analysed through paying attention to what it makes "normal" and how it compels us towards that normativity – how it narrows the choices available to us and then coerces us to act and exist in regulated ways, often under a threat of structural violence. This violence can include physical or psychological assaults but can also be the withholding of resources or care that are necessary to our survival and well-being.

The recurring description of things as compulsory in social justice works and critical theories points to an awareness of the ways in which systems of oppression seek to constrain agency as we navigate a society and world constructed to reinforce pervasive inequity and injustice. To define something as compulsory is to recognize that the choices we make, as well as the range of choices available to us, are mediated by a power that is greater than us as individual people. This power manifests in the form of punishments or rewards that compel us to make decisions that are deemed "good" in place of decisions that are deemed "bad." Depending on how we live our lives relative to the logics of power, we may be invited to participate in or be excluded from communities; we may be granted access to safety/security or threatened with violence; we might experience tenderness, love, and belonging or we might be shamed, rejected, and cast out.

Compulsory becomes an accurate signifier for our life choices when those choices become what protect us from and/or subject us to inequity and injustice – when the choices we make determine our livelihood because of the ways that systems of power have warped "humanity" into something that can be shared and withheld. The notion of compulsory, then, recognizes that being seen as fully human and receiving the privileges connected to humanity depends on our ability to conform to normative social expectations. Oppressive systems compel us into these expectations to limit expressions of difference, imposing in their place a social order that supposedly works for everyone when, in fact, it only truly works for a small number of people.

Oppressed people are exposed to systemic inequity/injustice and ordinary traumatic harm for simply existing out of alignment with expectations we are compelled to follow: for making the *wrong* movements, or doing the *wrong* things, or wearing the *wrong* clothes, or living our lives in the *wrong* ways. Advantaged people depend on compulsory normativity to rationalize harm, so in defying the compulsory, either actively or just by existing, oppressed people are rendered abusable, exploitable, violable. Access to the ranks of the fully human is reserved for people whose lives fit into the "mythical norm" (Lorde 1984: 116), for people who actively and successfully position themselves as "normal," and the rest of us who are compelled towards this mythical norm that we cannot reach are punished according to our degrees of deviation. The more we deviate, the more we are harmed and the less we are seen as worthy of care and social support.

Herein lies the catch: the *unattainability* of that which we are compelled to think, be, and do makes it so that oppressed people nearly always exist outside of normativity and, therefore, are nearly always marked as abusable, exploitable, violable. Marilyn Frye (1983: 2) describes this problematic dilemma as one of being in a double-bind:

> One of the most characteristic and ubiquitous features of the world as experienced by oppressed people is the double bind – situations in which options are reduced to a very few and all of them expose one to penalty, censure or deprivation.

Given that the mythical norm is ever out of our reach, it seems as if everything that oppressed people do cannot ever be enough to please the people around us; we are always seen to be failing because the systems and structures surrounding us leave us without passable routes to be successful and productive in the ways we are expected to be. Aligning with the compulsory for harmed people is, in itself, a kind of double-bind where we must choose between being true to ourselves and our lived experiences and sacrificing the pieces of ourselves that don't fit for a chance at fitting in.

Moreover, the notion of oppression being a matter of living through a series of double-binds exemplifies how the things we are compelled to do conflict with and contradict one another. Indeed, at the same time that we are compelled to do one thing, we may also be compelled to do its opposite, forming a complicated situation in which oppressed people must decide on the sorts of harm we are going to protect ourselves from and expose ourselves to, all the while carrying knowledge that we are not safe from violence either way. The double-bind of oppression is often especially real for people navigating ordinary trauma as we confront the competing and often contradictory logics and practices of compulsory survivorship: on the one hand, some people pressure us into various sorts of action, such as leaving our abusive partners, going to therapy, and/or calling the police. These people may even take the power of choice away from harmed people altogether (e.g. by calling the police for them without/against their consent). On the other hand, some people may pressure us out of various sorts of action, often into states of silence, complicity, and, as I explain momentarily, forgiveness.

No matter what harmed people do in these situations, we are often unable to make everyone happy, for the things we are compelled to do pull us in different directions, each of which is offered up as the thing which we *should* be doing. Competing compulsions work against the agency and well-being of harmed people who, rather than being supported as we make the decisions that are best for us, are punished no matter what we do. Given that compulsory survivorship so often pulls harmed people in opposing directions, we have to recognize that the multiple forces contributing to this phenomenon do not neatly map onto one or the other side of power. People in different social positions and expressing diverse political ideologies help to animate this compulsory force. Survival is a political endeavour that all kinds of people may seek to appropriate/control for their own benefit. Advocates and activists, for instance, even as they may be well-meaning, often pressure harmed people to visibly hold harm doers accountable through public demonstration, whether that be in court or drafting open letters or speaking at activist events.

Part of the compulsory survivorship that harmed people ordinarily experience is the painful belief that if we do not speak up and speak out, then it must be because we are still stuck in our oppression/victimization. This expectation is grounded in a reductive binary of speech and silence that constructs silence as the antithesis of liberation and social justice. Yet, as Amato (2018) writes, being made to speak about harm can also be a source of pain and further trauma:

> [T]alking about pain and trauma can actually cause pain and trauma . . . [We have a high regard] for employing narrative as cure. Verbalizing events in our lives that may be troubling, shaming, guilt inducing, violent, or traumatic is seen as a way through. . . . What if it's not? What if talking about it makes it worse?. . . . The truth is, sometimes talking about it is self-harm.

Part of what compulsory survivorship does, why it so detrimental, is to subordinate harmed people's genuine healing/agency beneath a co-opted vision of healing that promotes power elsewhere (i.e. outside of the harmed person most in need of solidarity) – it steals away our agency of expression by mandating that we express ourselves in particular and ordered ways, such as openly talking about pain and trauma or publicly acting out against the people who caused our pain and trauma. I call on this example because it is important to recognize that compulsory survivorship comes from all directions in which power is moving, not just those we identify as oppressive, silencing, or stifling.

Further, compulsory survivorship emerges intersectionally within the lives of harmed people, which means that its power is more complex than a simple dichotomy of progressive pushes to action and voice verses conservative calls for inaction/silence. The forces of compulsory survivorship are mediated by interactional, mutually constitutive logics of White supremacy, ableism, fatphobia, transnational capitalisms, heteropatriarchy, xenophobia, queerphobia, transphobia, and other systems of power. The same people who, for instance, encourage oppressed people to be silent about their experiences of harm at the hands of straight, White men readily promote the voice of people harmed by poor, Brown men in the borderlands (the *bad hombres*) or dangerous Brown men in the Middle East. In this way, forces of compulsory survivorship can simultaneously contribute to male dominance, violence against immigrant communities, and militarism or imperialism.

Relatedly, the complicated histories of White supremacist heteropatriarchy have often led oppressed people to pressure harmed people within their communities to be silent in order to prevent the continuation of destructive stereotypes, such as the idea that sexual violence is a "minority" issue (Crenshaw 1989), and also to limit further violence against them (e.g. to protect themselves from governmental agencies, especially ICE, the police, and military). Conditions of compulsory survivorship are not as a fixed checklist but are always contextual and dynamic in response to the shifting needs of power. How people are expected to survive or heal from harm shifts based on the social and political landscapes surrounding them.

While I recognize here that conditions of compulsory survivorship are collectively generated, I do not think that the people contributing to it cause harm in the same ways or even that the harm they inflict is comparable. While it is true that all aspects of compulsory survivorship revolve around the disempowerment of harmed people through interference in or curtailing of their decision-making power, it is also true that the reasons for doing so are complicated and depend on histories of experience and the social positions they occupy. In some cases, people have a genuine investment in supporting and showing up for harmed people that they express in harmful, but well-intentioned ways, which is hardly comparable to those people who act in their own self-interest or purely for the improvement of their social position. This distinction is vital to maintain as a tool to inform actions, but I do not mean for it to become a justification that makes some kinds of compulsory survivorship ok. Indeed, it is only useful insofar as it helps us to understand the ways we can expand beyond harmful expectations based on our specific contexts and relationships.

Compulsory Forgiveness and Forgivability

In earlier chapters, I wrote about the concept of integration and how trauma is often defined as an experience or encounter which refuses integration, one that stands out and continues to manifest in harmful, often debilitating ways. I argued that ordinary trauma is a reversal of this claim because it manifests when integration comes too readily, because the experience of harm is not extraordinary and because the systems and structures of society have been set up intentionally to perpetuate and to *anticipate* harm. In composing this chapter about compulsory survivorship, I also think about how expectations relating to integration become a piece of the performance of the Good Survivor™. In particular, I think about how forgiveness operates as a tool of oppressive integration employed to coerce harmed people (and anyone supporting them) into letting go of anger or resistance and to subdue calls for accountability, thereby preserving systems of oppression.

Compulsory survivorship describes how life following ordinary traumatic experiences often becomes fraught with competing expectations about how people will reclaim control, heal/restore themselves, and either liberate themselves from conditions of oppression or force themselves back on to the normative paths laid out before them. Among the more insidious facets of compulsory survivorship that traumatized peoples often experience is *compulsory forgiveness*, which broadly speaking refers to how decisions to grant or withhold forgiveness come to feel out of our control, as if the choice has always already somehow been made for us. Social pressure toward forgiveness, as with the fostering of resilience, is a way of placing blame and responsibility back onto the harmed person rather than the people who caused harm or the social context in which that harm occurred. In place of accountability and social justice, the expectation of forgiveness often becomes a weapon of silencing, shaming, and victim-blaming that stalls relational and social growth. People who refuse to accept ordinary trauma through forgiveness are frequently punished through an expectation to let go of their anger, their sadness, their hurt. This punishment comes from friends, family, communities, religious authorities, courts, and so on.

As with other compulsory things, forgiveness can come to seem like the only sensible option because refusing to forgive so often leads to ordinary punishment, violence, or further injury. Compulsory forgiveness emerges in response to harmed people's refusal to let things go as they *should*; it is a method for undermining resistance that comes from harmful experiences. The relational and sociopolitical forces pushing people into compulsory forgiveness start to affect us early on in life. For example, compulsory forgiveness becomes a lesson for children when children are forced to make up with and hug one another, often regardless of their own feelings about the matter or what was done to make the situation better. From this early age, many of us are taught to believe that forgiveness is more important than accountability and repair, especially considering how often the children who cause harm are made to apologize, regardless of whether they comprehend the meaning of that apology or truly understand the impact of their actions. Accordingly, children who cause harm, usually advantaged children, are conditioned to expect that saying sorry in itself merits forgiveness while harmed children, typically from oppressed or disadvantaged groups, are conditioned to give forgiveness, even in the absence of genuine remorse or change.

Compulsory forgiveness usually operates beneath the level of conscious awareness in the form of assumptions we make about how we are supposed to exist in the world. In an essay titled "Why I Don't Use the Word 'Forgiveness' in Trauma Therapy," mental health counsellor Anastasia Pollock (2016) writes about how an expectation of forgiveness can be detrimental to healing and result in revictimization:

> The people I work with in the therapy room are resilient and courageous. They are able to work through their traumas, but many get caught up on one point: They believe they are supposed to forgive the perpetrator but can't seem to get there. . . . Even if the intention is coming from a good place, trying to get someone who has been

> violated to forgive can feel like being victimized all over again.

Through compulsory expectations of forgiveness, which are embedded within constructions of humanity, morality, and spirituality, harmed people can become hindered in their healing. Many harmed people are conditioned to believe that not forgiving the person or people who caused them harm makes them a bad person deserving of pain and suffering. Consequently, many attempt to bury their anger and their hurt feelings, and they attempt to make amends without being granted the space to honestly and meaningfully work through their emotions or arrive a space of real understanding from which they can express their needs. In part, the feeling of revictimization, of being pushed to prioritize forgiveness over genuine repair, which is often reinforced by friends, families, and communities, is the point. I will not use the word *intentional* (though sometimes it most certainly is) because I believe that people advocating forgiveness, or some variation of it, often come from a space of love and support, but I will assert that it is one of the intended outcomes of power, for dominance thrives when harmed people do not name or resist what they have survived.

The danger of compulsory forgiveness lies not so much in the act of forgiving itself, but rather in the theft of agency that occurs when people no longer have control over who we forgive or the conditions of our forgiveness. Compulsory forgiveness actually has very little to do with how we feel or our well-being; rather, it is concerned with upholding particular sorts of power relations that benefit advantaged people and oppressive systems. Compulsory forgiveness is a *distortion* of the imagined human virtue of forgiving others for the harm they cause to us: those who practice forgiveness are seen as virtuous or admirable, role-models to look up to for strength and inspiration, while those who choose to withhold their forgiveness are often portrayed as selfish, hateful, unreasonable in their actions. This biased distribution of virtue and shame is present even – perhaps especially – when forgiveness is most difficult or least desired by the harmed person; compulsory forgiveness exists independently from the actual costs and benefits of forgiveness because it is disconnected from the lived experiences and needs of harmed people.

This disconnect is ultimately at the crux of the issue: because compulsory forgiveness is not concerned with the welfare of harmed people or the honest repair of damaged relationships, it cannot be a tool of healing, relational change, or justice; it can only be a tool of oppression. Ana Clarissa Rojas Durazo (2010: 85), citing Martha Minow (1998), distinguishes forgiveness from accountability:

> Accountability is not the pursuit of redemption or forgiveness. 'To expect survivors to forgive is to heap yet another burden on them' (Minow 1998). Forgiveness is not a right to be claimed; it is a *gesture* from the survivor.

Compulsory forgiveness collapses this distinction, and it creates a context in which harmed people are pressured to resolve situations and conflict by releasing those who harmed them from any need for accountability. It may be helpful here to think of accountability as actions taken in the present that are informed by the memory of past harms and the anticipation of harms to come. Compulsory forgiveness manifests as a silencing of memory – a method of selective remembering that pressures people to leave inflicted harms in the past or, at least, keep silent about them. Forgiveness as a tool of oppression urges harmed people to release advantaged people and social institutions from the need to remember past harms and, thus, from the needs to be accountable to them. Forgiveness is a way of letting people off the hook. Traits of good and bad survivors underlying compulsory survivorship and forgiveness emerge from the politics of memory, for the act of remembrance incites action and sounds a call for accountability in the form or reparations and/or substantive changes in behaviour.

Negative images associated with unforgiving people (e.g. "scornful women") and pervasive beliefs about the requirement to forgive reveal a lot about the importance of forgiveness for upholding systems of oppression. As a tool of dominance, compulsory forgiveness provides advantaged people and social institutions with a clear method to undermine, defer, reduce, or eliminate calls for accountability and to take support away from social justice movements. When oppressed, traumatized people are compelled to forgive, the impetus is no longer on harm doers to change themselves or repair their relationships with the people they harmed; the impetus gets shifted onto harmed people to accept the world as it is, to just let go of their anger, resentment, blame, etc. towards other people. Compulsory forgiveness is inherently about getting people to let go of their desires to hold other people accountable for the harms they committed.

Moreover, centring forgiveness distorts perceptions of the situation so that harmed people start to be seen as the unaccountable ones – the people perpetrating and perpetuating harm For instance, Sophie King (2019) writes:

> Men often use the status of an unforgiving woman to avoid accountability for their actions by disregarding whatever women accuse them of, by saying they're 'just bitter'. What he did was wrong but she's worse for not being the better person and forgiving him. . . . No one wants the reputation of being a 'bitter' woman, so this manipulates women into keeping silent and the perpetrator remains protected and their behaviour remains unchallenged.

Bitter, scornful, and other value-laden descriptors suggest that even if there was some initial harm, the person holding onto it is now *unreasonably* making a situation worse through their resentment; their actions are supposedly subjecting another person/people (the ones who actually caused harm) to unfair or harmful experiences. These adjectives create an image of the harmed person as volatile and overreacting, so that not only does accountability for the harm disappear from the conversation, but also the harmed person gets made out to be the source of continued harm that can be maligned.

When forged into a compulsory practice, into something that we are punished for not readily supplying, forgiveness morphs into one of the master's tools for maintaining and replicating systems of oppression. Consequently, liberation from the oppressive conditions leading to ordinary trauma will not and could never come from acts of forgiveness which compel us to stop demanding accountability and justice in favour of uncritical acceptance of the world as it is. Compulsory forgiveness furthers systemic silencing of harmed people in order to shield the perpetrators of harm, whether individuals, groups, institutions, or systems. Furthermore, compulsory forgiveness hinders oppressed people from seeking out reconciliation – that is, the restoration or realization of harmonious relationships that generate authentic humanity (Lee 2019).

In place of liberation or reconciliation, compulsory forgiveness coerces traumatized people into accepting ongoing harm/suffering and to privilege advantaged people's feelings above our own. In this way, the politicization of forgiveness comes to resemble or complement that of resilience, which, drawing on Ahmed (2017: 189), I defined as a conservative technique of power: "Resilience is the requirement to take more pressure; such that the pressure can be gradually increased." Forgiveness is an acceptance of this requirement, an acceptance that gradually increases as we are expected to bear more and more. A resilient person is, in many ways, a forgiving person who, instead of demanding accountability, adapts to environments of ordinary traumatic harm. It becomes urgent to ask: What have we been forgiving? For how long? What good has our forgiveness led to, if any at all?

As a part of compulsory forgiveness, one of its deepest-growing roots, ordinary trauma often develops in a context where oppressed people are expected to comfort advantaged people before ourselves *because* of what they have made us out to be (i.e. how they perceive us). Meredith Talusan (2019), for instance, writing about the emotional labour of interacting with loved ones as a trans person, states:

> I've come to find it deeply unfair that trans people are often left with the burden of assuaging their loved ones' grief. . . . Not only does this expectation posit that being transgender is a trans person's fault, but it also fails to account for the fact that transitioning is likely to be many

> times more difficult for the trans person than for any loved one. Most important, grief as a reaction to transition is a form of transphobia; it reduces a person's very being to their gender, and reveals that a loved one cares more about a phantom image than for the trans person they supposedly love, who is right in front of them.

Talusan goes on to write: "Expecting us to comfort them promotes the transphobic idea that cisgender people's feelings must be prioritized over ours, even when we are clearly dealing with so much more, and those expressions of grief are harmful to us." The hard reality of the matter is that compulsory forgiveness/survivorship marginalizes, neglects, and diminishes oppressed people's wellbeing relative to advantaged people and, in doing so, continues our ongoing dehumanization. While forgiveness that is consensually given as part of healing has transformative and humanizing possibilities, forgiveness coerced from us is constraining; it reduces us to hardships to get around and marks us as burdensome – as always needing to apologize for *who we are*. The secret of compulsory forgiveness is that it is most often based in the assumption that we somehow deserved to be harmed, that *we* incited or provoked the violence to begin with, and that oppressed people should always be atoning for our imagined transgressions, such as daring to express our genders and sexualities in ways that we desire. Compulsory forgiveness and compulsory survivorship, in this way, are just another tactic of victim-blaming.

Since compulsory forgiveness is ultimately about harmed/oppressed people, it also creates the conditions for *compulsory forgivability*, which refers to a socially constructed perception that particular people – people within the "mythical norm" (Lorde 1984) – should be readily forgiven for the actions. While other people existing outside this norm ought to be subjected to additional violence in the forms of surveillance, policing, incarceration, and/or other sorts of punishment, systems of oppression condition us to believe that advantaged people as a whole are more deserving of forgiveness. The notion of forgivability is, of course, deeply and historically racialized, gendered, classed, enabled, and otherwise made through oppressive forces. It's why White rapists like Brock Turner can cry their way out of serious punishments while the list of murdered Black people is too long to recount here. It is also why convicted felon Donald Trump continues to have cult following despite repeatedly lying to and stealing from the American people.

Which people are seen as forgivable is filtered through carceral logics of innocence and guilt, based on their relationship to groups/communities that have been criminalized to the point of being presumed guilty of transgressions that they may not have even committed (Hemphill 2017). Forgivability comes from acting in alignment with systems of oppression because the acts of dominance have already been justified and normalized – they often already have an infrastructure and a script. Boys will be boys, for instance. Compulsory forgiveness coerces oppressed people and just as notably other advantaged people to forgive those determined to be forgivable, which is once again a method that power uses to reproduce itself by limiting resistance. Forgivability makes it easier to side with people causing harm because they are granted a sheen of innocence that too often isolates them from accountability.

Each of the three terms I have been thinking about in this section of Chapter 5 – *compulsory survivorship, compulsory forgiveness,* and *compulsory forgivability* – are oppressive tools of silencing harmed people. In preventing oppressed peoples from genuinely expressing needs or sharing experiences, in telling them how they should survive the structural violence aimed against them rather than creating space for them to lead and resist, these compulsions work as well as tools for obstructing the radical practice of love through authentic dialogue. Paulo Freire (2000 [1970]: 89) writes:

> Dialogue cannot exist, however, without a profound love for the world and for people. The naming of the world, which is an act of creation and re-creation, is not possible if it is not infused with love. Love is at the same time the foundation of dialogue and dialogue itself. . . . Because love is an act of courage, not of fear, love is commitment

> to others. No matter where the oppressed are found, the act of love is commitment to their cause – the cause of liberation.

Love is the deepest, most sacred source of human connection that can guide us toward our authentic humanity. When we love others, we actively listen to them with the goal of learning from them; we help to share their struggles and join them in the quest of collective liberation; we allow them to recreate us through their consciousness of the world at the same time as we recreate them through ours. Love as a spring of liberation refuses compulsory practices, except for those compelling us toward freedom and just relationships. For love requires that we accept people as fully human beings with complex emotions and ways of navigating their existence. Paulo Freire (2000 [1970]: 90) goes on to say: "Only by abolishing the situation of oppression is it possible to restore the love which that situation made impossible."

Notes

1 The belief that women menstruate while men do not is inaccurate. Gender is neither as fixed nor as straightforward as the gender binary claims it is. Some men do menstruate, some women do not, and many other genders have their own relationship to menstruation.

2 See bell hooks (2013) for an important and useful critique of Sandberg's neoliberal feminist theory, especially how it props up dominant oppressive ideologies and harmful structures of race, class, and nation.

References

Ahmed, Sara. "Feeling Depleted." *FeministKilljoys*. https://feministkilljoys.com/2013/11/17/feeling-depleted/ (published November 17, 2013).

Ahmed, Sara. *Living a Feminist Life*. Durham: Duke University Press, 2017.

Amato, E. "#MeToo: Why I Don't Want to Talk about It: When Sharing Becomes Self-Harm." *Thebodyisnotanapology*. https://thebodyisnotanapology.com/magazine/why-i-dont-want-to-talk-about-it-when-sharing-becomes-self-harm/ (published September 29, 2018).

Arielle, Rousse. "Beyond the Binaries: Exclusive Dichotomies in the Anti-Sexual Violence Movement." In *Queering Sexual Violence: Radical Voices from within the Anti-Violence Movement*, edited by Jennifer Patterson, 39–48. Riverdale: Riverdale Avenue Books, 2016.

Bancroft, Lundy. *Why Does He Do That: Inside the Minds of Angry and Controlling Men*. Berkeley: Berkeley Trade, 2003.

Carter, Angela. "Disabling Trauma: Toward a Crip Critique of Post-Traumatic Stress Disorder." Ph.D. Dissertation. University of Minnesota, 2019.

Coulter-Thomson, Emilee. "Queering Healthy Sexuality." In *Queering Sexual Violence: Radical Voices from within the Anti-Violence Movement*, edited by Jennifer Patterson, 75–82. Riverdale: Riverdale Avenue Books, 2016.

Crenshaw, Kimberlé. "Demarginalizing the Intersection of Race and Sex: A Black Feminist Critique of Antidiscrimination Doctrine, Feminist Theory and Antiracist Politics." *Chicago Legal Forum* 1989, no. 1 (1989): 139–167.

Cvetkovich, Ann. *An Archive of Feelings: Trauma, Sexuality, and Lesbian Public Cultures*. Durham: Duke University Press, 2003.

Du Bois, W. E. B. *The Souls of Black Folk*. Edited by Brent Hayes Edwards. Oxford: Oxford University Press, 2008 [1903].

Durazo, Ana Clarissa Rojas. "In Our Hands: Community Accountability as Pedagogical Strategy." *Social Justice* 37, no. 4 (2010): 76–100.

Fassler, Joe. "How Doctors Take Women's Pain Less Seriously." *The Atlantic*. https://www.theatlantic.com/health/archive/2015/10/emergency-room-wait-times-sexism/410515/ (published October 15, 2015).

Freire, Paulo. *Pedagogy of the Oppressed*. New York: Bloomsbury, 2000 [1970].

Frye, Marilyn. *The Politics of Reality: Essays in Feminist Theory*. Trumansburg, New York: Crossing Press, 1983.

Hedva, Johanna. "Sick Woman Theory." *Mask Magazine*. http://www.maskmagazine.com/not-again/struggle/sick-woman-theory (published 2016).

Hemphill, Prentis. "Healing Justice Is How We Can Sustain Black Lives." *Huffington Post*. https://www.huffpost.com/entry/healing-justice_b_5899e8ade4b0c1284f282ffe (published February 7, 2017).

Herman, Judith Lewis. *Trauma and Recovery*. New York: Basic Books, 1992.

hooks, bell. "Dig Deep: Beyond Lean In." *The Feminist Wire*. https://thefeministwire.com/2013/10/17973/ (published October 28, 2013).

Kafer, Alison. *Feminist, Queer, Crip*. Bloomington: Indiana University Press, 2013.

Kandaswamy, Priya. "Innocent Victims and Brave New Laws: State Protection and the Battered Women's Movement." In *Nobody Passes: Rejecting the Rules of Gender and Conformity*, edited by Matt Sycamore, 83–94. Emeryville: Seal Press, 2006.

Kauer, Keri. "Yoga Culture and Neoliberal Embodiment of Health." In *Yoga, the Body, and Embodied Social Change: An Intersectional Feminist Analysis*, edited by Beth Berila, Melanie Klein, and Chelsea Jackson Roberts, 91–108. Lanham: Lexington Books, 2016.

King, Sophie. "How the Concept of Forgiveness is Used to Gaslight Women." *Medium*. https://medium.com/@kingsophiesworld/how-the-concept-of-forgiveness-is-used-to-gaslight-women-8d6e4a04e07e (published June 13, 2019).

Koyama, Emi. "A New Fat-Positive Feminism: Why the Fat-Positive Feminism (Often) Sucks and How to Reinvent It." *Eminism*. https://eminism.org/readings/fatpositive.html (published May 5, 2004).

Lee, Tiffany. "Radical Accountability: Navigating the Abusive Habits We May Perpetuate Towards Ourselves." *Thebodyisnotanapology.com*. https://thebodyisnotanapology.com/magazine/radical-accountability-navigating-the-abusive-habits-we-perpetuate-towards-ourselves/ (published April 1, 2019).

Levins Morales, Aurora. *Medicine Stories: History, Culture and the Politics of Integrity*. Cambridge: South End Press, 1998.

Lorde, Audre. *Sister Outsider: Essays and Speeches*. New York: Ten Speed Press, 1984.

Lowry, Lois. *The Giver*. Boston: Houghton Mifflin, 1993.

Luhmann, Susanne. "Queering/Querying Pedagogy? Or, Pedagogy is a Pretty Queer Thing." In *Queer Theory in Education*, edited by William Pinar, 141–156. Mahwah, NJ: Lawrence Erlbaum Associates, 1998.

Mahan, Jolie. "Children Don't Belong in Cages." In *Much Madness: A Survivor's Guide to Extreme States and Self-Advocacy for Young Adults*, edited by Calvin Rey Moen and Kaz DeWolfe, 13–22. Brattleboro, VT: The Hive Mutual Support Network, 2019.

McRuer, Robert. *Crip Theory: Cultural Signs of Queerness and Disability*. New York: NYU Press, 2006.

Millbank, Lisa. "The Ethical Prude: Imagining An Authentic Sex-Negative Feminism." *A Radical TransFeminist*. https://radtransfem.wordpress.com/2012/02/29/the-ethical-prude-imagining-an-authentic-sex-negative-feminism/#sexiscompulsory (published February 29, 2012).

Mingus, Mia. "Forced Intimacy: An Ableist Norm." *Leaving Evidence*. https://leavingevidence.wordpress.com/2017/08/06/forced-intimacy-an-ableist-norm/ (published August 6, 2017).

Minow, M. *Between Vengeance and Forgiveness: Facing History after Genocide and Mass Violence*. Boston: Beacon Press, 1998.

Moen, Calvin Rey and DeWolfe, Kaz. "Introduction." In *Much Madness: A Survivor's Guide to Extreme States and Self-Advocacy for Young Adults*, edited by Calvin Rey Moen and Kaz DeWolfe, 5–12. Brattleboro, VT: The Hive Mutual Support Network, 2019.

Piepzna-Samarasinha, Leah Lakshmi. "Not Over It, Not Fixed, and Living a Life Worth Living." In *Whatever Gets You Through: Twelve Survivors on Life after Sexual Assault*. Greystone Books, 2019.

Pollock, Anastasia. "Why I Don't Use the Word 'Forgiveness' in Trauma Therapy." *GoodTherapy.org*. https://www.goodtherapy.org/blog/why-i-dont-use-the-word-forgiveness-in-trauma-therapy-0120164 (published January 20, 2016).

Rich, Adrienne. "Compulsory Heterosexuality and Lesbian Existence." *Signs* 5, no. 4 (1980): 631–660.

Sandberg, Sheryl. *Lean In: Women, Work, and the Will to Lead*. Knopf, 2013.

Stewart, Terah J. "About Fat Campus." *About Campus: Enriching the Student Learning Experience* 23, no. 4 (2018): 31–34.

Talusan, Meredith. "Celebrate Your Kid's Transition: Don't Grieve It." *The New York Times*. https://www.nytimes.com/2019/10/18/opinion/sunday/gender-transition-death-grief.html (published October 18, 2019).

Taylor, Astra and Hunt-Hendrix, Leah. "One for All: To Avert Global Catastrophe, We Urgently Need to Resurrect the Ancient Ideal of Solidarity." *The New Republic*. https://newrepublic.com/article/154623/green-new-deal-solidarity-solution-climate-change-global-warming (published August 26, 2019).

Taylor, Sonya Renee. *The Body Is Not an Apology: The Power of Radical Self-love*. Oakland, CA: Berrett-Koehler Publishers, 2018.

Voronka, Jijian. "Storytelling Beyond the Psychiatric Gaze: Resisting Resilience and Recovery Narratives." *Canadian Journal of Disability Studies* 8, no. 4 (2019): 8–30.

6

Resistant Reclamations: Thoughts on Healing Against Ordinary Trauma

Ordinary Suicide: Western Medicine Cannot Keep Us Alive

As I begin this chapter on healing against ordinary trauma, I want to consider suicide and the implications it has for thinking about traumatic harm and trauma response. For some people, suicidal thoughts and actions might be the outcome of purely internal conditions, yet a more common reality for oppressed people is that suicidality emerges in response to the ordinary traumas of living through interlocking systems of oppression. Circumstances of inequity and injustice simultaneously and purposely generate feelings of helplessness, self-hatred, self-doubt, fear, self-loathing, and isolation – each of which promotes the destructive belief that ending one's life is preferable. Oppression also forms barriers that make it harder for people to access the things they need to feel love, cared for, belonging to community, and deserving of life. Surviving systems of oppression often feels like being told to "pick up the pace" when you are struggling to get through an obstacle course that everybody else seems to know the trick to navigating.

My argument here is that suicide is more than just an individual, psychological problem that can be cured through medical

DOI: 10.4324/9781003716198-6

or therapeutic interventions provided to people on their own; quite to the contrary, suicide is a sociopolitical problem borne from capitalism, queerphobia, transphobia, sexism, racism, ableism, sanism, colonialism, and other interrelated systems of oppression. And, as Sarah Mariann Martland (2018), explains:

> If we're not talking about trauma and oppression (in all its guises), about marginalization, about access to healthcare, community care and all manner of support systems, about systemic injustice and harm, then we're not really having a full conversation about suicide prevention.

Indeed, rather than being an isolated or out of the ordinary phenomenon, oppressed peoples are subtly encouraged, sometimes even instructed, to embrace and pursue our own deaths in one form or another. Suicidal thoughts and tendencies are beaten, whipped, screamed, implanted, carved, or otherwise conditioned into oppressed people precisely because, to remember the words of Audre Lorde (1984: 41), "we were never meant to survive." The reality of the matter is that suicide can appear to be a rational choice in a world characterized by systemic inequity and injustice – a world that is built upon the unhealth and unwellness of oppressed people (Barlow 2018).

For example, disproportionate rates of suicide among Indigenous peoples across the planet tell a compelling story about the ordinariness of suicide in the wake of historical and ongoing settler colonial violence – a violence which I described in earlier chapters as systematically traumatizing to Indigenous peoples, communities, nations, lands, and cultural memories or traditions. Suicide is an ordinary outcome of intergenerational colonial trauma in the context of historical suffering under capitalism, colonialism, White supremacy, and other structures of power that maintain colonial occupation of Indigenous lands and settler dominance over Indigenous peoples. Psychologist Pat Dudgeon, for instance, remarks:

> It is this lack of self-determination [arising from Australia's histories of colonial relations] that continues to cause

> a higher incidence of suicide in Aboriginal people. It is a sense of hopelessness passed from one generation to another.
>
> (cited in Kenyon 2019)

I want to recognize and maintain the distinctions between Indigenous communities across the world because they have unique histories and experiences, and, at the same time, I want to name the ways in which structures of settler colonialism depend on Indigenous death and disappearance (Monaghan 2015). Even as histories of colonial violence and occupation take unique forms across time, space, and nation, a widespread impact of colonial trauma is the increased ordinariness of suicidal thoughts and actions connected to the profound sense of loss and hopelessness that things will get better.

Writing about suicide among Indigenous communities in Canada, Jeffrey Ansloos (2018: 23) calls for decolonization as a necessary tool for nourishing Indigenous life:

> Indigenous communities face the ongoing effects of historical colonialism, and the contemporary effects of neocolonial violence. We need to begin to articulate an approach to research that can recognize the social and structural foundations of suicide in a way that goes beyond mere acknowledgement, towards material practices which promote holistic wellbeing for and with Indigenous peoples. This is a bold and necessary call in Indigenous suicide and prevention research–for us to become emboldened in our critical concern for addressing the complex forms of violence which make life unlivable, and to implicate our life in the pursuit of the type of justice that nourishes Indigenous life.

There is a great power in recognizing suicide as an outcome not of deficits among Indigenous peoples or cultures, but of the traumatic violation of settler colonialism. Not only does such recognition destabilize colonial logics and settler myths of superiority, but it also creates a critical sociopolitical method of organizing against suicide instead of a purely individual one. By identifying connections between decolonization and suicide, Ansloos also shares with us an invitation to consider its connections to other outcomes of colonial occupation, such as the theft and destruction of land and sexual violence against Indigenous peoples, especially women and two-spirit folks (Smith 2005). Indeed, all of these issues intersect because they emerge from a common oppressive system.

In addition to Indigenous peoples, we can also think about ordinary suicide in connection to disabled folks, whose treatment within an ableist and sanist world creates a culture in which death and disappearance become normalized. Lydia Brown (2014: 41) claims that disabled people are often praised for desiring/pursuing death while enabled people are encouraged towards life:

> Even today, disabled people who wish to kill themselves are more frequently praised as brave and courageous, and offered the option of euthanasia, while non-disabled people who express the same suicidal ideations are referred to anti-suicide counseling and support.

I do not reference this quote to argue that we should remove autonomy from disabled people desiring to end their lives – that would be another example of medial paternalism – nor do I believe we should start to praise enabled people for doing so; I have my own private thoughts on this matter that I will keep to myself. Rather, I draw on Lydia Brown's words here because they capture the complicated truth that our willingness as a society to recognize suicide as a problem, to intervene against suicide or to focus our attentions elsewhere, is inseparable from inherited beliefs about what makes life worth living and whose lives can be meaningful. Mainstream movies, such as the 2016 Box Office hit *Me Before You*, advocate understanding and acceptance for disabled people who choose to end their lives, yet popular culture lacks comparable representations of disabled people celebrating or enjoying their lives – disability is rarely portrayed as anything more than an impediment to life in need of cure (Clare 2017), and cure can mean death.

Yet, these and other accounts of suicide as a consequence of systems/structures of power do not enter into most discussions of suicide – what few there are. Writing about depression, but equally relevant to the discussion here, Ann Cvetkovich (2012: 116) writes that much of the difficulty in understanding such issues emerges from biases in medical literature and a lack of a systemic analysis of power:

> [M]ost of the literature, both medical and historical . . . often without acknowledging it directly, tends to presume a white and middle-class subject for whom feeling bad is frequently a mystery because it doesn't fit a life in which privilege and comfort make things seem fine on the surface.

Unwellness in the medical model of suicide becomes inevitable as bodyminds diverge from this normative presumption; that is, when people belonging to the "mythical norm" – people that are White, heterosexual, male, economically privileged, young, thin, etc. – are placed at the centre and used as a model for understanding health and wellness, the experiences and needs of people outside of this norm, which might naturally differ, become coded as deviant and excessive. Unwellness and unhealth develop both because systems of power normalize inequity and injustice and because they define such terms in relation to particular groups of people that are not representative of humanity as a whole. If the way we understand suicide exists in relation to advantaged people, then of course issues of race, ability, class, sexuality, and so on will be notably absent from the conversations we have about it as well as the sorts of interventions/practices of care we participate in. This erasure is an intentional effect of oppression working to keep itself invisible as it distributes life and death.

Furthermore, at stake here is the question of which people's lives are seen to matter enough for intervention and whose are seen as disposable enough to make their deaths acceptable and unremarkable to the broader society. Indeed, the ordinariness of suicide is reflected in the fact that only some people's stories are regarded as worth telling. The refusal to address the systemic/structural sources of suicide is part of what Angela M. Carter (2019: 27) refers to as "the citizenship project of traumatocracy" through which normative constructions of trauma determine "who can claim trauma, what counts as trauma, and what narratives of trauma are recognized." The traumatocracy generates the pervasive "refusal to consider or critique – let alone work to change – any of the systemic, institutionalized causes of trauma." Political, relational, and material conditions preceding suicide (i.e. the collection of ordinary traumatic experiences making death desirable) as well as the traumatizing action of suicide itself are filtered through discourses that obscure the impact of oppression. In doing so, they promote the medicalized and pathologized narrative amenable to medical models of health. Thus, rather than being an understandable if regrettable response to unliveable conditions of inequity/injustice, portrayals of suicide become a method of associating particular people with pathology and a tool for validating, instead of critically questioning, oppressive systems and the dominance of medical/psychological institutions.

Medical and psychological interventions cannot adequately address the problem of suicide for oppressed people because they are privatized responses to a socially produced issue. If the circumstances leading someone to end their life are bound up in the ordinary trauma of inequity and injustice, then interventions failing to address the violence of systems of power leave the underlying or root causes of suicide unaddressed. Without addressing root causes of suicide, interventions can only even provide a temporary solution: we might convince our people to stay alive for a while longer, but the forces pulling them toward death will continue to assert an influence. For this reason, medicine and therapy could be seen to resemble self-defence courses: they give people some hopefully useful tools to fight back, but they do not work to dismantle the sources of harm people have to defend themselves against.

My purpose here is not to discredit or devalue the empowerment that medicine and therapy provide for many people; rather, I am arguing that medicine and therapy are, by themselves, inadequate solutions because suicide is much of the time not about individual people. Like trauma in general, systems of power make suicide ordinary in the lives of oppressed people, so our responses to suicide have to address not only impacted person(s), but also all of the social forces that are converging around and inside them. In surviving inequity and injustice, death by choice can easily become a path of least resistance for oppressed people because dying might easier than living. I recall adrienne maree brown's poem that reminded us "that death might be the only freedom" (2014). Promoting liberation requires that we open up alternative paths that celebrate all our lives and fill them up with pleasure, worth, and deeper meaning. This work has to take place across all levels – personal, relational, communal, and societal. Otherwise, we will fail.

Despite these limitations of medicine and therapy for addressing suicide, the most common responses when suicide enters into popular discourse continue to emphasize these sorts of individualistic interventions. People share suicide hotline numbers or name the importance of mental health, for instance, before and often to the exclusion of any systemic issues that contribute to suicide, such as hunger or homelessness. The consequence of such efforts is that the conversation remains eternally fixed on what is *wrong* with individual people rather than the harm done to them by a society built on and around ordinary trauma. The individual who completed or attempted to end their life is effectively removed from their social context, treated as exceptional or out or the ordinary, and their story gets reinterpreted through a lens of power that masks ongoing issues of inequity and injustice. I refer to this tendency as the "hotline approach" – give people a number to call, and you have done your part; no need for further action.

I believe that suicide prevention hotlines, emergency rooms, and related things are essential sources of care and support for a lot of suicidal people, and sharing these resources can be a life-saving act, but there is a significant danger when we permit conversations to stop there. In focusing on individuals and removing them from their social context, the hotline approach pathologizes people and fails to recognize that, as horrible as it sounds, suicide can feel like the most *logical* response to our oppression when the weight of survival becomes too heavy. We are all as humans seeking in one way or another to reduce the harms we experience, so when social systems fail to protect us, kinship networks fail to care for/about us, institutions fail to serve us, and/or loved ones fail to love us – basically, when harm seems inevitable and restoration seems impossible – ending it all can start to make sense.

Medicine and therapy, even when social justice-oriented and attuned to the lived realities of ordinary trauma that oppressed peoples experience, are fighting an uphill battle against this conditioned impulse toward death. As an analogy, think about a potted plant running out of water: the hotline approach is like nourishing the plant with a cup of water, but doing nothing to close up the holes in the pot that let the water spill out. Even if the plant was able to absorb some water and survive for a bit longer, it quickly dehydrates again because the surrounding environment is not conducive to its sustained life. The practical response for the plant is to shrink down so that it needs less water to survive in a pot that can't sustain it, and if it spends enough time shrinking, eventually it disappears altogether. To truly address the problem of suicide, we need to locate holes in the pot of our society that leave people without nutrients they require to sustain themselves. Poverty, discrimination, violence, neglect, isolation, and so on are the social precursors to ordinary suicide that leave people starving and dehydrated, and these are things which medicine and therapy cannot fix. We all share a responsibility for dismantling harmful and oppressive conditions that steal life away, and we all have a stake in refusing the death of people around us.

While it may seem responsible and accountable, the "hotline approach" is actually a way of not seeing and un-seeing broader social problems, for by reducing suicide to something that can be solved through individual-level interventions like giving someone a crisis line number, social conditions become less relevant to the conversation. The "hotline approach" enables people to convince ourselves, however partially, that we are not complicit in the conditions leading someone to the decision to end their life. Dissolving ties to contemporary systemic issues also dissolves advantaged people of accountability for the high rates of suicide – they can continue to use their privileges in ways that exploit, violate, abuse, neglect, or otherwise mistreat oppressed people without feeling responsible for their lives because they don't see how suicide is about dominance and the behaviours of people in power. Medicalization and pathologization, in this sense, are political manoeuvres that have direct implications for how we live together with our relatives and how we understand what it means to be in relationship with them.

Western medicine has for centuries sought to redefine social problems as private issues for which individual people can be blamed and punished, and the hotline approach is a strong example of how we have collectively become complicit in this misdirection. Even as it makes suicide more visible, more spoken, more named, the hotline approach creates a silence on which systems of oppression nourish themselves. Of course, the pervasive tendency to rely first and foremost on medical and psychological institutions is not coincidental: systems of oppression actively contribute to the *medical industrial complex* which exists to mask social problems and weaken resistance through appropriation of concepts like health or wellness into a medical model centred on individual people instead of broader systems/structures. Mia Mingus (2015) writes:

> The Medical Industrial Complex is an enormous system with tentacles that reach beyond simply doctors, nurses, clinics, and hospitals. It is a system about profit, first and foremost, rather than 'health', wellbeing and care. Its roots run deep and its history and present are connected to everything including eugenics, capitalism, colonization, slavery, immigration, war, prisons, and reproductive oppression. It is not just a major piece of the history of ableism, but *all* systems of oppression.

Through the medical industrial complex, systems of oppression sideline critical analyses of social problems by advancing narratives that justify different forms of inequity and injustice. The cooptation of health, wellness, and care is connected to a capitalist imperative towards profit that requires ongoing ordinary trauma and inequitable distributions of resources away from oppressed people. Ana Clarissa Rojas Durazo (2006: 181) asserts that "[t]he structured goals of the medical industrial complex are to heighten profits, legitimate the state, and maintain the dominance of the western medical model, which, in turn, perpetuates racism, classism, and heterosexism." So, if suicide is a social phenomenon grounded in unbalanced power relations, what then does it mean for us to put trust in medical institutions that have historically participated in White supremacy, settler colonialism, heteropatriarchy, ableism, and other systems or structures of power? Doing so can prevent us from addressing broader issues in need of rectification, and, in being conditioned to always direct people elsewhere, we often fail at one of the most important things we can do in our relationships: show up for each other. As a social problem, ordinary suicide needs to be addressed socially, politically, and historically.

Before I move on to the following portion of this chapter, I want to make one final comment about ordinary suicide: the problem is not simply that oppressed people are exposed to conditions that cause suffering; indeed, Clint Smith (cited in Murphy 2016) reminds us that oppressed people "are not singularly defined by the things that kill us." We are greater than the sum of our advantages and disadvantages. Yet a critical danger emerges in the presence of systems of oppression that we become, personally and culturally, obsessed with trauma and death to the exclusion of other narratives about the desirable aspects of life – things like hope, joy, love, and community. Leah Lakshmi Piepzna-Samarasinha (2019: 175), for instance, writes:

> We have narratives that focus on how hard it is not to die when we are young and queer, trans, or Two Spirit. And those are very necessary. But maybe we should also be getting real about what it takes to keep queer and gender-variant and Two-Spirit adults alive too.

Naming harm and discussing the systemic/structural forces underlying ordinary suicide is urgent to be sure, but so too is the action of creating alternative stories in which life, however messy, prevails over death and disappearance. We need counternarratives that instil hope, genuine hope not hollow platitudes, and that take suffering seriously while also transporting us beyond suffering. Counternarratives which refuse to leave us in suffering with no hope for something more pleasurable and sustainable. What we need are stories and communities that recognize and honour our complexity, that truly value our lives, and that reject the things or people that reduce us to no more than what we have survived.

From Un-Health to Dis-Order: Healing Against Oppression

In February 2019, I participated in a day long "Mental Health First-Aid" training hosted by my previous university. The training was geared towards an introductory audience, people with limited experience responding to mental health crises, and the presenters' objectives were to describe some best practices for support, de-escalation, and intervention. Although the presenters did provide several helpful strategies to care for other people, I struggled to really engage with the training because it failed to connect mental health to the broader social and political context that shapes the sorts of experiences people are likely to encounter and care they are likely to receive. The strategies they offered were, therefore, centred on individuals and neglected the need for social change and social justice.

Like trauma in general, the presenters and the generalized content they were sharing talked about mental health or mental illness as something that individuals experience more or less the same, regardless of their relationships to power. Aside from a few fleeting moments, this training did not include substantive information about the ways that mental health or illness are formed through racism, ableism, queerphobia, sexism, transphobia, settler colonialism, xenophobia, or other systems of power. One presenter did strive to bring poverty and police violence into the conversation, but not as part of a systematic critique of capitalism or state violence. As a participant, I was led to an erroneous conclusion that who we are and how we are positioned socially does not matter when thinking about mental health/illness.

Furthermore, the manner in which the presenters led this training was not trauma-informed or healing-centred and actually gave me a pretty clear impression that they were operating under the assumption that no traumatized people or mentally ill people would be present in the space. In addition to not addressing the effects systems of power have on mental health and illness, the presenters also failed to recognize their advantaged positions, especially as seemingly able-bodied/minded people. I arrived at this conclusion based on the presenters' overall demeanour as well as the learning activities they used throughout the training. At one point, to practice suicide intervention, members of the audience split up into pairs and took turns asking each other "Are you thinking about killing yourself?" to which the other person had to answer "No." Then the presenters asked the audience "Are you thinking about killing yourself?" and we collectively had to respond "No." This activity assumed that no one in the room would say "yes" or have a history of suicidal thoughts or actions. I was triggered for the rest of the day.

At another point, we had the opportunity to "experience" schizophrenia: in groups of three, two people had a conversation while the third person played the part of "voices" whispering paranoia into the ears of one of the others. This activity also made a lot of assumptions about who would be present/not present in the room, and it advanced a particularly harmful belief that non-schizophrenic people could comprehend that experience through such a debasing exercise. As a Women, Gender, and Sexuality Studies scholar, this activity reminded me of the problematic book *Nickel and Dimed* by Barbara Ehrenreich (2011) in which the author seeks to understand poverty and worker oppression by "becoming poor" and working at minimum wage jobs. I could spend several hours discussing the problematic aspects of this training (and I did with my partner afterwards), but it is only one part of a much broader problem – a "symptom," if you will – within mental health discourses and practices.

From my experiences, what worries me the most is the fact that this training is, for the most part, not out of the ordinary; quite the opposite, it is typical of what I have come to expect as someone who thinks and writes about trauma and healing. How we are often conditioned to understand mental health and mental illness reflects a pervasive belief that these things are individualized and disconnected from the oppressive social conditions and histories around us. Similar perceptions also exist for other dimensions of health and well-being. Goodkind et al. (2012: 1026) observe:

> Within western medicine and psychology, healers have tended to focus on treating specific symptoms and/or eradicating disease, as opposed to holistic healing of a person within the context of their family and community.

Mental health in particular is often treated pathologically as something wrong with individual people to be cured through therapy and medication. Furthermore, Paulina Helm-Hernandez (2013) writes:

> There are two different ways of looking at disease 1) the clinical model, i.e.: you have a really bad diet, you don't exercise enough, etc. or 2) the historical roots of why people of color are more susceptible to certain things.

This claim can be extended to disabled people, queer and trans folks, impoverished people, and other oppressed groups as well, though of course with attention to historical differences between them. What these theorists are identifying is the separation of health and wellness, and by extension unhealthy and unwell people, from the social contexts, communities, and histories that shape them. As I have argued elsewhere in this book, this privatized approach changes healing from something that happens in communities through caring relationships, something that people can share accountability for, into something which individuals alone are responsible for resolving and that they can more often than not be blamed for. Systems of oppression are altogether removed from this narrative.

Where people are willing to acknowledge the impact of systems of oppression, conversation often does not go beyond the important but insufficient observation that unequal access to healthcare privileges some people at the expensive of others. The extent of this system-level analysis tends to focus on how we respond to mental unwellness rather than the systematic political determinants of mental unwellness itself. However, just like trauma, mental health and illness are not randomly occurring or equitable across differences – they are distributed unjustly. This statement does not claim that only some people will experience mental health concerns in their lifetimes, but rather that our relationships to mental health, mental illness, and healing are shaped by our positionalities – that they are more than just individual internal conditions. For as Jameta Nicole Barlow (2018: 901) writes: "Trauma rooted in racist, sexist, and classist policies and perpetuated by systems of power on a daily basis is simply not healthy."

Cara Page (2013) poses the urgent question of "[h]ow do we remain well inside systems that do not want us to be well or already associate us to disease?. . . . How can we move forward to make a better world if we're not understanding the impact of long-term oppression?" Through systemic/structural oppression, the socio-political order directs and cultivates (un) wellness to ensure a normal distribution of resources and health outcomes in favour of advantaged peoples. Similarly, just as with our lived experiences more broadly, our experiences of (un) wellness are historically grounded. For instance, Cvetkovich (2012: 132), reflecting on the ordinariness of depression, poses the following critical, cutting question: "What if depression, in the Americas, at least, could be traced to histories of colonialism, genocide, slavery, legal exclusion, and everyday segregation and isolation that haunt all of our lives, rather than to biochemical imbalances?" Essentially, Cvetkovich is naming unwellness as something grounded in histories of slavery, White supremacy, and colonial violence instead of imbalances within the individual. Moving towards wellness, then, entails grappling with histories as they manifest in our present-day intimacies, families, and communities as well as within individual bodies and minds.

In a society built on systemic inequity and injustice, mental health and healing are entwined with ongoing conflicts between advantaged and oppressed people over access to resources that allow us to meet our needs and live good, meaningful lives. Health inequities in people's experiences of mental health/healing across sites of difference serve a necessary function in maintaining systems of power – in ensuring advantaged people remain in dominant social positions. Writing about healing in the context of the Black Lives Matter movement, Jameta Nicole Barlow (2018: 897) contends that the health and healing of Black people transgresses systems which benefit from Black death and illness:

> Prioritizing the healing of individual and collective black bodies, minds, and spirits is a subversive notion. To be Black, Brown, healthy, and whole in the United States can be viewed as a *threat* to a system that benefits from *unhealthy* populations.

The state and the intersecting systems of oppression on which it relies, according to Barlow, benefit when people of colour and other oppressed peoples suffer from the lack of health and healing – when they are kept *unhealthy*. In other words, the problem is not just that the state neglects or fails to care about oppressed people living in the country, though it does do those things; the actual problem is that we have built a system of governance that cannot continue to exist without the ordinary suffering and un-health of particular dehumanized or devalued people. Accordingly, to really support mental healing, we need to promote take seriously the psychic, spiritual pain and suffering of people of colour as well as others who experience trauma as an ordinary part of their lives.

Recognizing the necessity of un-health shows that there is a critique to be made of much of the language surrounding mental illnesses and disorders, especially from an intersectional, disability justice lens. The occurrence of mental illness under oppressive systems might be better understood as socially manufactured *dis-ease*.[1] Just as the social model of disability declares that bodies are not the problem so much as inaccessible social arrangements, this concept of dis-ease recognizes how people's lives are made more difficult through oppressive social realities instead of purely internal conditions. Traumatic stress, anxiety, depression, and other experiences typically included within the umbrella of "mental illness" are each facets of ordinary trauma that come into being as people survive, recover from, and resist systems of oppression; they are not accidental, but enforced to the point of presumption, and in this recognition of enforcement, the workings of power become visible as sources of dis-ease in need of healing.

Similarly, the language of mental "disorders," while typically used to diagnose what is *wrong* with individual people, provides another meaningful lens for thinking about power in relation to mental health and well-being. The concept of dis-order exposes the reality of compulsory able-mindedness – that is, the expectation that we condition ourselves to think and mentally experience the world in specific, normative ways (Kafer 2013). Thinking about dis-order and the people it gets applied to makes visible how oppressive systems impose expectations on the minds of people who unavoidably exist outside of compulsory able-mindedness – those of us who cannot meet expectations of mental productivity, rationality, and sanity. It names the power of containment used to judge, regulate, punish people who transgress the narrow boundaries of normativity. This is the alternate meaning of dis-order: "to disturb the regular or normal functions of" (Merriam-Webster). Dis-orderly people threaten social control and suggest the possibility of other social arrangements; that is, they are dis-ordering.

Through individualizing, medicalizing, and pathologizing discourses, socially generated un-health, dis-ease, and dis-order are depoliticized/privatized, thereby promoting the erasure of critical consciousness and socially responsible healing practices and institutions. As with the ordinariness of trauma, the ordinariness of these realities gets stripped away from the common knowledge of people engaging in care work. For example, Dom Chatterjee (2017) explains how guidance offered in *The Post-Traumatic Stress Disorder Sourcebook* (Schiraldi 2009) misses an important aspect of the mental health experiences of people of colour:

> [According to the sourcebook], we just have to realize we're safe now, and then the trauma responses can slow

> down. We're supposed to accept that trauma is in the past. But what if it's not? When trauma is tied to systemic oppression such as racism, leaving it in the past can be and often is impossible. Given that safe spaces are an ideal, not a reality for most of us, these kinds of statements are invalidating. If feeling safe is a required condition for healing, that makes any kind of recovery inaccessible to those of us enduring chronic trauma from the world around us.

While Schiraldi's sourcebook asserts that safety is a necessary piece of the healing process, Chatterjee makes an important recognition that people of colour and other oppressed people are never actually "safe" and that the danger of trauma is never in the past because sources of harm emanating from systemic oppression continue to exist all around us. Consequently, mental health is always contested when surviving oppression, which means that oppressed people get excluded or marginalized within these dominant ideas about healing. Chatterjee goes on to write: "That's not to say there's no space to heal in my life, but that the conditions of my healing involve not having access to safety or stability. And that's ok because there are always opportunities to heal." Healing outside of safety or stability is a necessary aspect of survival when people's un-health is vital to the functioning of systems of power.

This recognition of the simultaneity of healing and danger is important because it challenges assumed binaries within dominant medicalized and pathologized discourses about healing as well as the normative assumptions upon which dominant discourses are formed. Healing frameworks tend to centre around idealized constructions of "normal," healthy bodies that, as Leah Lakshmi Piepzna-Samarasinha (2018: 103) writes, people are presumed/expected to yearn for:

> Mainstream ideas of 'healing' deeply believe in ableist ideas that you're either sick or well, fixed or broken, and that nobody would want to be in a disabled or sick or mad bodymind, Unsurprisingly and unfortunately, these

> ableist ideas often carry over into healing spaces that call themselves 'alternative' or 'liberatory'. The healing may be acupuncture and herbs, not pills and surgery, but assumptions in both places abound that disabled and sick folks are sad people longing to be 'normal', that cure is always the goal, and that disabled people are objects who have no knowledge of our bodies.

Furthermore, Loeser et al. (2018: 257) maintain: "Constructions of this 'normal' body have historically invoked binary notions about gender, class, 'race' and sexuality." Instead of true recognitions of harm and movements toward accountability and repair, healing becomes a technology of *curing* individual people into their proper positions in these false, constructed binaries: from what is imagined as sick to what is imagined as well, from "broken" to "fixed," from "deviant" to "normal," and so on.

Much of the time, practices of healthcare, both mainstream and alternative, reinforce what Alison Kafer (2013) describes as a *compulsory nostalgia* – the socially enforced longing for a time prior to disablement or difference which ultimately marks disabled bodies or minds as inferior, undesirable, or detestable markers of failure, loss, harm, etc. For example, disabled people who undergo some major change to their experiences of the world (e.g. losing a limb, having a stroke, living through a traumatic brain injury) are expected and even compelled to remember their lives before the change as better or more desirable, as if becoming disabled has reduced their capacity to lead meaningful, joyous lives. While processing and adjusting to change certainly takes time, and although disabled people might reasonable feel a sense of loss, the danger of compulsory nostalgia comes from keeping people trapped in memory, and in foreclosing possibilities for a future not defined by what is missing. Such nostalgia, in itself, advances a false binary in which disabled and enabled peoples are distinct from each other with the former being marked as lesser than the latter. When we unlearn these binaries, healing can then enter a more expansive space where collective access is prioritized above making people "normal."

Joining Chatterjee, Piepzna-Samarasinha, and Kafer with Barlow's assertion that oppressed people's healing is *threatening* to power, I arrive at the following conclusions: when healing becomes threatening to systems of oppression, healing becomes dangerous to advantaged people, and oppressed people who dare to heal themselves in line with their own definitions of well-being gain a power to transform the world. Systems of oppression need the un-health and dis-ease of oppressed people to maintain existing distributions of power for social order. This need in part arises from the process of manufacturing consent and complacency within oppressed people but also originates from deep-seated fear of the power oppressed people as a collective hold within our dis-orderly bodies and minds. Indeed, just as the dangers in oppressed people's lives never go away, the threat of our existence will never go away – we will unrelentingly persist and resist. Such is the eternal flaw of power: its enactment over us makes us dangerous, gives us the tools to challenge and negate it.

Moreover, enactments of power in the realm of health, as a source of un-health and dis-ease, mean that our healing comprises a resistance in itself, for if as Audre Lorde (1984: 41) said, "we were never meant to survive," then our survival represents a refusal of power's will and a recognition of the possibility for alternative futures filled up with our life. To heal is to love ourselves, and to love ourselves is to resist the hatred of systems of oppression, and to find pleasure in that which is supposed to be ugly and undesirable (brown 2019; Mingus 2011). Furthermore, when oppressed people refuse to merely survive and choose to heal our lives outside of dominant practices and social institutions – for instance, when we locate healing in restorative practice, community-building, or collective resistance – we challenge many of the structural foundations advantaged people have formed their fragile self-esteem around. Rhiana Anthony (2019) states, "It's a security threat to the safety of our movements when our folks are not getting healed," but the opposite is also true: when we take care of our people, when we create spaces for genuine healing and transformation, then our movements realize a wellspring of radical potential to carry us forward.

The systemic dehumanization of oppressed people comprises the constructed social space against which advantaged people imagine themselves into an imagined position of mental health and well-being. That is, by associating unhealthiness or pathology with dehumanized, oppressed people, advantaged people can differentiate themselves into a mental space of wellness – they can dislocate and project anxieties, fears, self-doubt, and the like onto those oppressed people who are subjected to inequity and injustice. The un-health of oppressed people, then, reaches down to the very foundation of how advantaged people conceptualize themselves and go through their lives. When oppressed people engage in healing practices, especially on our own terms, it threatens to undermine the well-being of people benefitting from systems of power who regard themselves as better and more-fully human. Ultimately, this observation reveals the immense power oppressed people acquire as the result of their positions within an inequitable and unjust society. This power reflects the psychological and emotional manifestation of advantaged people's "fragility."

As somebody who is personally and politically invested in movements for disability justice, which include chronic ill people and those with health-related disabilities, I have never really liked the language of mental illness. So, even though it might seem accurate to think about fragility as a form of "mental illness" manifesting in the anxieties and terrors of advantaged people, I think it makes more sense to conceive of fragility in terms of a relational politics of belonging through which people bring into existence particular kinds of mentalities/internal realities. Aimee Carrillo Rowe (2008) argues that loving is a political act that determines who and what we become, that our sense of belonging to and with other people is embedded in our shifting understandings of "self." Indeed, the issue at hand is not that advantaged and disadvantaged people are "mentally ill" according to prevailing discourses, but instead that we have fallen out of relationship with one another, that we have not been good relatives or ancestors. Fragility becomes a common social reality precisely because advantaged people come to love themselves through feelings and practices of hatred for or non-loving of people they see as less-than-fully human. The self-love and self-esteem that come from dominance depend on the ongoing suppression of the health/well-being of oppressed others.

Further, fragility is also connected to a feeling within advantaged people that their identities lack substance or distinctiveness. So much of dominance is about the ongoing rejection of othered people – for example advantaged people demonstrating that they aren't like people of colour, queer people, women, disabled people – that the "self" can start to feel like absence or emptiness. If advantaged people are defined by what they are not, then their fragility could also be an outcome of always pushing others away, of constantly differentiating themselves instead of building their identities through connections and communities. Much of the time, advantaged people seek to remedy this feeling by encountering the other. These encounters allow for excitement while simultaneously reinforcing differences and shoring up power.

For instance, bell hooks (1992) writes about White people's need to "enhance the blank landscape of whiteness." The pursuit of normativity and the privileges associated with it is largely about occupying the same social positions and identities as other "normal" people, an endeavour which at the same time threatens to erase individuality, fashion boredom, and reduce memorability. hooks goes on to write that "Difference can seduce precisely because the mainstream imposition of sameness is a provocation that terrorizes" (1992). Thus, since advantaged social positions are defined by the rejection of the other, rejection of difference, advantaged people come to depend upon flash encounters with othered people to *spice* up their lives, to save them from the terrifying realization of sameness or lack of individuality, to ensure they do not disappear totally in the continuous rejection of others. hooks writes:

> To make one's self vulnerable to the seduction of difference, to seek an encounter with the Other, does not require that one relinquish forever one's mainstream positionality. When race and ethnicity become commodified as resources for pleasure, the culture of specific

> groups, as well as the bodies of individuals, can be seen as constituting an alternative playground where members of dominating races, genders, sexual practices affirm their power-over in intimate relations with the Other (1992).

Importantly, the commodification and consumption of others preserves rather than disrupts relations of power as intimacy becomes a space for domination and theft. However, there is also a fragile aspect to this sort of encounter, for even as advantaged people reclaim power-over the other, the impetus to do so is bound up in a fear of being "normal" – of being always "the same." Seeking out the other in these conditions moreover shows advantaged people's internalized vulnerability. This vulnerability makes control feel slippery, and it increases the need to reassert dominance. Fragility comes into being as a result of perceived threats, both real and imagined, to the ordering of power in intimate relationships.

***

Considering the complex, frictional interactions between systems of oppression and health makes it necessary to explore methods of healing that go beyond curing what's "wrong" with individual people. Whereas "curing" roots the problem within individual bodyminds, a more expansive approach to healing looks at how individuals are positioned relative to each other and in relation to oppressive systems. This relational component of health is where popular discourses about wellness – particularly in not only educational institutions but also spaces shaped by the for-profit wellness industry – tend to miss the mark. Beth Berila (2016: 8) argues that even though "college campuses often talk of wellness, it is important to situate the wellness of marginalized groups within the context of structural oppression and violence." As a facet of health discourses, wellness has been co-opted into a hyper-individualized concept which removes individuals from social contexts and swaps conversations about oppressive social conditions with capitalistic practice (e.g. buying the right health products or memberships). As with resilience, wellness transforms the awareness of structural vulnerability/harm into an expectation to care for ourselves so that we can continue to provide profit to systems and advantaged people.

While wellness always emerges from our relationships with other people and broader social contexts, the privatization of health naturally leads to a focus on individual interventions, so that typical responses to "illness," especially mental illness, revolve almost entirely around individual people and nearly never around the conditions in which people live. I return briefly to the workshop I discussed earlier on in this chapter: as the presenters described a version of mental health which was devoid of social context, and as they treated the learning space of the workshop as an apolitical, detached location, it became clear that the recommended interventions would be more of the same. Rather than sharing tools for community-building, accountability, solidarity, or social justice, the presenters solely focused on individual-level solutions, such as not being judgmental or guiding people into therapy. Promoting wellness, in this sense, was only about connecting people with resources they could use on their own; it had nothing to do with building health-promoting practices into communities and societies.

If we think about health and wellness as tools of belonging and being in relationship with one another, then lasting healing and growth can only ever occur where we centre the individual *as well as* the communities and societies the individual is a part of. Insofar as mental health concerns are born out of social conditions – not only but especially the ways we (fail to) care for each other – interventions like therapy will miss a vital piece of what is going on. We need more holistic approaches that integrate the personal, social, political, and historical. What if instead of classifying people as mentally "ill" as our first response to mental difference or neurodiversity, we started by exploring how our actions, behaviours, relationships, and social systems contribute to the conditions affecting people's lives? In other words, what if our first response was not to pathologize people and decrease their involvement in our communities and lives but instead to figure out ways to open our communities up and more meaningfully care for and about the people around us?

In this framework of community-based healing, I draw from Phillips and Taylor's explanation of *kindness* as "the ability to bear the vulnerability of others" (2009: 8). What would it mean to think about kindness in the context of building communities that are radically welcoming (Ford 2016), inclusive, and accessible to people across embodied or enminded differences? How might we express kindness through a commitment to be in just relationship with people around us? These questions are useful in thinking about healing beyond dominant framings of medicine/therapy and in opening up possibilities for defining healing as a daily practice of promoting one another's belonging.

Despite the availability of diverse approaches to healing, medical/psychological discourses have tended to fall back on the idea of curing individuals, but a more viable, meaningful, and liberatory way forward is rooting individual care within broader social movements to restore and transform communities and social systems. I am advocating for an integrated approach to healing that prioritizes neither the individual nor the social, the personal nor the political, but endeavours to recognize their interconnectedness: individual healing cannot happen with social transformation, and social transformation cannot happen without individual healing. Building a better, more connected, more authentically human world demands that we work for both at the same time. Approaches to individual healing must focus, in part, on repairing people's harmed or weakened capacities for relationship-building and genuine connection. Movements for liberation must focus on creating space for diverse people to be present and form relationships with one another, for as Freire (2000 [1970]) reminds us, liberation is "the process of humanization" through which we learn to embrace one another as equals.

I value the words of Jolie Mahan (2019: 20) who, in speaking of their traumatizing experiences of psychiatric institutionalization as a child, advocates for *radical togetherness* in the place of isolation and containment:

> We should be creating community-based institutions that don't involve caging and forced treatment, where kids are encouraged to help each other and form supportive

> networks to collectively better their social and mental positions. We should be promoting spaces that involve skill-sharing and cooperation to build foundations for growth instead of insisting on 'self-care', therapy, and medications as panaceas for mental health. To be a truly mentally healthy person at any age, we need the autonomy to choose who we spend our time with, and the freedom to do so.

While I would not entirely refuse self-care, therapy, and medication, I would like to see them tempered and situated within a more holistic approach to healing that starts with an ongoing critique of the ways that our mental health is impacted by existing social arrangements. For transformative healing to become accessible, we have to practice intentionally and tenderly listening to harmed peoples, following their guidance, and prioritizing their needs. Moreover, we need to expand and share transformative skills for working with people who have caused harm in order to promote accountability and meaningful change that prevents further harm. Social justice demands that we can no longer simply expect people to bear the weight and expectations of healing; we must work to understand why such healing becomes necessary and what we can do to alleviate the burdens of restoration through returning to responsibility for our people.

Without making an effort to integrate the individual with the social, practices of healing often squander their reserves of restorative and transformative possibilities. Notably, practices of healing are not inherently restorative/transformative and often cause further harm through the reproduction of logics of domination and a continuation of inequity and injustice. Rather than being about the betterment of people's lives, healing as a tool of dominance more often conditions people to accept oppressive social conditions and to follow the normative paths laid out for them. Accordingly, what is presented as healing is actually perpetuating people's un-health and un-wellness. Many of the metrics used to determine mental health in popular and psychological discourses, for instance, revolve around the logic of productivity – we are "well" if and when we are able to be productive.

Conversely, "illness" or lack of mental well-being becomes relevant within a capitalist society because we fall out of productivity (Hedva 2016). In this sense, healing as a tool of dominance is not about empowering individuals or transforming oppressive conditions of their lives; to the contrary, it exists to preserve power relations and condition people back into their respective social positions.

Because dominant approaches to healing are so often disempowering for oppressed people and so frequently push us back into harmful situations or relationships, we can easily forget what healing is actually supposed to feel like. For many of us, a genuine sensation of healing can emerge from involvement in activism or resistance movements. Jess Stohlmann-Rainey (2019: 86) writes that "[m]ore than anything, I believe activism saved my life. I was liberated by the recognition that the oppressed are not broken or flawed, but living in a world that was never designed with them in mind." At the same time, however, dominant notions of healing can lead to confusion and further harm, especially among change makers, as we neglect to care for ourselves. Yashna Maya Padamsee (2011) says that

> [w]e are burning out faster and at higher rates – unable to do the work we love. How can we win when our bodies individually and collectively can't keep up? We are risking not just burn-out, but organizer loss and movement fragmentation. We cannot afford this.

The danger of burn-out is one reason why we must urgently bridge the gap between individual healing and social transformation.

The more subversive approach to healing, the kind of healing that Barlow (2018: 896) defines as threatening to power, gets at the *root* of the problem in order to simultaneously help people regenerate from harm and dismantle systemic/structural sources of suffering:

> Uncovering intergenerational trauma requires digging toward the root of trauma and addressing this root through

> personal narrative, collective practices, and healing strategies. This action is essential to movement-building, social justice, and any ethic of care.

For healing to be subversive or liberatory, its purpose must include refusing oppression and it must define health and wellness based on how fully we experience the wonders of life and practice kindness as we live together in solidarity. In this version of healing, our well-being is never the function of our productivity or alignment with power, but of the care we show to each other and to ourselves. If, as Aimee Carrillo Rowe (2008) says, we are becoming who we love, then healing is truly a matter of loving and being loved by people that empower us to grow and move into the best versions of ourselves that we can be.

Loving others and receiving love from others are not always easy, especially where we cross over constructed "power lines," so healing won't always feel good or be energizing for us in the moment. In fact, given that radical healing demands that we take accountability for our lives/actions, it is often painful and difficult. Yet, this work is what needs to be done to repair the human spirit that connects us to each other. Until we go through the difficult process of healing together and re-claiming our relationships to one another, our well-being will remain temporary at best and always connected to a practice of ignoring what we desperately need to change. Prentis Hemphill (2023) maintains that "Healing . . . increases our capacity for authentic relationships with one another, and therefore opens us up to a power inside of our movements that we have not seen before."

Embracing this community-centred model of healing shifts the conversation entirely, for it defines healing as community-based and always rooted in interdependence, empowerment, and liberation. Whereas "curing" the individual most often revolves around capitalist, White supremacist, heterosexist, sanist, and ableist imperatives toward productivity, the intention of community-based healing is to put people back into just relationship with each other, and its success grows as we find better, more lasting ways to care for ourselves and other people across sites of difference. Consequently, this version of healing never arrives at an end point as might version of healing as "cure." So long as we pursue healing relationships with other people, we will have work left to do – work that includes attuning ourselves to the care other people need from us and figuring out how we can be responsible, accountable, honest, and generous to those people with whom we find belonging.

I think it is useful here to think about Daniel Heath Justice's (2018) four questions of critical kinship as they are very much in line with the community-based, socially just, and relational model of healing I have just been describing:

1. How do we learn to be human?
2. How do we behave as good relatives?
3. How do we become good ancestors?
4. How do we learn to live together?

As much as these questions are directed outward in terms of forming just relationships with other people, so too might they be powerful questions for exploring how we can begin to heal ourselves internally. They are reflective questions that move us in the direction of accountability and honesty. I do also want to recognize that these questions are based in Indigenous knowledge, so as we use and learn from them, settler colonialism and the ongoing historical trauma of Indigenous communities must remain a centre point of our consciousness. As I hope to have shown throughout my work, transformative healing towards authentic humanity cannot take place without participating in the work of decolonization.

It is easy to fall into the trap of viewing this transformative healing as extra burdensome work, especially given that so many of us are constantly exhausted and grappling with the ordinary trauma of oppression. This reluctance to practice radical healing is exactly what systems of power need to keep functioning, and it is something we must overcome as we move forward. I find energy, hope, and faith to pursue transformative healing in the work of disability justice advocates/activists, who describe collective access not as another *burden* to get past, but as a form of *love* pulling us closer together (Mingus 2018; Piepzna-Samarasinha

2018; Taylor and Duguay 2016). Radical love calls for critical shifts in our thinking and relational practices that allow us to reclaim the pleasures of togetherness (brown 2019). We must disentangle the complicated knots of healing and justice to re-weave them in a pattern that is legible for our lives. Kai Cheng (2018) writes:

> there is a distinction between punishment, justice, and healing. punishment is a gratifying process of enacting revenge that also perpetuates cycles of violence. justice is a slow process of naming and transforming violence into growth and repair that is also frustrating and elusive – and it rarely ends in good feelings. healing is the process of restoration of those who have been hurt.

Healing can occur individually and for some of us it must, but establishing the conditions for healing involves building communities of caring people invested in accountability and social justice. Such communities are a necessary part of moving towards collective well-being, for healing carries little value if we are not, at the same time, working to address the sources of harm we are healing from and refusing to participate in oppressive systems. Our wellness, I deeply believe, comes from unlearning the harms in which we are/have been complicit. For if there is truth to be found in Dr. Gabor Mate's claim that "in every case, mental illness is an outcome of traumatic events. . . . Fundamentally, it has to do with whether human needs are being met or not" (cited in Nerenberg 2017), then moving toward well-being is inseparable from the task of promoting collective access and striving to meet one another's needs in our splendid interdependence.

The Emotional Knowledge of Ordinary Trauma

One of the deepest and most impactful harms of oppression is the damage that it inflicts on our emotional well-being and emotional knowledge. Just as ordinary trauma can disconnect people from their bodies (e.g. avoiding certain physical sensations associated with harm or neglecting physical needs like food), so too can experiences of ordinary trauma disconnect people from their emotions, making it more difficult to process feelings and learn from them. Much of the time, harmed people are conditioned to believe that their suffering is normal, or that they deserve to suffer, or that they are not really suffering at all. Systems of oppression empower social institutions and advantaged people to manipulate the emotions/emotional knowledge of oppressed people to their benefit, such that oppressed people often become complicit and/or complacent in their own suffering. Therefore, the reclamation of emotions and emotional knowledge can be a resistant act as well as a healing act – one that contains the power to both transform systems of oppression and restore, at least partially, the health and well-being of oppressed people.

For the remainder of this chapter, I explore the practices/process of emotional reclamation through the works of Audre Lorde, making special note of how her teachings may inform our collective liberation/healing against the ordinary traumatic harm of systems of oppression. The life and creative works of Audre Lorde, like so many other queer women of colour, convey the intersectional traumas of socially sanctioned hatred, violence, and suffering. Yet, at the same time, radical women of colour and other multiply marginalized folks have brought to life some of the greatest and most inspiring legacies of resistance that continue to motivate and inform social justice organizing today. From these legacies have arisen invaluable tools not only for surviving inequity and injustice but also for imagining and building different worlds liberated from the ordinary trauma of oppression. Several of Audre Lorde's writings from the *Sister Outsider* collection (1984) reveal the restorative and transformative possibilities that surface in the wake of ordinary trauma.

I want to look at three essays here which I view as most profoundly exposing the possibilities for radically different futures that are informed by trauma but not complicit nor complacent in it: *The Transformation of Silence into Language and Action*, *The Uses of the Erotic*, and *The Uses of Anger*. These essays not only speak to the deep, lasting suffering that comes from traumatic experiences, but they also reveal an agency that systems of power can never take away from oppressed people – an agency that is, in fact, given life through those same forces that seek to take life away from us. In this sense, the faith I have in Lorde's work derives from her ability to hold mourning together with celebration, to make space for the recognition of harm while at the same time advocating for personal and political transformation. My use of faith in this context is meant to be in line with James Fowler's definition of faith as a "dynamic quality of human meaning making" (1991: 31) that allows us to find sense from the chaos of existence. My faith in the works of Audre Lorde, then, is an expression of how her essays, stories, and poems have helped me figure out what to make of trauma as it related to lived experiences of oppression.

The Transformation of Silence Into Language and Action

In this first essay, Lorde (1984: 41) recounts how an experience of being confronted with her own mortality led her to the realization that silence was not and could never be a source of life: "I was going to die, if not sooner then later, whether or not I had ever spoken myself. My silences had not protected me. Your silence will not protect you." Silence, many of us have been conditioned to believe, provides safety from harm: it keeps us out of the crosshairs and sightline of violence; it reduces the risk that people will lash out at us; it allows us to go about our day without having to account for ourselves or apologize for something that other people will blame us for. The problem with silence is that harm is unavoidable when trauma is made ordinary by inequity and injustice. There may be moments when silence is necessary for our safety and well-being, but as a habitual practice, silence can never produce a foundation for liberation or the end of ordinary trauma.

While for some recognizing that harm is unavoidable in our current historical moment might result in feelings of despair, for Lorde, it yields the opposite: if harm is inevitable, then there is no reason to remain silent and reclaiming our voices becomes thinkable. Put another way, accepting that trauma has already been made ordinary in oppressed people's lives can be a source of empowerment to take part in political action or resistance to inequity and injustice. The threat of violence and trauma loses so much of its power when we realize that systems of oppression never meant to keep us safe: oppressed peoples' existence will be assaulted, maligned, and violated no matter what we do with ourselves or how we behave, so we might as well pursue the lives we want to live. In many ways, the pressure to be silent is internalized victim-blaming: it is a conditioned belief that not speaking out means we are behaving, and behaving keeps us safe. Unlearning silence or reclaiming our voice is the practice of refusing this belief, externalizing it and removing blame from ourselves for the harm done to us. Doing so is a humanizing act.

Lorde, writing about her experience as a Black, lesbian, mother, warrior, poet, goes on to say, "For to survive in the mouth of this dragon we call america, we have had to learn this first and most vital lesson – that we were never meant to survive." Silence is equated with safety because not speaking out supposedly puts us in line with normative ways of being – through silence, we create a socially legible image of ourselves as deserving of love and compassion because we are like everybody else. The issue with this equation, however, is that oppressed people are always already perceived as different, less-fully human to a point where our lives are scratched out of the future, our existence in a state of perpetual crisis. Talking about the politics of living a feminist life, Ahmed (2017: x) explains: "to name the problem is to become the problem" – that is, to break the silence is to become threatening – but many oppressed people are made into problems long before they voice dissent; they are made into problems regardless of what problems they name because their very being is seen as dangerous. For this reason, Ahmed's comparison needs a counterpart: to become oneself is to become the problem that should not have been named. When people who are seen as the problem name themselves, the silence cannot be unbroken.

I think here of people that actively dissent from or transgress normative ways of being: queer and trans people that exceed the limited categories of the gender binary; disabled, Mad, and crip folks that refuse to assimilate to compulsory able-bodiedness/mindedness; Black and Brown people that *speak in tongues* and celebrate their colour. Their existence and presence in spaces give names to the problems that were supposed to be contained and silenced. For those eternally forced to the margins, the magnitude of Lorde's lesson – "that we were never meant to survive" – is followed by the refrain, "but we did." And it is through this survival that histories of ordinary trauma become wells of knowledge from which oppressed peoples can learn to radicalize ourselves, for in the sheer fact of our still being alive, we have witnessed a betrayal so great that we must speak out against it. Indeed, coming to understand that we are always already marked for death frees us to live outside the boundaries that have been prescribed for us by those who benefit from our collective suffering. If staying silent does us no service, then we have no reason to cling to it; rather than being too dangerous or costly, learning to speak and act are transformed into thinkable, worthwhile endeavours.

The final point I want to draw from this essay is that silence does more than just not protect us; silence causes us harm. Lorde (1984: 44) writes, "For we have been socialized to respect fear more than our own needs for language and definition, and while we wait in silence for that final luxury of fearlessness, the weight of that silence will choke us." So, in some ways, the notion that "silence will not protect you" is misleading, for there is more at stake in being silent than many of us realize: silence does not stop other people from harming us, and also, silence as a habit harms us. The words that keep getting stuck in our throats fill up dangerous amounts of space; the air we swallow to force them back down is poisonous. Silence about the exploitation, abuse, and violation other people perpetrate against us leaves us exposed to future assaults as much as speaking out can make us targets for impending violence. But silence comes with the additional weight of internalized victim-blaming that leads us to feel ashamed, depressed, and insecure, and it leads many people to punish themselves through acts of self-harm. For silence cannot last forever, it will be broken one way or another; either we express it outward at the sources of our suffering, or we break ourselves as we try to hold it in. And, as Zora Neale Hurston teaches us, "If you are silent about your pain, they'll kill you and say you enjoyed it."

Thus, the transformation of silence into language and action is ultimately about learning to practice self-care and community-care in a stolen land that does not and never intended to care for oppressed people. During the past several years, I have struggled to internalize this message and realize its implications for my own life; I am still struggling to learn that silence can be just as harmful for me as all the dangers I associate with the reclamation of my voice and acting in my own best interests. The fears I have built up around being authentically and unapologetically myself were so *intense* that they stopped me from noticing the tightness of my throat and difficulties I had with breathing. I was choking from a mixture of the silences pressing me down into submission and the words inside of me pushing up, suffocating from a lack of oxygen. One thing presumptive trauma does especially well is make the future feel more important than the present; we can often ignore the pain we are in now if we focus hard enough on the suffering that we may face later. What is remarkable about this fact is that for me, the pain I was already experiencing was just as bad as the pain I was afraid of. I listened to my fear of pain more than the pain itself, and so I remained silent and complicit in my own suffering for many years. It is only though breaking with silence that I have been able to feel the breath start to move freely through my body again.

The Uses of the Erotic

The other two essays I want to explore here are *The Uses of the Erotic* and *The Uses of Anger*. In many ways, Lorde's descriptions of the *erotic* and *anger* are in direct response to ordinary traumas familiar to her as a Black lesbian mother warrior poet: she frames anger as a logical, necessary response to inequities/injustice produced by systems of oppression, particularly the hatred and violence of racism; she names the erotic as a power residing deep within the spirits of oppressed people that has been twisted and distorted by those in power who fear its realization. In the context of my work here, we might consider the uses of the erotic to be tools for restoration from traumatic harm and, as I explain in the final chapter, a component in our *self-actualization*. Similarly, the uses of anger are strategies for personal, social, and political transformation that centre reclamation of our emotional knowledge. The reverse pairing also makes sense – recovering the erotic demands fundamental transformations in how we understand ourselves and live with others, while tapping into our anger may restore a connection to our emotions and senses that has been long buried under the weight of other people's expectations. Both concepts are relevant for conversations about ordinary trauma, and critically engaging with them leads to deeper appreciation for the intersections between *feeling*, *knowing*, and *understanding*.

In *The Uses of the Erotic*, Lorde (1984: 54) writes that erotic knowledge has been traumatized in order to preserve patriarchal power, distorted into something ugly, horrible, and villainous as a way to punish and contain the "feminine":

> The erotic has often been misnamed by men and used against women. It has been made into the confused, the trivial, the psychotic,[2] the plasticized sensation. For this reason, we have often turned away from the exploration and consideration of the erotic as a source of power and information, confusing it with its opposite, the pornographic. But pornography is a direct denial of the power of the erotic, for it represents the suppression of true feeling. Pornography emphasizes sensation without feeling.

The erotic lives in our deepest and most chaotic feelings; it is the love and unfiltered joy we experience from demanding the most of ourselves at all times and from pursuing the fullest potential of the life we are in control of. Systems of oppression, such as men's domination of women through patriarchy, breed fear of the erotic to disconnect oppressed peoples from the indestructible, uncontainable power dwelling within them. Through various enactments of power, pleasure in all of its forms is twisted into pornographic sensations, which are then smeared through a weaponization of consumption – we are punished for experiencing too much pleasure or for experiencing pleasure at the wrong times. When oppressed people find too much joy in their lives, they are often accused of living beyond their means, of not caring enough for their families, or of taking resources away from people who truly need them. For example, the controlling image of the "welfare queen" that has repeatedly been used to turn public opinion against welfare policies is based on the belief that poor people should not be able to access nice things that wealthy people have – that they should not be able to find joy or pleasure in the same ways.

In some ways, everyone is punished for experiencing what is seen as too much pleasure, but the pleasure experienced by oppressed people is seen as especially suspect. For instance, people are usually allowed to enjoy food until they start to be perceived as fat, at which point fatphobic ideologies/practices come into play. *Hetero*sexual pleasure is welcomed in public spaces and displayed on billboards across the country, but queer p.d.a. as simple as a kiss is often regarded as excessive or too much. Wealthy people point to poor people's pleasure as reason enough to justify the elimination of welfare or social security programmes or to justify further exploitation because they are not "working hard enough." The erotic is subjugated in all these situations among many others because the erotic is what allows oppressed people to transgress the narratives of oppression that have been judiciously crafted by systems of power to govern or control them.

At the same time, suppression of the erotic and erotic knowledge has to do with the borders advantaged people construct to differentiate themselves from dehumanized others. Lorde says, the erotic functions through a sharing of joy and excellence between people that "can be the basis for understanding much of what is not shared between them, and [lessen] the threat of their difference" (56). If this is true, and I believe that it is, then the pursuit of erotic knowledge threatens to undermine the entire social order, which is built on the construction, regulation, and containment of human difference into an *us versus them* mentality. Where erotic encounters with dehumanized people do occur, advantaged people risk experiencing a cognitive dissonance between their oppressive beliefs about, for example, women of colour and their newfound understandings of another person. If too many such encounters happen, systems of power start to collapse in on themselves. Most of the time, advantaged people are able to see the other person as exceptional (i.e. not like *those* other people), but this kind of segmentation is only possible because of the systemic suppression of erotic knowledge, because erotic encounters across power lines have been made *extra*ordinary. As it turns out, the misnaming and failure of advantaged people to use or learn from the erotic also keeps them in a particular narrative that stalls social change.

I want to pause and note here that the erotic and erotic knowledge do not just mean sex, but rather the entire expanse of our emotions and emotional connections with other people. The erotic encapsulates the ways we experience the world around us on an emotional level, that is, how we realize the "true feeling" that accompanies our sense of reality. Erotic knowledge refers to both our awareness of the erotic within ourselves – our emotional intelligence and our willingness to process the depth of emotions we are capable of – and to the growth and understanding that can emerge from that awareness. We develop erotic knowledge over time as we experience the world and process the emotions that rise from those experiences. Sex and sexual pleasure are one potential pathway to the erotic, but so too are the numerous other things that fill our emotional capacities: rigorous discussion about a topic that carries emotional relevance, witnessing unfiltered creativity in the artwork of ourselves and others, and achieving life's milestones or our long-term goals, to name just a few, are also pathways. Similarly, erotic knowledge is not just related to sex; it is our profound consciousness of the world rooted in our lived experiences of joy, grief, accomplishment, loss, belonging, anxiety, and other emotions.

The erotic and erotic knowledge empower advantaged and oppressed people alike to move in the direction of our collective liberation because "[t]he erotic is the nurturer or nursemaid of all of our deepest knowledge" (Lorde 1984: 56). This metaphor means that how and what we feel, our internal senses of right and wrong, good and bad, create a path toward knowing and understanding not only ourselves but also the world around us. Consequently, Lorde is articulating a vision of knowledge as not independent of but born through the awarenesses we have of our emotions and embodied sensations. What we now *know* to be true started as something we *felt* could be right – the erotic is what delivers us through feeling to knowing to understanding. When our feelings for people different from us are suppressed, contained, and distorted, we become less able to know or understand them; in our minds, they become fragments of people, reducible to stereotypes or "controlling images" (Collins 1990). At the interpersonal level, systems of oppression maintain and reproduce themselves through the ongoing interruption of this learning cycle: our erotic knowledge and feeling are suppressed so that violent metonymies and hateful social moods can develop and take hold. Simply put, prejudice festers where erotic encounters with other people are curtailed to the point where we have such limited understandings of *them* that *we* become afraid of the differences we imagine to exist between people.

Lorde argues that this suppression comes from confusing the erotic with the pornographic. There are many injuries that emerge from conflating the erotic with the pornographic, one of the most harmful of which is that we stop understanding the erotic as a source of knowledge we can turn to throughout our lives. Since the pornographic is defined by sensation without feeling, we start to doubt what we could possibly learn from our erotic senses, and we try to restrict them to specific times and places; private spaces removed from others. Systems of oppression actively condition us to be suspicious of erotic knowledge, but in reality:

> Our erotic knowledge empowers us, becomes a lens through which we scrutinize all aspects of our existence, forcing us to evaluate those aspects honestly in terms of their relative meaning within our lives. And that is a grave responsibility, projected from within each of us, not to settle for the convenient, the shoddy, the conventionally accepted, nor the merely safe.
>
> (57)

Being suspicious of the erotic/erotic knowledge creates fear about the depths of feeling and the dangers of moving past what we are comfortable and familiar with; restricting our erotic and the possibilities for understanding it contains keeps us from knowing the fullness of our lives, traps us in the ordinary, mundane, mediocre. Through the erotic, we can demand more and pursue better relationships, communities, institutions, and systems. When the erotic is suppressed, we become more complicit or stuck in the world as it is, and we miss out on the fullness of life. This loss of full life is bound up in a learned reluctance to look too closely at our lives for fear of what we are missing out on. Embracing the erotic knowledge within us is inherently transformative, for learning not to settle challenges the complicity/complacency systems of oppression have sought to fill us up with. Instead of bursts of excitement – most often excessive moments of consumption that allow us to squeeze out as much pleasure as we possibly can – that are surrounded by days, months, years of commonplace living, the erotic is a force that calls on all of us to find sources of pleasure in our everyday lives and to push ourselves to know joy and fulfilment whenever such an opportunity arises.

Ordinary trauma all at once keeps the erotic from us and gives us new, unparalleled ways of understanding the erotic sense within our bodies, minds, and spirits. Dissociation and other common symptoms of trauma that people use to protect themselves can often make it more difficult to tap into erotic knowledge, especially when the places where feelings come from have been assaulted. Sometimes, ordinary traumatic harm makes it difficult to tell the good feelings from the bad ones, so our brains trigger our defences whenever we feel anything at all from the damaged parts of ourselves. Figuring out how to pull the good from the bad is a long process that can often feel impossible. However, when we manage to arrive at a space where feeling is possible and even comfortable, we may realize that our erotic has become something different. A lot of the time, this change feels like *loss*, as if something was stolen from us that we can never get back from the people that dealt us harm. However, this change can also inspire feelings or sensations we did not previously know existed – for many people, trauma coupled with restorative practices can fundamentally alter the erotic and grant us access to heightened levels of joy, intimacy, love, respect, and so on. Trauma changes our lives profoundly, causes deep, lasting pain and suffering, but so too does it change what we can attain from our lives.

I am not attempting to valorize trauma; the pain and suffering are truly beyond words. Nor is my intention to reinforce the compulsory survivorship that I detailed in the previous chapter. I am attempting to convey my belief that trauma does not just "break" people or make them into "worse" versions of themselves. Additionally, I am not trying to argue that trauma makes people "better" or that it is redemptive and necessary to help people grow – "post-traumatic growth," a concept used by psychologists to explain changes witnessed in people following experiences of trauma, is never without significant grief, loss, and many other harms. What I am expressing here is that when subjected to ordinary trauma, the erotic knowledge buried within us does not just shrivel up or disappear. To the contrary, it swells and adapts, so when traumatized people are able to once again return to their erotic knowledge, they may come upon opportunities and possibilities for knowing and understanding themselves that did not previously exist.

In my mind, I envision erotic knowledge speaking back to trauma in much the same way as eucalyptus trees respond to forest fires: it is only after a great burning that eucalyptus seeds will be released into the soil to grow and replenish a forest; similarly, when erotic knowledge encounters trauma, it is instantaneously harmed (as is our connection to it), but so too does it release "seeds" that eventually flourish into our new understandings about our bodies and the ways to bring emotional fulfilment to them. The ordinary trauma oppressed peoples are made to know, in this sense, can lead us to the erotic knowledge we need to survive and fight back, to demand our own liberation in the face of ordinary trauma and structural unwellness.

The Uses of Anger

As with the other two essays I explored earlier, *The Uses of Anger* is an expression of ordinary trauma that names the potential for resistance in the wake of harms caused by inequity and injustice. Lorde begins *The Uses of Anger* by listing several illustrative experiences of racism she survived in the years of her life, and by asserting that anger is the natural and appropriate response to racism. The need to assert such a thing points to a long history of people being conditioned to distrust and suppress their anger. This distrust and suppression of anger may be especially present for women of colour who, more so than White women, are expected to show grace, deference, and kindness to others, especially advantaged people (Magnet et al. 2014). Systems of oppression actively distance people from their anger to control resistance, and they dehumanize and criminalize people who claim their anger as a tool of liberation. In doing so, they reveal the power of anger and the threat it poses to dominant systems, for if it weren't threatening, then it would not need to be contained. Lorde's anger is simultaneously directed at the systems of oppression that have impacted her life and the White women with whom she shares in a history of suffering under patriarchy that will not listen to her critiques of racism within feminist organizing or take seriously her call for solidarity across differences. Her expression of anger then is both external and internal; she is speaking against the harms not only of a shared oppressor but also of the people who should be her sisters in struggle.

The central intervention Lorde is making in this essay is to shift how we understand and use anger. Lorde's most urgent premise is that anger can be directed towards and made useful for liberation movements. Speaking about women's experiences of patriarchal oppression, Lorde writes:

> Every woman has a well-stocked arsenal of anger potentially useful against those oppressions, personal and institutional, which brought that anger into being. Focused with precision it can become a powerful source of energy serving progress and change. And when I speak of change, I do not mean a simple switch of positions or a temporary lessening of tensions, not the ability to smile and feel good. I am speaking of a basic and radical alteration in those assumptions underlining our lives.
>
> (127)

While it is common to observe advantaged people and media dismiss or attempt to discredit activists based upon their anger (such as the woman Lorde recalls in this speech that asked her to speak less harshly), Lorde is offering a different understanding of anger, as something that can fuel social change, as a tool to support social and political transformation. As with Foucault's argument that the enactment of power always creates resistance, Lorde is telling a story of anger as the ever-expanding "arsenal" within us that can dismantle the sources of harm that made us angry to begin with. Similar to erotic knowledge, oppressed people have been and continue to be distanced from anger in an effort to constrain our resistance, for in producing that distance, systems of oppression leave behind subdued feelings of complicity and apathy, and we are left less able to articulate our needs for social change.

If we revisit Ahmed's description of privilege as an "energy-saving device" (2013) and Ford's account of oppression as an experience of "energy lost" (2016), then Lorde's notion of anger as a "source of energy" become even more insightful and useful. The systemic suppression of anger saves energy for advantaged people and social institutions that benefit from stalled resistance and slowed social change. Similarly, when oppressed people are distanced from their anger (as well as the erotic), they are less energized to pursue liberation and authentic human connection. Accordingly, when oppressed people reclaim their anger and apply it in the pursuit of collective liberation, it reverses the script: advantaged people must put more energy into maintaining their control over a people who have discovered a "source of energy" to propel them forward. Thwarting anger then is a necessary part of making people docile or complicit in their own oppression. Docility is a mental state of oppression that is most easily maintained because docile minds are not resistant to the influence of power. Foucault (2012 [1975]: 136) maintains that a "body is docile that may be subjected, used, transformed and improved." It is one that power can most readily penetrate and wield. Separation from anger is a vital component of docility.

Yet, even beyond generating docility, the vilification of anger is just as much about hindering the growth of particular sorts of knowledge or understanding that precede the emergence of critical consciousness. When systems of oppression restrict access to anger, we lack much needed clarity:

> anger expressed and translated into action in the service of our vision and our future is a liberating and

> strengthening act of clarification, for it is in the painful process of this translation that we identify who are our allies with whom we have great differences, and who are our genuine enemies.
>
> (Lorde 1984: 127)

Lorde's claim here is that focused anger – anger channelled into the humanizing practices of collective liberation – is, among other things, an intellectually generative force that enables us to distinguish between the people committed to sharing in our struggle for liberation, the people acting in collusion with the sources of our trauma, and, I would add, the people who fail to support our well-being by doing nothing to resist inequity and injustice. Anger, then, is or can be a tool for sharpening our awareness of the world, an emotional teacher we start to carry inside us following our earliest experience of ordinary trauma. Focused anger provides clarity because in order to translate it "into action in the service of our vision and our future," we have to become adept critical thinkers who continuously question the assumptions that guide our lives. And when we think about our lives through a critical lens, we then acquire a unique power to "read" our surroundings and differentiate between what brings us joy and what pisses us off, what contributes to our continued life and what poisons us.

Critical thinking and remembering are necessary to focus our anger because trauma often distorts our perceptions and memories, which means that without focus and precision, we may feel anger towards the wrong people or the wrong things. The process of understanding out trauma through critical reflection is how we arrive at more nuanced understandings of power and the willingness to stand against injustice and inequity, for as Lorde says, the uses of anger become clear to us through the process of translating rage into something that we can use. Critical thinking and reflection are the hammer and chisel with which we sculpt the clay of our anger into the shapes of our desires. Moreover, translating anger is also how we figure out its deeper meaning and relationships to our lived experiences. Untranslated anger results in isolation as we lash out against all sorts of people, friend and foe, and push them away from us. Untranslated anger is also something systems of oppression regularly exploit to discredit advocates and activists (e.g. consider how the atrocious term "feminazi" has been used against feminists). Systems of power don't really respond to translated anger any better, but if they are going to come for us, we should be sure that we can fully own our words and actions. For "[R]age in response to injustice opens up radical potential" (Tiffany Lee 2019).

It is important to understand that our "hatred and our anger are very different. Hatred is the fury of those who do not share our goals, and its object is death and destruction. Anger is a grief of distortion between peers, and its object is change" (129). No matter where it comes from, hatred can never be generative because it can only ever lead us to inflict greater harm against people who we see as different to us; hatred is a primary weapon utilized by systems of oppression to build up mental borders between *us* and *them*. Anger, on the other hand, is a reasonable response to being treated unfairly or unjustly; it is a primary device of activists pursuing change or transformation. When advantaged people disparage activist efforts with comments like "you can't stop violence with violence," they are, maybe unintentionally but often purposefully, ignoring the differences between hatred and anger in order to deny their accountability and the need for social change. While some activists may inflict unnecessary harm, most of the time there is a clear delineation between the people intent on furthering destruction and those organizing for a more equitable and just future.

When we critically reflect on our traumatic experiences, they can become the foundation of a generative anger that transforms ourselves and our societies. When accompanied by the consciousness of our erotic knowledge and awareness of the cost of staying silent, learning to be angry and learning from being angry can help us to rediscover a wholeness of self that systems of oppression steal to give themselves life. We can learn to understand ourselves in a more complete sense, to embrace that which our bodies and minds need to feel whole and cared for on a deeper level. Without this emotional awareness, however, we will remain stuck in repetitive cycles of violence and oppressive conditions that keep us unhealthy and unwell. Overcoming our silence, reconnecting with the erotic and our erotic knowledge, and reclaiming our anger are crucial for ending ordinary trauma through collective liberation. The humanizing work of liberation must include our emotional and psychological selves, for how can we learn to love one another without creating space to love ourselves?

Notes

1 In critiquing the language of mental illness, my intent is not to invalidate people that identify with this term or to suggest in any way that people's experiences of "mental illness" are not "real." When we finally achieve the dismantling of oppressive systems of power, things like anxiety and depression will likely continue to exist, but not as a normalized part of social/political projects of domination, which is the distinction I mean to draw here. I use dis-ease in this instance to refer to those social forces that purposefully make people's lives harder in order to secure particular kinds of "power over."

2 In 2013, Sami Schalk published a crucial article describing and critiquing the use of ableist metaphors in writing by feminists, such as Lorde's use of "psychotic" here or "crazy" in other parts of her writing. The use of such metaphors is a good example of how what is liberating and transformational for some people can actually be a kind of ordinary trauma for others. As a disabled/crip activist scholar, I have found great value in Lorde's writing, but I also feel compelled to hold it accountable for such rhetorical sleights against Mad or neurodivergent people.

References

Ahmed, Sara. "Feeling Depleted." *FeministKilljoys*. https://feministkilljoys.com/2013/11/17/feeling-depleted/ (published November 17, 2013).

Ahmed, Sara. *Living a Feminist Life*. Durham: Duke University Press, 2017.

Ansloos, Jeffrey. "Rethinking Indigenous Suicide." *International Journal of Indigenous Heath* 13, no. 2 (2018): 9–28.

Anthony, Rhiana. "35 Destigmatizing Mental Health with The Icarus Project (Agustina Vidal & Rhiana Anthony)." *Healing Justice Podcast*.

https://www.pandora.com/podcast/description/irresistible-fka-healing-justice-podcast/35-destigmatizing-mental-health-with-the-icarus-project-agustina-vidal-and-rhiana-anthony/PE:2207265 (published April 23, 2019).

Barlow, Jameta Nicole. "Resorting Optimal Black Mental Health and Reversing Intergenerational Trauma in an Era of Black Lives Matter." *Biography* 41, no. 4 (2018): 895–908.

Berila, Beth. "Mindfulness as a Healing, Liberatory Practice in Queer Anti-Oppression Pedagogy." *Social Alternatives* 25, no. 3 (2016): 5–10.

brown, adrienne maree. "Change is Divine: How Sci Fi Visionary Octavia Butler Influenced This Detroit Revolutionary." *Yes Magazine*. https://www.yesmagazine.org/issues/the-power-of-story/how-sci-fi-visionary-octavia-butler-influenced-this-detroit-revolutionary (published June 27, 2014).

brown, adrienne maree. *Pleasure Activism: The Politics of Feeling Good*. Chico: AK Press, 2019.

Brown, Lydia. "Disability in an Ableist World." In *Criptiques*, edited by Caitlin Wood, 37–46. Minneapolis: May Day Publishing, 2014.

Carrillo Rowe, Aimee. *Power Lines: On the Subject of Feminist Alliances*. Durham: Duke University Press, 2008.

Carter, Angela. "Disabling Trauma: Toward a Crip Critique of Post-Traumatic Stress Disorder." Ph.D. Dissertation. University of Minnesota, 2019.

Chatterjee, Dom. "Mental Health is Different for People of Color in These 3 Ways." *Restforresistance.com*. https://restforresistance.com/zine/mental-health-is-different-for-people-of-color (published April 29, 2017).

Cheng, Kai. "I Hope We Choose Love: Notes on the Application of Justice." *Medium*. https://medium.com/@ladysintrayda/notes-on-the-application-of-justice-5a058a209599 (published May 5, 2018).

Clare, Eli. *Brilliant Imperfection: Grappling with Cure*. Durham: Duke University Press, 2017.

Collins, Patricia Hill. *Black Feminist Thought: Knowledge, Consciousness, and the Politics of Empowerment*. New York: Routledge, 1990.

Cvetkovich, Ann. "Depression Is Ordinary: Public Feelings and Saidiya Hartman's Lose Your Mother." *Feminist Theory* 13, no. 2 (2012): 131–146.

Durazo, Ana Clarissa Rojas. "Medical Violence against People of Color and the Medicalization of Domestic Violence." In *Color of Violence: The Incite! Anthology*, edited by Incite! Women of Color against Violence, 179–190. Durham: Duke University Press, 2006.

Ehrenreich, Barbara. *Nickel and Dimed: On (Not) Getting By in America*. Picador, 2011.

Ford, Jillian Carter. "'I'm Feelin' It': Embodied Spiritual Activism as a Vehicle for Queer Black Liberation." In *Yoga, the Body, and Embodied Social Change*, edited by Beth Berila, Melanie Klein, and Chelsea Jackson Roberts, 29–40. Lanham: Lexington Books, 2016.

Foucault, Michel. *Discipline and Punish: The Birth of the Prison*. New York: Random House, 2012 [1975].

Fowler, James W. "Stages in Faith Consciousness." *New Directions for Child and Adolescent Development* 1991, no. 52 (1991): 27–45.

Freire, Paulo. *Pedagogy of the Oppressed*. New York: Bloomsbury, 2000 [1970].

Goodkind, Jessica, Meredith, Hess Julia, Gorman, Beverely, and Parker, Danielle. "'We're Still in a Struggle': Diné Resilience, Survival, Historical Trauma, and Healing." *Qualitative Health Research* 22, no. 8 (2012): 1019–1036.

Hedva, Johanna. "Sick Woman Theory." *Mask Magazine*. http://www.maskmagazine.com/not-again/struggle/sick-woman-theory (published 2016).

Helm-Hernandez, Paulina. "Interview" *Kindred Southern Healing Justice Collective*. http://www.healingcollectivetrauma.com/paulina-helm-hernandez.html (published February, 2013).

Hemphill, Prentis.—. "Transforming Our Systems, Transforming Ourselves: The Pivotal Role of Healing in Social Change Work." *Non-Profit Quarterly*. https://nonprofitquarterly.org/transforming-our-systems-transforming-ourselves-the-pivotal-role-of-healing-in-social-change-work/ (published February 13, 2023).

hooks, bell. *Black Looks: Race and Representation*. Boston: South End Press, 1992.

Justice, Daniel Heath. *Why Indigenous Literatures Matter: Indigenous Studies Series*. Waterloo, ON, Canada: Wilfrid Laurier University Press, 2018.

Kafer, Alison. *Feminist, Queer, Crip*. Bloomington: Indiana University Press, 2013.

Kenyon, Georgina. "'If the Land Is Sick, You Are Sick': An Aboriginal Approach to Mental Health in Times of Drought." *Scroll.in*. https://scroll.in/pulse/921558/if-the-land-is-sick-you-are-sick-an-aboriginal-approach-to-mental-health-in-times-of-drought (published April 28, 2019).

Lee, Tiffany. "How Rage is Radical." *Thebodyisnotanapology.com*. https://thebodyisnotanapology.com/magazine/how-rage-is-radical-tiffany-lee/ (published April 1, 2019).

Loeser, Cassandra, Pini, Barbara and Crowley, Vicki. "Disability and Sexuality: Desires and Pleasures." *Sexualities* 21, no. 3 (2018): 255–270.

Lorde, Audre. *Sister Outsider: Essays and Speeches*. New York: Ten Speed Press, 1984.

Magnet, Shoshana, Mason, Corinne L. and Trevenen, Kathryn. "Feminism, Pedagogy, and the Politics of Kindness." *Feminist Teacher* 25, no. 1 (2014): 1–22.

Mahan, Jolie. "Children Don't Belong in Cages." In *Much Madness: A Survivor's Guide to Extreme States and Self-Advocacy for Young Adults*, edited by Calvin Rey Moen and Kaz DeWolfe, 13–22. Brattleboro, VT: The Hive Mutual Support Network, 2019.

Martland, Sarah Mariann. "Instagram." https://www.instagram.com/p/BpcqIwHHzzH/?utm_source=ig_twitter_share&igshid=1xklnlunf78du (published October 27, 2018; November 4, 2018).

Mingus, Mia. "Finding Each Other: Building Legacies of Belonging." *Leaving Evidence*. https://leavingevidence.wordpress.com/2018/04/10/finding-each-other-building-legacies-of-belonging/ (published April 10, 2018).

Mingus, Mia. "Medical Industrial Complex Visual." *Leaving Evidence*. https://leavingevidence.wordpress.com/2015/02/06/medical-industrial-complex-visual/ (published February 6, 2015).

Mingus, Mia. "Moving Toward the Ugly: A Politic Beyond Desirability." *Leaving Evidence*. https://leavingevidence.wordpress.com/2011/08/22/moving-toward-the-ugly-a-politic-beyond-desirability/ (published August 21, 2011).

Monaghan, O. "Dual Imperatives: Decolonising the Queer and Queering the Decolonial." In *Colouring the Rainbow: Black Queer and Trans Perspectives*, edited by D. Hodge, 195–206. Wakefield Press, 2015. http://ebookcentral.proquest.com/lib/unimelb/detail.action?docID=4604754

Murphy, Alison. "'We Are Not Singularly Defined by the Things That Kill Us': A Conversation with Clint Smith." *Grub Street*. https://grubstreet.org/blog/we-are-not-singularly-defined-by-the-things-that-kill-us-a-conversation-with-clint-smith/ (published October 28, 2016).

Nerenberg, Jenara. "Why Are So Many Adults Today Haunted by Trauma?" *Greater Good Magazine*. https://greatergood.berkeley.edu/article/item/why_are_so_many_adults_today_haunted_by_trauma#:~:text=There's%20nothing%20about%20any%20mentally,don't%20mean%20dramatic%20events (published June 8, 2017).

Padamsee, Yashna Maya. "Communities of Care, Organizations for Liberation." *Naya Maya*. https://nayamaya.wordpress.com/ (published June 19, 2011).

Page, Cara. "Kindred Collective: Cara Page." *Kindred Southern Healing Justice Collective*. http://www.healingcollectivetrauma.com/cara-page.html (published 2013).

Phillips, Adam and Taylor, Barbara. *On Kindness*. New York: Farrar, Straus and Giroux, 2009.

Piepzna-Samarasinha, Leah Lakshmi. *Care Work: Dreaming Disability Justice*. Vancouver: Arsenal Pulp Press, 2018.

Piepzna-Samarasinha, Leah Lakshmi. "Not Over It, Not Fixed, and Living a Life Worth Living." In *Whatever Gets You Through: Twelve Survivors on Life after Sexual Assault*. Greystone Books, 2019.

Schiraldi, Glenn. *The Post-Traumatic Stress Disorder Sourcebook: A Guide to Healing, Recovery, and Growth*. McGraw-Hill, 2009.

Smith, Andrea. *Conquest: Sexual Violence and American Indian Genocide*. New York City: South End Press, 2005.

Stohlmann-Rainey, Jess. "Much Madness is Divinest Sense." In *Much Madness: A Survivor's Guide to Extreme States and Self-Advocacy for Young Adults*, edited by Calvin Rey Moen and Kaz DeWolfe, 83–92. Brattleboro, VT: The Hive Mutual Support Network, 2019.

Taylor, Kara and Duguay, Jennie. "Can Broken Be Whole?" *Guts*. http://gutsmagazine.ca/broken/ (published November 15, 2016).

7

Self-Actualization: From Meeting Needs to Becoming Ourselves

Limitations of Maslow's Hierarchy of Needs

In 1943, Abraham Maslow published his "Theory of Human Motivation" in which he claimed that humans become motivated to action based upon a universal hierarchy of needs. At the base of this hierarchy are our physiological needs (food, water, shelter) – the basic things we require to function as living beings. Next are safety needs (protection from danger, wellness), followed by our needs for love (care, connection, belonging), and then esteem needs (belief in one's ability to undertake tasks, self-respect). Finally, atop this pyramid sits our need for self-actualization, which Maslow defines as "the desire to become more and more what one is, to become everything that one is capable of becoming" (382). The hierarchical positioning of needs in Maslow's theory asserts that human's motivation to attain our "higher" needs is dependent on the attainment of each of our "lower" needs – motivation for love and esteem, for instance, is severely limited when an individual lacks nourishment and/or is made to feel unsafe.

In this sense, his arrangement of needs into a hierarchy is meant not so much to order needs in terms of their relative importance, although it certainly does that; rather, his hierarchy is meant to demonstrate how human needs build upon one another, so

DOI: 10.4324/9781003716198-7

that the attainment of our "lower" needs is what makes possible the pursuit of our "higher" needs – meeting baser, more "animal" needs is what enables us to pursue that which makes us more fully human – things like creative or cultural express, answers to unanswerable questions, or the height of our experiential capacities. For instance, it is exceedingly difficult to think about something like self-actualization when we are struggling to find food to eat or safe places to sleep, when we don't believe that people care for us or when we don't believe in ourselves, but receiving such nourishment frees us to attend to higher needs as we are no longer struggling to attain our lesser physiological needs. As another useful example: my decision to enrol in graduate school was made significantly easier because of the ongoing support my family has provided me, because they helped to ensure that my "lower" needs were consistently met.

Since its publication over 80 years ago, Maslow's hierarchy has evolved to be one of the most widely taught and heavily cited theories of human motivation. At the same time, it has been the subject of great controversy and critique, and with good reason. In constructing his hierarchy, Maslow seemingly neglected to expand beyond his own social position, centring and privileging the experience of advantaged people like him as if they could stand in for the rest of humanity. While this critique does not necessarily undermine Maslow's work, it does raise valid concerns about both the content and arrangement of the hierarchy. Socialization into different cultures, for instance, might cause belonging in a community to become more important than self-actualization, or it might shift what self-actualization looks like (Merriam and Bierema 2013). This difference may also result from social disadvantage if marginalized or oppressed peoples come to believe that their health and well-being are connected to the livelihood of their communities. Moreover, individual needs do not remain static throughout their lifetime given that the contexts they live in are ever changing. Children and adolescents will likely understand their needs differently than adults – they may have different needs than adults – and needs gain different levels of importance depending on the surrounding social and political environments. For instance, imagine how individuals' needs for safety and love have transformed under the violence of the Trump administration as well as how many of us have come to long for different kinds of esteem or different understandings of ourselves.

Critiques of Maslow's hierarchy have also questioned whether human needs are accurately represented within his theory. Feminist theorists, for instance, generally oppose hierarchies because of the ways they consolidate power and authority, and queer theorists tend to resist universal approaches that advance singular narratives applied equally to all people. Thus, a hierarchy of needs is quite problematic for feminist and queer theorists alike: a hierarchy of needs privileges certain needs above others – needs that have been historically associated with men and masculinity, as well as White supremacy, colonialism, and ableism, and it reduces human difference into one simple arrangement leaving little to no room for variation. Are men's needs really the same as women's or as genderqueer or non-binary people's? Are White people's needs identical to the needs of Black, Indigenous, and other people of colour, especially transnationally? Are enabled people's needs no different from disabled people's needs? How much does the social construction of difference factor in (e.g. dominant ideas about masculinity vs. femininity)? How do experiences of dominance and oppression affect our needs?

Importantly, Maslow's hierarchy is far from intersectional – it does not at all account for how difference and power shape people's needs, and it supports normativity in a way that erases the lived experiences of oppressed people. Lack of attention to power becomes particularly clear when we consider that the safety needs of oppressed people are never truly met when living under the terror of systemic/structural oppression (Chatterjee 2017) – true safety for folks existing outside the "mythical norm" (Lorde 1984) is a fable, a myth, an illusion, or, at best, a transitory state ever nearing its end. The physiological needs of oppressed people as well are perpetually under attack as food is made scarce, healthcare is stripped away for all who aren't productive enough to be seen as deserving, and housing becomes increasingly unattainable. Yet, despite the systemic barriers, oppressed people continue to achieve self-actualization – they create culture and art; they generate incredible knowledge that benefits the world; they set new records of achievement. If a hierarchical arrangement of needs was accurate, then people like Dorothy Allison, Alice Walker, Patti Berne, Frida Kahlo, and Leslie Feinberg would have been too busy meeting their "lower" needs to have become the writers, poets, artists, or activists we know them to be. Maslow's assumption that self-actualization comes only after meeting our "lower" needs is one that erases the creativity and imagination of oppressed peoples.

Hierarchies are also problematic because they establish false divisions between things that are in fact deeply interconnected. Maslow's hierarchy does more than just classify different kinds of human needs; it represents such needs as if they exist independently of one another and can be theorized in isolation. For Maslow, it seems, the only relationship between these different human needs has to do with their positions in the hierarchy. Yet, drawing from the disability justice principle of interdependence (Mingus 2017; Sins Invalid 2016), it becomes necessary to recognize how different needs interact with and depend upon each other – and not just from our "lower" to "higher" needs. The hierarchical arrangement Maslow proposes constructs barriers to thinking about how, for instance, satisfying esteem needs might be an important part of feeling safe or like we are part of a community that loves and cares for us. Because esteem is positioned above safety and love, our thinking is restricted to movement in that one direction, yet there is value in taking on a different approach. Queering needs and breaking them out of a hierarchy, then, are a necessary step for understanding the complexity of human life, for such a simplistic arrangement fails to accurately represent the diversity of existence.

One final critique of Maslow's hierarchy before moving on: the segregation and hierarchical arrangement of needs makes it difficult to think about how the selves we are (becoming) are defined against and through other people. For Maslow, the very pinnacle of human existence is the individual assertion of difference – the achievement of independence – rather than the understanding of our collectivity, community, and interdependence. Yet, people do not have naturally occurring identities outside of our relationships to other people and to systems of power; indeed, there is no neat division between self and other, or personal and political, for the self comes into being as a result of its ongoing interactions with many different peoples and systems. Who we are and who we become, then, are to a large extent the consequences of how we are positioned socially and how we respond to our social positioning – a fact that leads Aimee Carrillo Rowe (2008) to advocate for a "politics of relation" in place of a "politics of identity." This observation is why I use the term *social position* intentionally and frequently throughout this text.

As an example of this alternative understanding of the self, consider my use of "non-binary" to describe my experiences with gender. Non-binary is not a naturally occurring identity, for it points to the social construction of a gender binary with two accepted categories that both fail to represent me; my gender is a product of not belonging with other gendered people that see themselves as either male/man or female/woman. This description of who I am cannot exist outside of the social landscapes around me. Furthermore, what I have long aspired to become – the self I seek to actualize – is intimately connected to what I have been subjected to as a queer, trans, and disabled person. The vision I hold for my future is not innate but the fusion of my self with my socially situated experiences. So, in order to more fully understand the "self" in relation to motivation, we have to understand how people are situated relative to one another – how we are brought together and how we are kept apart.

Many feminist, anti-racist, anti-capitalist, anti-ableist critiques of motivation theories, such as Maslow's hierarchy, come from this understanding of the self as intimately connected to other people and to social contexts. As part of this understanding, the concept of motivation itself can be critiqued because of concerns about its explanatory usefulness and theoretical responsibility within contexts of inequity and injustice. On the one hand, advantaged people repeatedly use motivation to explain their dominance and the hoarding of social/material resources: they depict their economic privilege as an outcome of their effort, rather than the ordinary exploitation of oppressed peoples, such as disenfranchised workers in factories or undocumented

migrants working on farms. In this sense, the idea of motivation becomes a multi-purpose tool to stifle resistance and legitimize unbalanced distributions of power. The rhetoric of motivation marginalizes conversations about inequity and injustice by presenting power as the outcome of individual behaviours.

On the other hand, motivation has time and time again been harmfully applied to rationalize and justify the subordination of oppressed peoples: through gendered, ablest, colonial, and capitalist logics that create an image of oppressed people as lazy, incapable, and otherwise unproductive, advantaged people have used the frame of motivation to normalize everything from the elimination of welfare/the war against the poor to the racialized economic system of slavery to the astounding rates of pay inequity between people of different genders, races, and abilities. Through a rhetoric of motivation, economic injustice and exploitation often get represented as problems of motivation, meaning that poor people and those who earn less can only solve their problems through taking on more work or working harder. Broader social contexts constraining oppressed people are not factored into this equation of motivation, or they get reinterpreted as an obstacle to be overcome through an individual effort. Motivation lies at the core of the fictional, victim-blaming narrative of the "American Dream."

The Needs Chart: A Tool for Understanding Ourselves

Despite the abundance of criticism against theories of motivation, and Maslow's hierarchy in particular, they remain an important consideration when exploring the issues of systemic or structural oppression and ordinary trauma. I believe that motivation does not have to be defined solely as a private resource – something that resides within individuals and is tied to capitalist logics of productivity. Instead, I maintain that we can re-imagine and re-construct motivation as a *liberatory resource* co-generated between people through the desire to hold ourselves accountable to one another as we organize against inequity and injustice. We can claim motivation as the energy bringing people together in pursuit of collective liberation. In other words, motivation can lead us to ask the following questions: How are we energized to pursue social transformation towards healing and authentic humanity? How can we expand our desire to build anti-oppressive relationships across difference? What will urge us toward deepened capacities for collective creativity or radical imagination? In short, how do we find motivation to pursue collective liberation when we are continually exhausted and depleted?

This alternative understanding of motivation reveals that in addition to offering an individual resource for survival, motivation can inform and be formed through transformative practices of community-building, intersectional accountability, and practices of love and care across difference. Given this alternative way of thinking about motivation, I want to devote the next several paragraphs to reformulating Maslow's hierarchy of needs into something that better aligns with the liberatory impulse of social justice as well as the difficult realities of ordinary trauma. Figure 7.1 below, like Maslow's hierarchy, is one possible representation of human needs as they connect

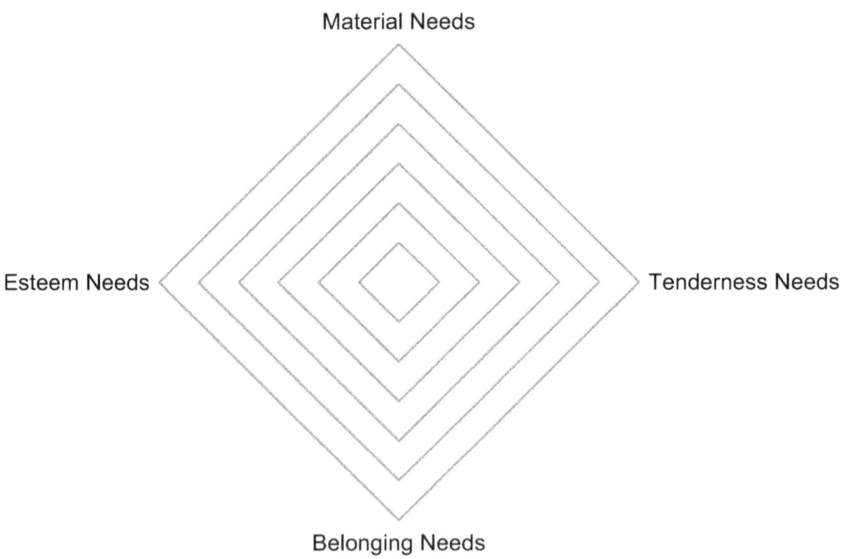

FIGURE 7.1 The Needs Chart.

to one another. This "Needs Chart" contains four categories: Material needs, Tenderness needs, Belonging needs, and Esteem needs. Like a compass, this chart can be turned on its side or even flipped upside down – the location of material needs at the top, for instance, does not indicate that it is any more or less important than belonging needs, which sit down at the bottom. Furthermore, the arrangement and positioning of the categories does not carry a deeper meaning as it would in a hierarchy; the motivation to meet particular needs is not dependent on how fully others needs have been met, though, as I describe a bit later, they do not operate wholly independent either. Self-actualization, which is the highest need in Maslow's original hierarchy, is not represented as an independent need for reasons that I explain later on in this chapter.

Because people are all made differently and socially positioned differently, this Needs Chart should be contextualized based on lived experiences and adapted to the particular needs of individuals, families, and communities. As a disability justice scholar, advocate, and activist, I encourage you to break apart the shape of this chart: just as disabled bodies and minds are not always symmetrical or linear, this chart does need to be composed into a single "perfect" form – too short, too long, and unbalanced sides are both welcome and informative. People completing their own needs chart should feel free to retain their creativity and make changes to better represent their self-perceptions.

My intention is for this Needs Chart to align with teaching from queer and anti-ableist politics, both of which refuse to accept singular normative accounts of human experience by instead prioritizing difference/marginality. Indeed, where Maslow's Hierarchy uncritically centred around advantaged people's needs, I intend for this chart to be more useful to the "misfits" (Garland-Thompson 2011) – those queer and disabled people who are too often expected to conform themselves to representations or models created for people who *fit* into dominant spaces, systems, and institutions. So, the interpretation above is just a starting point to help people imagine what kind of needs chart to make for themselves. In addition, do not feel bound to a single chart – your needs right now will probably be different from your needs at a different point in your life. Any chart you construct later on can be a different shape, its arms and legs different lengths relative to one another. We do not stay the same across our lifetimes, so why should we limit ourselves to one figure?

Before exploring what each of the four needs categories contains and how they are affected by trauma, I need to explain how the Needs Chart works and what it tells us about motivation. The Needs Chart takes the form of a *spider chart*, also known as a *radar chart*. Basically, it combines four separate scales into one representation, which allows them to be viewed and interpreted together for a more complete image of the individual's needs. To fill in the Needs Chart, start from the centre and plot four points, one in the direction of each needs category. Points closer to the centre indicate less met needs, while points closer to the outside of the chart indicate that an individual's needs are being more fully met. Then, connect the points so they form a single shape with four sides, and fill in the area. The figure below is an example of what a completed needs chart might look like:

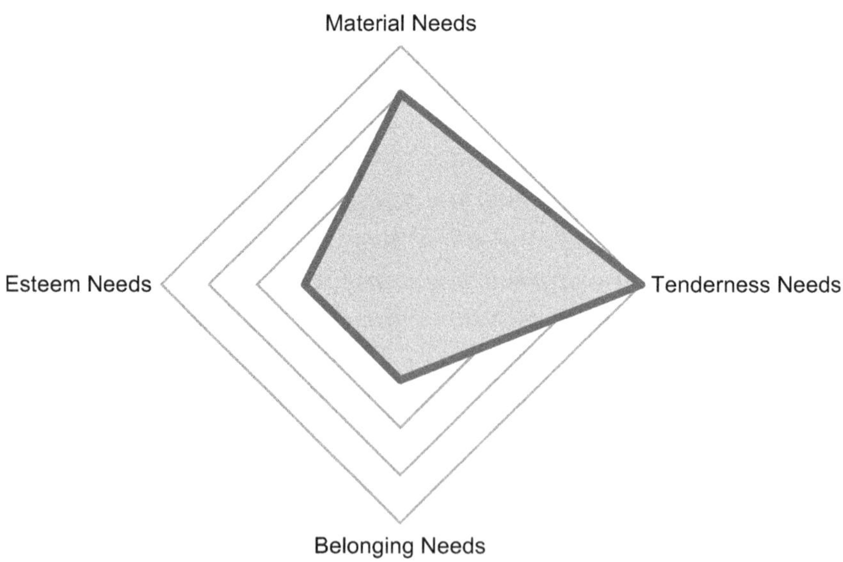

FIGURE 7.2 An example of a completed Needs Chart. This chart shows a person whose materials needs and tenderness needs are relatively well met, but whose belonging needs and esteem needs require greater attention.

To interpret the meaning of a needs chart, look at the distance of each individual point from the centre – the closer to the edge of the chart, the more fully a need is being met – but look also at the area the shape fills, as this gives a more holistic representation of the individual's needs where they are or are not being met. In a perfect scenario, the area of this shape would be equal to the area of the chart, with each of the individual's needs being consistently cared for.

When interpreting a needs chart, remember to bear a few things in mind. First, the chart is a subjective evaluation of needs at a unique moment. Its accuracy depends on the individuals' awareness of their own needs/the awareness of the person making it for them. Mindfulness practices like grounding and reflective meditation can help individuals become more tuned into their needs, but how people understand their needs over time is likely to change as they learn more about themselves and world they exist in. Second, a single needs chart does not necessarily represent anything more than a solitary moment in an individual life. Completing several needs charts over a longer period of time may provide more information, but any and all attempts to make long-term evaluations of needs requires much caution. Third, this tool is meant to cultivate reflective self-awareness rather than medicalization/diagnosis. While we can potentially identify growth areas from our own and other people's charts, we should do so as part of an open dialogue that promotes solidarity and transformative relationships. Finally, this tool should never be used punitively, non-consensually, or to undermine agency, for its purpose is to humanize and connect people.

The following several paragraphs each accomplish two things: they elaborate on what goes into each of the four needs categories and then briefly consider how ordinary trauma interferes with the attainment of those four needs. Please note that while I focus on trauma's negative impacts on human needs, it is important to also think about the potential for the opposite to occur. For example, many people harmed by acts of queerphobic and transphobic violence develop a greater sense of community and connection with other queer and trans folks who share similar experiences. In this sense, even as the trauma of a violent act may cause great harm, so too might it guide people to a space where they can more fully meet their belonging needs. The sections following this one explore more of these positive outcomes. I make this statement to keep in mind that trauma is not just a deficit/loss but also disruptive possibility and an occasion for transformation.

Material Needs

Material needs include all of the things that we need to keep our bodies alive and functioning, such as food, water, and shelter. Material has two relevant meanings in this context: (1) "the matter from which a thing is or can be made"; and (2) "important; essential; relevant" (Oxford Dictionary). Material needs, then, are those things our bodies require to thrive and adapt as we move through life, pursuing all our different desires/longings and becoming the versions of ourselves to which we aspire. Attaining material needs is how we build ourselves up and sustain ourselves across time. Material needs can be specific to individual people, and they can change depending on our present circumstances, past experiences, and perceptions of the future.

Ordinary trauma interferes with the attainment of material needs in multiple ways, such as:

- Through dehumanization and systemic violence, ordinary trauma makes food, water, and other sources of nourishment scarce for oppressed people. Economic injustice, environmental racism, settler colonialism, and the privatization of lands and natural resources ensure that advantaged people regulate the means by which other people meet their material needs. Regulation also occurs in intimate relationships when, for example, harm doers exert power and control over what their partners eat or how they live in their bodies.
- For most oppressed people, survival under systems of power entails regularly leaving our material needs unmet. Oppressed people are repeatedly punished for nourishing ourselves, which results in health disparities, like higher rates of eating disorders and self-harm; dangerous medical,

surgical, or other bodily practices; and degraded self-esteem. Importantly, when oppressed peoples are shamed for meeting their material needs, it can directly interfere with the attainment of all other needs.

- Capitalist logics of productivity, like the victim-blaming myth of the American Dream, subject oppressed people to criticism or violence when they seek assistance, to the point where they may become fearful of the consequences of taking "hand-outs" or feel immense shame over acts of charity. Many people choose to forgo meeting their material needs because their fear/shame is greater than their hunger, thirst, or need for shelter. Ordinary trauma makes it difficult to ask other people for support.
- As an internally disruptive force, ordinary trauma interferes with individuals' capacity to fulfil material needs. A consequence of learning to disassociate from their bodies and minds in response to overwhelming experiences of hurt, traumatized people can often become less aware of their material needs and/or less inclined to take care of themselves. For example, they may not eat enough, get too little sleep, stay at home more than usual, or avoid exercising their bodies. They may not put off getting much needed care if their experiences of ordinary trauma are tied to medical/psychological professionals.

Tenderness Needs

Educator Becky Thompson (2017: 1) defines tenderness as a practice of being together that prioritizes deep, patient, and attentive listening in order for people to "do their best work, to go beyond the given, the expected, the status quo." Tenderness needs include all the things that make us feel safe, cared for, and listened to. Our tenderness needs are met when other people treat us with love, kindness, and compassion, and/or when we do this for ourselves. When we have experienced tenderness, we discover willingness to share parts of ourselves that we typically keep hidden or private, to make ourselves vulnerable to the people around us. Everyone experiences tenderness based on their own social location and individual spirit, which is why being tender with other people requires deep and attentive listening (O'Reilley 1998). Expressions of love and care that fill my needs may look and feel different from those that fill other people's needs.

Ordinary trauma interferes with the attainment of tenderness needs in multiple ways, such as:

- Socialization into positions of dominance can lead advantaged people to feel safe as oppressed people are made unsafe through repeated exposure to ordinary harm and injustice. Under systems of oppression, which inevitably cause presumptive trauma, the tenderness needs of oppressed peoples are difficult to truly meet beyond fleeting moments; there will always be the concern for what might happen in the future. When the loss of safety is a presumptive reality, fulfilling tenderness needs becomes partial and precarious, like a pot leaking too much water.
- The inequitable distribution of resources leaves oppressed people in a near constant state of danger. Resources necessary for maintaining a decent quality of life – access to healthcare, for instance, and the ability to afford housing – are made overly scarce. Oppression often assume a form of being dominated by concerns about maintaining a certain level of safety amidst always present inequity and injustice; oppression can feel like existing in a perpetual state of crisis management. Speaking to racial trauma, Prentis Hemphill (2019): asserts: "Unprocessed trauma disturbs our sense of safety, belonging, dignity, and purpose."
- The violence embedded in vital social institutions and the internalization of hatred by advantaged people often isolates oppressed people from the love/care readily given to others. When oppressed people are able to access tenderness from loved ones or compassionate strangers, it often seems exceptional or extraordinary since it occurs within a broader social context of hatred and normalized violence. Ordinary trauma makes tenderness extraordinary,

but it can also make tenderness we do receive feel that much deeper, more empowering, and transformative.

- All forms of trauma but ordinary trauma especially tend to precede feelings of anxiety that make fear of harm/loss exceedingly familiar. Experiences of anxiety grounded in trauma often feel like a voice in your head constantly saying, "You better watch out." As a result, the sensations of anxiety can keep individuals in a perpetual presumptive state of readiness for the next assault. The pursuit of safety might come to dominate their actions, often to the exclusion of tenderness from other people.

Belonging Needs

Tenderness needs have to do with the way other people care for and about us, and belonging needs have to do with the way we come to understand ourselves in and through other people. Belonging needs include all the things we require to feel connected to the people around us and to the fabric of the human spirit. A lot of people try to fill their belonging needs by building a family, or by participating in social events (e.g. sports or clubs), or by doing volunteer work. Oppressed people often find belonging with others who have been harmed by similar forms of inequity and injustice, and advantaged people seek out similarly situated individuals who have access to familiar privileges and have been socialized into dominance. Less commonly, people seek to find belonging across difference by building community with those who have not shared a similar experience of the world. In either case, filling belonging needs help the individual overcome isolation through the knowledge that their beliefs, values, and desires resonate at the same frequency as somebody else – they are not on their own because they belong to a family, group, or community. Describing the value of relationships and belonging, Nora Samaran (2019: 3) maintains that: "Contrary to many Western conceptions of the self as disconnected and atomized, it turns out that close-knit connections to others are in large part how we grow into our own, fully expressed, autonomous selves."

Ordinary trauma interferes with the attainment of belonging needs in multiple ways, such as:

- Ordinary trauma manifests through a repeated failure of other people to care for and about us. Most oppressed people at some point in their lives must learn to accept the fact that their experiences are a consequence of a deep and pervasive hatred running throughout their society. It is particularly difficult for people to fulfil belonging needs following ordinary traumatic harm because they oftentimes do not have a supportive environment to counteract the injustice they have experienced – an injustice which is, in many cases, an assertion that the individual does not belong. Frequently, harms come from the families, groups, and communities we thought we belonged to, which means that a significant part of the trauma can come from realizing that other people did not think the same – that they saw us as different, as outsiders, as less-than-fully human others.
- Many encounters with trauma are the direct consequence of seeking belonging with other people. Intimate forms of trauma (e.g. sexual and domestic violence) construct harmful associations between love, care, and pain; in some cases, individuals learn to accept violence as part of being loved by other people (hooks 2000) or of belonging to a community. At other times, oppressed people stop attempting to find connection with other people altogether. Either way, their belonging needs are not authentically met, and in lacking the connections that come from belonging become vulnerable to additional harms – both external harms (e.g. more dangerous or risky relationships) and internal harms (e.g. unhealthy practices like drinking or self-harm).
- Whatever else it is, dehumanization is a decisive assertion of non-belonging. To view someone as less-than-fully human is to view them as inferior because of their real or imagined differences from social norms. To be regarded as less-than-fully human is to be told that others will not care for you because you matter less. Dehumanization is a theft of community and all of those things that come from belonging, and ordinary trauma serves as a deep

reminder of that systematic isolation from authentic human connection.

Esteem Needs

Finally, esteem needs include everything that inspires us to have confidence and trust in, as well as care for, ourselves. Esteem needs are how we develop self-love and how we practice self-care. Belonging is a measure of how we witness ourselves in other people, while esteem is our sense of individuality that gives our lives purpose and the self-assurance that enables us to believe that we are deserving of other people's affections and attention. Paradoxically, our esteem needs are frequently filled through the love and compassion we receive from the other people to and with whom we belong, an observation which supports a view of the self as an extension of the relationships we build with others (Carrillo Rowe 2008). Esteem needs also are met through overcoming challenges, developing skills and knowledge, and reaching key milestones or surpassing the goals we set for ourselves. In short, esteem needs underlie a willingness to believe that we are important and worthwhile members of our communities.

Ordinary trauma interferes with the attainment of esteem needs in multiple ways, such as:

- Systems of power continuously question the self-esteem of oppressed people, using an assortment of tactics to send the message that other people are more important, more worthy, and/or more desirable. From eugenics and scientific racism, to lack of representation, to stereotypes that oppressed people are "lazy," "ugly," and "dumb," dehumanization advances a narrative of inferiority that bombards oppressed people, often to a point where they internalize the sense of themselves as substandard. And, as I said earlier, I agree with Berila (2015) that internalizing these hateful messages is traumatic in itself.
- As advantaged people portray themselves not only as desirable but also as "normal," dominant ideas about humanity come to mark oppressed people as different,

most often as less capable. Oppressed people often have a harder time filling their esteem needs because they are told to measure themselves against a disciplinary rubric built for somebody else. Moreover, biased rubrics are everywhere – they are systematic – affecting everything from healthcare and psychology to education to contributions in the workplace. Rarely are oppressed people permitted to exist and feel confident or good about themselves on their own terms. More often, as Sonya Renee Taylor (2018) states, they are expected to apologize and account for themselves.

- Ordinary trauma often includes harder critiques or lack of acknowledgement for work done well. How many times have you read a book, or watched a movie or television show, or talked with someone and heard the line, "x group has to work twice as hard to get half the credit"? The difficulty of earning recognition is compounded by the long history of advantaged people taking credit for the accomplishments of people they view as less-than-fully human. In doing so, advantaged people simultaneously take praise away from people who deserve it and deny future generations the opportunity to feel inspired by their ancestors. This can lead to things like imposter syndrome, or the feeling of non-belonging that comes when people doubt the ability to succeed or question whether they should have been included in the first place.

Having now elaborated upon each of these four needs categories, I want to make two critical observations. First, the needs categories are not completely separate: they co-exist, inform, and strengthen each other. Tenderness and belonging, for instance, overlap in recognizable ways, as is demonstrated by the difference in feeling when we receive love and support from someone whom we are deeply connected to versus someone whom we are less familiar with. Similarly, we often need less praise or positive evaluation when we have strong community connections nourishing our confidence; we feel esteem more readily if our belonging needs are consistently met. In the Needs Chart, the elevation of one need actually raises the others around it, increasing the overall area covered. Similarly, fulfilling tenderness, belonging, and esteem need can each improve our chances of sustaining our materials needs: we will likely be more willing to take more chances (e.g. applying for better jobs), to share resources, and to seek out support because we come to trust that our lives matter and that others care for us.

The second observation is that the same or similar things can fill up multiple needs because our needs are interdependent. However, some actions might also fill one need while leaving another unmet or, worse, while depleted. This contradiction can be a normal part of life, but it can also indicate the presence of abuse and violence. For instance, sex leaves us needing food/water (i.e. with increased material needs) even though it can also fulfil our tenderness, belonging, and/or esteem needs. Pursuing those other needs involved making the choice to expend energy and require more sustenance later on, which is an understandable trade-off. However, in instances of harm, the denial of our needs results in a sort of collapsing in which all our needs can become endangered. For example, when an abusive partner tells someone they will only love them if they do this or that (e.g. stay skinny by not eating or give up careers/hobbies), the fulfilment of love needs can become precarious, always ready to topple into itself, as do our other needs (e.g. if we stop eating enough food or if we stop doing the things that make us feel confident in ourselves). So even though I have broken these needs out into identifiable categories, it would be a mistake to assume they are isolated or self-contained.

Self-Actualization as Authentic Humanity and Erotic Knowledge

The need for self-actualization sits atop Maslow's hierarchy as the final source of motivation to which all people supposedly aspire: after individuals have filled their physiological, safety, love, and esteem needs, Maslow argues, they will be motivated to reach to the extent of their potential, whatever that might be. Like much of Maslow's work, critics have questioned this concept of self-actualization and its position as the pinnacle of human motivation. Over the next few pages, I reckon with this concept in an attempt to critically reclaim in relation to the theory of ordinary trauma and authentic humanity.

The concept of self-actualization is complex and nebulous, simultaneously deeply personal and socially constructed. As I wrote earlier, Maslow (1943: 382) defined self-actualization as "the desire to become more and more what one is, to become everything that one is capable of becoming." In a postmodern perspective, this definition is limited because it claims that who we are exists separate from the context in which we become, that it is possible to think of ourselves without seeing the innumerable webs that bind us to other people and systems of oppression. Moreover, this description of self-actualization falls back on understandings of our identities as stable and fixed things that persist absolutely. Meeting our needs for self-actualization, according to Maslow's account, entails moving closer to an inherent essence that encapsulates "what one is."

Yet, our identities are continuously reconstituted and reinterpreted over time and space; the essence of "what one is" does not exist apart from the creation and performance of a version of ourselves within a social context that has already instilled in us a sense of how we should/should not behave, who we should/should not be. Aimee Carrillo Rowe (2008: 3) explains that "[t]he meaning of 'self' is never individual, but is forged across a shifting set of relations that we move in and out of, often without reflection." Who we are depends on who we have been with or belonged with, both intentionally/consciously and unreflectively, accidentally, or uncritically. Accordingly, how we seek out self-actualization, in many cases, gets warped into alignment with normativity, for to be(come) something different, something deviant or transgressive, means putting all of our needs in danger.

Finally, many have questioned why Maslow's vision of self-actualization, which is inherently an expression of individuality, should be prioritized above relational connection within one's family/community. Indeed, it seems to expose Maslow's Western bias that he assumes all people would be motivated towards self-actualization as their highest need instead of caring for and elevating the people who are connected to them. This prioritization of individuality is filtered as well through logics of oppressive systems that promote dominance, competition, and productivity above connection, collaboration, and care. So, in addition to removing the self from the community and context, Maslow's framing of self-actualization also defines as lesser individual's contribution to the health and well-being of other people.

Despite these substantive criticisms, I still find value in the concept of self-actualization, so rather than a wholesale discarding of it, I think that it should be deconstructed and situated within a context of collective empowerment and resistance to oppression – reimagined and reassembled with a critical bias towards intersectional social justice. Self-actualization, as I reimagine it here, is an outcome of two central factors that are realized through each of our other needs. First, we move closer to self-actualization as we journey closer to our *authentic humanity*, which I defined earlier as a unification that empowers us to come together in the shared pursuit of life and radical love. Authentic humanity is inseparable from Paulo Freire's description of liberation as "the process of humanization" (2000 [1970]: 79). Understanding and reaching our true potential as individuals is in the end a matter of developing meaningful relationships with other people and with the more-than-human world around us. Authentic humanity is the unmaking and healing of ordinary trauma though reclamation of our internal and external connections – reclamation that is accomplished through the transformation of our relationships away from harm towards love.

Since all life is interdependent, our potential as individuals is profoundly influenced by how we learn to coexist with people like and not like us; how we create families and communities. In his original paper, Maslow offered the example of self-actualization through painting – the artist is self-actualized when they can skilfully express their individuality through artwork, but I would argue that painting is only a means to an end. For artists, painting or sculpting or photographing are *methods* of meaning-making that allow them to share their awarenesses, however partially, with others in a way that draws them closer together. Thus, the true self-actualization of the artist comes from drawing ever closer to the human spirit and authentic humanity. What leads someone to utilize artistic methods in place of others has to do with their socialization and the nurturance of their unique capacities, which again may be innate to a certain degree, but are always socially produced.

The accomplishment of self-actualization depends on the successfulness of these methods in achieving our authentic humanity, but that is not the whole story. The second component of self-actualization is the exploration and realization of that which is *erotic* to us, that which brings us to the height of our sensations so that we know our full potential for feeling. I wrote about Lorde's conceptualization of the erotic in the previous chapter, but a few of her words are especially relevant here:

> The erotic is a measure between the beginnings of our sense of self and the chaos of our strongest feelings. It is an internal sense of satisfaction to which, once we have experienced it, we know we can aspire. For having experienced the fullness of this depth of feeling and recognizing its power, in honor and self-respect we can require no less of ourselves.
>
> (1984: 54)

To experience the erotic is to capture a fleeting glimpse of the climax of our aspirations, the magnitude of our desires as their power converges in our bodies and minds. Describing self-actualization as the exploration and realization of erotic knowledge means it entails learning to trust our emotions and our too often neglected sensory reactions to the world around us. It means that experiencing pleasure and other sources of emotional fulfilment are not base desires, but a final purpose of our being. Returning to the example of an artist, accepting the erotic as a second part of self-actualization explains why they would seek the restoration of their authentic humanity through painting: it grants them a sense of emotional fulfilment or pleasure that other paths do not. While they may be able to find deep and lasting connection just as easily by any number of other pursuits, painting is a source of erotic knowledge and fulfilment in their life. As someone who very much enjoys spending time alone or with a few close others, the things that bring me the greatest pleasure while still connecting me to the spirit of humanity are things that I can do on my own, such as reading or writing. Other people might find "the chaos of their strongest feelings" through gardening or sports or architecture or sexual intimacy or an infinite number of other activities.

To summarize:

Self-actualization = Authentic Humanity + Erotic Knowledge

Authentic humanity and erotic knowledge are two primary components of self-actualization because they swell the boundaries of what we are capable of becoming and they inspire us to continually pursue the limits of our potential for feeling and connection. Such is the push and pull of existence: we swell our potential outward by integrating ourselves into the human spirit that connects us to all other people while our erotic knowledge pulls us toward the ever-expanding edge of possibility. Accordingly, self-actualization is dynamic: like everything else, it changes across our lifetimes as we grow closer to and more distant from people we know, make friends and new commitments, and discover new and more complex pleasures in our constantly evolving bodies and minds. Changes in self-actualization are normal, especially when our lives are experienced in a society founded on inequity and injustice. Think about it like this: when we are forced apart or violently dragged together by unequal power relations, our attachment to the human spirit takes a beating, and we have to search for new remedies. Similarly, as much as the erotic may exist within us, so too can it come from encounters with ordinary trauma. Pleasures and emotional fulfilment we find in certain activities or pursuits are often connected to the ways we have been loved and harmed, which I explained more in the previous chapter.

In the theory of human needs I have been building here, self-actualization is not represented as an independent needs category on the chart. This is because self-actualization does not exist apart from the four main needs categories: rather than being something that we pursue when our "lesser" needs have been met as Maslow explains it, self-actualization is actually what becomes more and more clear to us when our needs are consistently met throughout our lives. Look again at the Needs Chart. Notice the outermost lines. This space is where the experience of self-actualization resides. It is always available to us, but pursuing it becomes easier as our needs get filled. Think about the area of the shape in your Needs Chart swelling when your needs are met, carrying you to the edge of your potential and to the height of your emotions. In this way, being able to nourish ourselves, experiencing tenderness, accessing belonging with other people, and believing in ourselves – each of these things propels us in the directions of highest capacities. They not only make life possible but also they make life joyous and memorable and worthwhile.

The peripheral position of self-actualization is purposeful: nourishing ourselves, being cared for, finding community and esteem are elevators moving us towards authentic humanity and erotic knowledge. For example, think about doing something that brings you to deep joy and sense of purpose; something that you feel driven to accomplish or contribute. Now consider how much harder it is to enjoy that activity when your stomach is growling. Or, when you just had a fight with your best friend/partner. Or, when your friends do not invite you somewhere. Or, when you have just received a harsh review of your work. Finding self-actualization is still possible at that moment, but it takes more work to find motivation to reach for it. Unfulfilled needs do not prevent us from self-actualization, but they do create barriers and roadblocks that sap our energy and slow us down.

Now, think about how systems of oppression normalize and distribute these barriers, so that oppressed people consistently have to put more energy in while advantaged people need to use less. Self-actualization is impacted by the politics of exhaustion – by the energy spent/saved through social institutions and systems that treat people differently across race, class, gender, ability, and so on. Inequity, injustice, and structural violence then, might be thought of as imposed obstacles that increase the required energy input or cost of self-actualization: oppressed people have to jump higher, reach farther, and expend more energy to attain self-actualization in a society that blocks their needs, but nothing can keep people eternally from their potential/their dreams. The humanizing process of liberation includes the removal of these barriers, so that self-actualization is challenging for the right reasons: we should have to work towards self-actualization, it should take great effort because realizing our potential is an incredible lifelong process, but it should be challenging in its own right and not because the path to it is designed to keep some of us down.

Moreover, the position of self-actualization on the periphery of the needs chart can make it precarious for traumatized people: when trauma enters our lives, it hollows out our needs, leaving behind sinkholes that pull us down whenever we are not paying enough attention. It becomes more arduous for traumatized people to seek out their self-actualization because the foundation holding us up is at risk of collapsing in on itself. It's like walking on quicksand or a thin sheet of ice above a deep lake. The holes trauma leaves behind – holes in memory, for instance, or lapses in time – estrange us from our bodies and minds, making it harder to remain aware of the things we need to survive/thrive. This is called *dissociation*, and it is the covering of sticks and leaves that can deceive us into thinking our needs have been met even when they are unsatisfied.

Traumatized people often struggle to understand or express our needs in words because we have learned to fear listening to what our bodies tell us. Since bodies are so often connected to the traumas we experience, especially ordinary traumatic harms, actively listening to our bodies can often lead to involuntary sensations or remembrances of how they felt during the worst moments. Gabor Mate (cited in Nerenberg 2017) explains that "The essence of trauma is disconnection from ourselves . . . separation from [our] body and emotions." Neglecting the body becomes a way of protecting ourselves from the things we are not yet ready to process, or things that we have spent too much time processing, but unfortunately it also means we might become less aware of our varied needs/less willing to fulfil them. However, as I have argued elsewhere in this text, when we are able to process trauma, to come back into our bodyminds following traumatic harm, we often have a deeper appreciation for our embodied and enminded needs as a result of our personal transformations (Levins Morales 1998). This is what I take away from Peter Levine's statement that the "paradox of trauma is that it has both the power to destroy and the power to transform and resurrect" (2010).

In addition to the foundation of self-actualization, it is also true that trauma messes with the two primary components of self-actualization in notable ways. First, as I have been asserting throughout this text, ordinary trauma splits people apart and takes away from us the sense of our own interdependence. In cases of incest and child sexual abuse, for example, harmed people are often reluctant to seek out family relationships and frequently find it challenging to ever fully trust other people. The trauma they experienced from a young age makes human connections feel dangerous and/or violent, which means that pursuing authentic humanity can become a source of profound fear, anxiety, and pain. For harmed people who have been violently isolated from the human spirit against their well (as opposed to advantaged people socialized into dominance), any efforts to build relationships and communities may include a greater need for reassurance, support, time, and/or space to process. They may cling more strongly to their own sense of independence because it feels safer and may mimic defensive mechanisms they used to protect themselves as children. Embracing interdependence may feel overwhelming or go against their learned disconnection from others.

Second, when trauma makes people reluctant to live in and listen to their bodies and minds, it interferes with their erotic knowledge. How can we experience the depth of our emotion or the fullness of our pleasure when we feel the need to endlessly dissociate from the parts of ourselves where those sensations reside? This learned fear of and distancing from the erotic can be especially real for those harmed people who experienced violence and trauma where they expected to find joy and satisfaction from someone or something else, such as when a sexual partner becomes a sexual assailant, or when a celebration or achievement becomes a source of punishment. For example, trans people transitioning into a body and identity that matches their internal sense of themselves should be a cause of relief and joy and hope, but it is so often warped into a matter of dealing with cisgender people's feelings of anger, loss, and/or grief (Talusan 2019). Part of the damage of ordinary trauma and structural violence is a loss of trust in our senses and embodied knowledge.

Interfering with these components of self-actualization leaves the equation unbalanced and may result in a different, less desirable outcome. For this reason, traumatic harm impacting tenderness, belonging, and esteem needs can be especially detrimental to psychological/spiritual well-being. Healing from these forms of trauma at both the individual and collective levels is an essential aspect of restoring justice to our relationships, for if justice is a matter of how we learn to live together, then it must centre around accountability, interdependence, and care. Doing so increases the capacity of people to become all that they can become – the versions of themselves that they dream of.

So, here's my radical conclusion: self-actualization is the process of inviting other people to care for us in a liberatory way, of sharing with them our interpretations of reality and listening to theirs, such that they might love us in the ways we so desperately need them to as sentient, living beings and recognize the fullness of our humanity. In the end, we self-actualization is a reciprocal process we undertake by figuring out how to respond to these calls for love and care, and by repeatedly accepting the invitations to encounter different people's paradigms of understanding and experience. The self is produced relationally, so true self-actualization must reach outward to the actualization of families, communities, and societies. Otherwise, how can we become the best versions of ourselves? How can we fulfil all our needs enough to experience the fullness of our deepest emotions? Indeed, the equation I posited earlier – *Self-actualization = Authentic Humanity + Erotic Knowledge* – requires us to ground our own development in the growth and well-being of others.

Caring for each other's needs as well as for our own is always an imperfect endeavour, but it is one which we should nevertheless strive to improve upon as we turn towards our relatives, neighbours, ancestors, and descendants. Berenice Malka Fisher (2001: 123) writes about the imperfectability of caring as arising both from the way our needs change over time and place and from the unique contexts of our lives:

> The *imperfectability of caring* stems from the fact that it is very difficult to fully meet the needs of others [and of ourselves]. Needs fluctuate and vary with the context. Many factors limit and constrain even the most devoted carer's efforts to do her job: the amount of work she has to do, the resources at her disposal, and her opportunities for self-care, such as getting enough sleep.

For this reason, self-actualization as the call-and-response of care must journey in multiple directions, and it must be personalized; anything less pulls us back down into the spaces of abuse and exploitation, the spaces of scarcity in which some people's needs get met at the expense of others. As we receive care, we have a responsibility to extend care back to other people in the ways we are able and in the ways that make sense to them. The process of self-actualization is an opportunity to become more practiced in the clear expression of needs and in the care-full nourishment of the people we love.

References

Berila, Beth. *Integrating Mindfulness into Anti-Oppression Pedagogy: Social Justice in Higher Education*. New York: Routledge, 2015.

Carrillo Rowe, Aimee. *Power Lines: On the Subject of Feminist Alliances*. Durham: Duke University Press, 2008.

Chatterjee, Dom. "Mental Health is Different for People of Color in These 3 Ways." *Restforresistance.com*. https://restforresistance.com/zine/mental-health-is-different-for-people-of-color (published April 29, 2017).

Fisher, Berenice Malka. *No Angel in the Classroom: Teaching through Feminist Discourse*. Lanham: Rowman & Littlefield Publishers, 2001.
Freire, Paulo. *Pedagogy of the Oppressed*. New York: Bloomsbury, 2000 [1970].
Garland-Thompson, Rosemarie. "Misfits: A Feminist Materialist Disability Concept." *Hypatia* 26, no. 3 (2011): 591–609.
Hemphill, Prentis. "Letting Go of Innocence." July 5, 2019.
hooks, bell. *All about Love: New Visions*. New York: William Morrow, 2000.
Levine, Peter. *In An Unspoken Voice: How the Body Releases Trauma and Restores Goodness*. North Atlantic Books, 2010.
Levins Morales, Aurora. *Medicine Stories: History, Culture and the Politics of Integrity*. Cambridge: South End Press, 1998.
Lorde, Audre. *Sister Outsider: Essays and Speeches*. New York: Ten Speed Press, 1984.
Maslow, Abraham. "A Theory of Human Motivation." *Psychological Review* 50 (1943): 370–396.
Merriam, Sharan and Bierema, Laura. *Adult Learning: Linking Theory and Practice*. Jossey-Bass, 2013.
Mingus, Mia. "Forced Intimacy: An Ableist Norm." *Leaving Evidence*. https://leavingevidence.wordpress.com/2017/08/06/forced-intimacy-an-ableist-norm/ (published August 6, 2017).
Nerenberg, Jenara. "Why Are So Many Adults Today Haunted by Trauma?" *Greater Good Magazine*. https://greatergood.berkeley.edu/article/item/why_are_so_many_adults_today_haunted_by_trauma#:~:text=There's%20nothing%20about%20any%20mentally,don't%20mean%20dramatic%20events. (published June 8, 2017).
O'Reilley, Mary Rose. *Radical Presence: Teaching as Contemplative Practice*. Portsmouth: Boynton/Cook Publishers, 1998.
Samaran, Nora. *Turn This World Inside Out: The Emergence of Nurturance Culture*. Chico: AK Press, 2019.
Sins Invalid. "Skin, Tooth, and Bone. The Basis of Movement is Our People: A Disability Justice Primer." *Sins Invalid*, 2016.
Talusan, Meredith. "Celebrate Your Kid's Transition: Don't Grieve It." *The New York Times*. https://www.nytimes.com/2019/10/18/opinion/sunday/gender-transition-death-grief.html (published October 18, 2019).

Taylor, Sonya Renee. *The Body Is Not an Apology: The Power of Radical Self-love*. Oakland, CA: Berrett-Koehler Publishers, 2018.

Thompson, Becky. *Teaching with Tenderness: Toward an Embodied Practice*. Chicago: University of Illinois Press, 2017.

Index

Note: Page locators in *italic* indicate a figure, and page locators in **bold** indicate a table on the corresponding page.

For Product Safety Concerns and Information please contact our EU
representative GPSR@taylorandfrancis.com
Taylor & Francis Verlag GmbH, Kaufingerstraße 24, 80331 München, Germany

www.ingramcontent.com/pod-product-compliance
Ingram Content Group UK Ltd.
Pitfield, Milton Keynes, MK11 3LW, UK
UKHW022350190926
475702UK00015B/2214
* 9 7 8 1 0 4 1 2 0 3 0 1 8 *